The Great Wheel

a commentary on the System of W.B. Yeats' *A Vision*

by Bob Makransky

Volume IV of the Introduction to Magic series

Copyright © 2013, 2017 by Bob Makransky

ISBN: 978-0-9677315-9-9

Published by Dear Brutus Press

Woodcut of 'The Great Wheel' by Edmund Dulac from *A Vision* by W. B. Yeats reproduced by permission of Hodder and Stoughton Ltd, Carmelite House, 50 Victoria Embankment, London imprint, EC4Y 0DZ.

Excerpts from THE THREE PILLARS OF ZEN: TEACHING, PRACTICE, AND ENLIGHTENMENT by Roshi P. Kapleau, copyright © 1989 by Roshi Philip Kapleau. Used by permission of Anchor Books, an imprint of the Knopf Doubleday Publishing Group, a division of Penguin Random House LLC. All rights reserved. Any third party use of this material, outside of this publication, is prohibited. Interested parties must apply directly to Penguin Random House LLC for permission.

Reprinted with permission of Washington Square Press, a division of Simon and Schuster, Inc. All rights reserved from:
  (1) Copyright © 1971 by Carlos Castaneda
  (2) Copyright © 1974 by Carlos Castaneda
  (3) Copyright © 1977 by Carlos Castaneda
  (4) Copyright © 1987 by Carlos Castaneda

© National Portrait Gallery, London

Table of Contents

Frontispiece: Mr. and Mrs. William Butler Yeats
Proem & Preface 5
Seven Propositions 12

I. Connecting to Your True Purpose 14
    Voices of the Ancestors 26
    Past Life Regressions 30
    Probable Reality Progressions 40
    Recapitulation 52

II. The Four Memories of the *Daimon* 64

III. The Phases of the Moon 95
    The Lunar Rhythm 95
    The Power of Symbolism 100
    The Phases of the Moon 105
        The Four Quarters 124
        The Seven Chaldean Planets 133
        The Rectangles 140
        The Influence of the *Faculties*
            Upon the Phases 141
        Table of Keywords for the Influence
           of the Faculties *Upon the Phases* 169
        Interpretations for Individual Phases 173

IV. The Nature of the *Daimon* 257
    Mind and Memory 257
    Waking and Dreaming 260
    Change 266
    Familiarity 271
    The Akashic Records 287

Glossary 303
Bibliography 308
Appendix I: W.B.Y.'s Keywords for the
    Influence of the *Faculties* Upon the Phases 309
Appendix II: The Critical Degrees 314
Books by Bob Makransky 326

Proem

**The Great Wheel is the wheel of karma;
of reincarnation – of death and rebirth.
It is the wheel of the law;
the wheel of retribution.
It is number and it is measure.
It consists of wheels upon wheels,
and wheels within wheels;
and it is symbolized by
the phases of the moon.**

☾

Preface

The present book is the fourth in the author's series of magical training manuals; and is the second book in the author's projected three-volume series on *The Astrology of Consciousness*. The first volume, *Thought Forms*, dealt with the symbolism of the synodic cycle of the planet Mercury; *The Great Wheel* deals with the symbolism of the synodic cycle of the moon; and the forthcoming volume on lucid dreaming will describe the symbolism of the synodic cycle of the planet Venus.

Where *Thought Forms* dealt with your social conditioning – everything you've learned since you were born, the present volume discusses your karma: your conditioning which arises out of past life / human / mammalian / vertebrate / animal / multicellular / unicellular evolution – in short, everything you bring into your present lifetime at birth. Every single act that you perform all day every day is being created and shaped and formed out of a mass of memory – of cognitive assumptions and evolutionary branching points – that goes back to the very first single cell of life on earth (and "before" it, actually; except there is no "before"). You are not just living in this moment, as you believe: you are living in an eternal *now* moment, glimpses of which you can discern beneath the surface of everyday life if you are attentive enough (if you are sensitive and intuitive to begin with; or at peak moments now and again; or if you have had magical training using techniques such as those described in this book).

Where *Thought Forms* discussed the issue of *importance* (your ability to focus your moment-to-moment attention, which in turn gives rise to your sense of being a discrete being embedded in linear time), the present volume will discuss the issue of *familiarity* (your sense of being oriented and sustained in physical space).

Where the concern in *Thought Forms* was on how to recognize and act on your true feelings in this lifetime, the concern in the present book is with your true purpose – the underlying feeling of all your lifetimes and incarnations – the reason you keep coming back for more (what we term "higher self" and W. B. Yeats termed "*Mask*").

The problem with trying to read *A Vision* is that it is incomprehensible to the intellect. The reason for this is that it is a message from the spirit world, and as such it is couched in "spirit language", which is far less linear than human language: *Those who taught me this system did so, not for my sake, but their own. They say that only the words spoken in trance or written in the automatic script assist them. They belong to the "unconscious" and what comes from them alone serves. My interpretations do not concern them.*

A Vision is more like a Bach fugue or a Van Gogh painting – or a poem, if you will – than it is a linear discourse. It means multidimensional things because it expresses feelings rather than concepts. As Carl Jung said in *Man and His Symbols*, "Dreams' contents are symbolic and thus have more than one meaning. The symbols point in different directions from those we apprehend with the conscious mind; and therefore they relate to something either unconscious or at least not entirely conscious."

However, it's not that symbols have more than one meaning – a symbol has but one meaning – but different rational interpretations of it are possible. A symbol is how feeling reveals itself to mind – symbols are to feeling what thoughts are to mind: they mean what they mean, but the manifoldness arises when you try to analyze, to use mind (thought forms) to try to describe feelings (light fibers). For example, the *Four Faculties* (discussed later in this book) might be considered to symbolize different things – but this is not exactly true: rather, what the *Four Faculties* symbolize can be approached from different points of view, each of which reveals a different facet of the symbolism (namely, as four levels of memory; or as four levels of communication between people; or as four ways in which the stream of thoughts which make up a person's moment-to-moment inner dialogue are molded, or nudged this way and that). You run into the same problem when you try to interpret the symbolism in *A Vision* that you do trying to interpret dreams: there is no way to "fit" what can only be known intuitively into a framework of concepts. The present book is an attempt to explain the System in everyday language; but it's just one way of looking at it.

The universe is not as simple as you are accustomed to believing (or perceiving) it to be in your everyday life. In fact, you can do a much better job of perceiving what is actually going on by using your feelings – your intuition – to process incoming information rather than your thinking mind (as society has trained you to do). The purpose of this book – and of all magic and astrology, actually – is to create a bridge or springboard to facilitate reaching a more profound and effective level of understanding and appreciating everyday life than can be grasped by intellect alone.

This involves reaching for meaning and understanding rather than relying on concepts and beliefs. All concepts and belief systems are going to become very, very irrelevant, very, very soon.

The question which the book *Thought Forms* proposed and never answered was why and how anything exists "out there" at all. *Thought Forms* did address (more or less) the question of why two people looking at the same thing can see the same thing: namely because they *aren't* really seeing the same thing at all, but are only paying attention to certain features on which they can indeed seem to get some agreement. It's more like an agreement to agree rather than the perception of some external "reality". But *Thought Forms* never explained why two people should see anything there at all; i.e., to what extent a rock, for example, has any self-existence apart from the beings apprehending it. Or, as Shankara put it, that a rope which is mistaken for a snake is not a snake; but on the other hand, neither is it unreal just because the person perceiving it is mistaken about what it is.

The answer to this question lies in the *persistence* of memory. Memory is that which endures and repeats, i.e., it symbolizes the eternality of the Spirit. Memory is as eternal as the Spirit – it *is* the Spirit, in its eternal aspect. Mind cannot arise until things repeat themselves – it's all just random thought forms until some kind of repetition or cyclic memory arises to tie certain thought forms into a continuity termed *mind* (individual, self-aware, separated sentient beings). In other words, cycles don't repeat as waves embedded in a matrix of linear time; rather, linear time (mind) only arises as something is repeating itself or perpetuating itself through cyclical repetition.

What sticks all this up is memory. If there were no memory, every transaction would be pure and free and aboveboard, with no hidden agendas or unacknowledged motives. Everything would happen spontaneously.

Memory is a heavy weight added to experience, but also what anchors it, gives it stability – a sense of duration and therefore *meaning*.

Ultimately, what the inexorable revolution of the Great Wheel symbolizes is *change*, and how different people handle it (how they give meaning to their experience). Change is one of the two facets of memory (the other is *stasis*). In this System, the principle of memory is symbolized by numbers (in particular, the numbers four, seven, and twenty-eight) because memory is so incredibly complex and infinitely ramified that there is nothing else in common experience which even remotely resembles it (which can be used metaphorically to model it) except for arithmetic. Astrology – the cycle of 28 lunar phases – is then projected on top as a way of interpreting the underlying numerical symbolism – as an allegory for interpreting the life purposes of different types of individuals.

The Great Wheel also symbolizes the evolution of life / consciousness as a whole: Phases 1 to 14 symbolize the descent into individuation: from inorganic life (dreamless sleep) through unicellular life (dream consciousness) to multicellular life (waking consciousness); and the Phases from 15 to 28 symbolize the return to union (lucid dreaming). It's a microcosm / macrocosm kind of thing.

This book is unquestionably the most enjoyable and intriguing piece of writing I've ever done. The thing basically wrote itself, and I was always surprised and amazed to see what would come next. As the pieces of the jigsaw puzzle fell into place and the overall picture began to emerge, I was astounded by its sophistication and complexity. Indeed, the System described in this book is but a rough sketch of a very small part of what is in fact an all-encompassing system of symbolism – a model of the entire universe: *all thought, all history and the difference between man and man* – which was revealed to and recorded by Mrs. and Mr. William Butler Yeats in *A Vision*. This book is in fact a *last act of defense against the chaos of the world* – a survival manual, if you will, with which to confront the impending collapse of society and the earth turning against us humans, by finding our own true purpose in life as individuals and as a species.

The exposition of the System given in these pages differs in certain important respects from that propounded by W.B.Y. in *A Vision*; and as a result it has been criticized in certain quarters as being inauthentic. The fact is that the System exists "out there" independent of human apprehension: W.B.Y. and his wife channeled it the way they channeled it; Busteed, Tiffany, and Wergin channeled it the way they channeled it; Chelsea Quinn Yarbro (in *Messages from Michael*) channeled it the way she channeled it; I channeled it the way I channeled it; and you, gentle reader, can channel it any way you please. In my purview, the matrix of rulerships of the lunar phases by the Chaldean planets is more aesthetically pleasing than that by the zodiac of signs; moreover it works well in practice. To my mind it is more suggestive than the zodiacal approach; and after all, what we are trying to do is open our intuitive channels and stimulate our imaginations. Similarly, the tetrapolar geometrical symbolism described in Chapter II is more congruent with the astrological map of consciousness propounded in the present series of books (which began with *Thought Forms*) than is the simpler dipolar geometry of *A Vision*. Whatever works is right.

Only a few facets of the System given to W.B.Y. are discussed here (the material in the first section of *A Vision*), namely the *Four Faculties* and the astrological symbolism. I have been told that the rest of the model (the geometrical and numerical symbolism, the *Four Principles*, the organization of world history, etc.) will be revealed to and published by other channels at some future time. I make no pretense to ought than having barely scratched the surface of *A Vision*. The present volume is not so much a commentary on *A Vision* as it is an approach to it or a way of getting a handle on it. Passages in italics are quotations from William Butler Yeats' writings (from *A Vision*, 1937 edition, unless noted otherwise). My own comments / interpretations on same are placed within square brackets []. Words and phrases in pointed brackets <> were crossed out in the original manuscripts.

B. M.

Seven Propositions

I. *Reality is a timeless and spaceless community of spirits which perceive each other. Each Spirit is determined by and determines those it perceives, and each Spirit is unique.*

II. *When these Spirits reflect themselves in time and space they <are so many destinies which> still determine each other, and each Spirit sees the others as thoughts, images, objects of sense* [i.e., thought forms]. *Time and space are unreal.*

III. *This reflection into time and space is only complete at certain moments of birth, or passivity, which recur many times in each destiny. At these moments the destiny receives its character until the next such moment from those Spirits who constitute the external universe. The horoscope is a set of geometrical relations between the Spirit's reflection and the principal masses in the universe and defines that character.*

IV. *The emotional character of a timeless and spaceless spirit reflects itself as its position in time, its intellectual character as its position in space. The position of a Spirit in space and time therefore defines character.*

V. *Human life is either the struggle of a destiny against all other destinies, or a transformation of the character defined in the horoscope into timeless and spaceless existence. The whole passage from birth to birth should be an epitome of the whole passage of the universe through time and back into its timeless and spaceless condition.*

VI. *The acts and nature of a Spirit during any one life are a section or abstraction of reality and are unhappy because incomplete. They are a gyre or part of a gyre, whereas reality is a sphere.*

VII. *Though Spirits are determined by each other they cannot completely lose their freedom. Every possible statement or perception contains both terms – the self and that which it perceives or states.*

(W.B.Y., *National Library of Ireland MS 30,280*)

I. Connecting to Your True Purpose

This book was written to explain the purpose of life. The purpose of life is to *feel feelings*. Period. Life has no other purpose. The rest of this book will enlarge upon this statement.

Along the way, you will learn how to connect to your true purpose in this lifetime – the reason why you incarnated upon the earth at this time – the reason you were born. In present-day society, people don't feel their true feelings much, or have much sense of connection to their true purpose in being here on earth. This book will explain some techniques for making these connections, and it will present some lessons. The main lesson to be learned here is that there is no time to waste; but there is no wasted time. Magicians say that nothing is lost; nothing is won; nothing defended; and nothing undone.

This book will also discuss the principle of *memory*. Memory is the most profound of the planetary principles. Memory reflects the primordial quality of the Spirit: its existence prior to time (mind) or space (desire). Memory is symbolized by wheels upon wheels, and wheels within wheels.

By memory is meant instinct, which means not only your learned reactions from this lifetime, but also all the instincts you developed as an individual in the sum total of all your past and future lives as a human; plus the instincts you have as a mammal, as a vertebrate, as a multicellular being, etc. etc. all the way back to your instincts from one-celled life.

I know now that revelation is from the self, but from that age-long memoried self, that shapes the elaborate shell of the mollusc and the child in the womb, that teaches the birds to make their nest; and that genius is a crisis that joins that buried self for certain moments to our trivial daily mind. (W.B.Y., *Autobiographies*)

For example, the most primordial instinct you have, which goes back to one-celled life, is hunger. And the most fundamental instinct on the next level up (above the unicellular level) is death. Ontogeny recapitulates phylogeny: this is a true symbol of who you are – the sum total of all the memories of the entire race of living beings from one-celled beings on up, all contribute to who "you" are. The human part of this "you" is called the *Daimon*, which encompasses not only your present self in this lifetime, but also the sum total of all of your human selves through all of evolution.

Note that this evolution does not occur in linear time – it's all happening *now*. It's not as if you had a life in ancient Greece and then you died; then you had a life in ancient Rome and then you died, then you had a life in the Middle Ages and then you died; etc. Rather, all your past and future lives are happening right now, this minute, in an eternal now moment; and they are all interacting on one another: *Eternity is not a long time but a short time. ... Eternity is in the glitter on the beetle's wing.* Linear time does not really exist. Your memories are not records of the past (because there is no past) but rather are tendencies or instincts.

Particular memories / instincts are proper to certain individuals; but any other individual in the system, namely all sentient beings, can access them (from the Akashic Records). A given individual's instincts differ from another individual's instincts – Joe's instincts differ from Sam's. The feeling of familiarity that you pick up when running past life regressions – the sense of identity with the "you" in the regression even though he or she may be very different from who "you" are today, is just this sense of individual instinct. It is a connection or sense of solidarity you share with all the other beings who make up "you" in all your incarnations, not to mention the connection you have with all other beings in the universe. All of this instinct weighs upon the present moment. It is the goal of the practice of magic to free yourself of this ponderous weight to be able to seize each moment anew.

We use the term "true feelings" to mean your intent in the present moment – the message of your inmost heart; your innate sense of what is right and true; of who you really are and what you must do. Similarly, by the term "true purpose" we mean your intent in a given lifetime – the reason why you incarnated; the lesson you are on this earth to learn; what you must witness and bear; what you must *feel*.

Modern humans have lost almost all touch with their true purpose, which is a sense of connectedness: to the earth, to the sky, to your forbears, to your descendants. Modern life – particularly in its urban manifestation – is fragmented and disconnected. Modern society is deliberately designed to make people feel isolated and alienated, at odds with their fellows, their environment, and their own hearts. Dissatisfaction is good for the economy, which is basically all anyone cares about anymore. Everyday life is no longer imbued with a sense of being part of an ongoing process of unfoldment – it has become sterile, vacuous, filled with noise and distraction.

When most people still were farmers, although they had already lost most of the intuitive / telepathic ability they had as hunter-gatherers, they were at least still connected to the earth's love, the rhythms of the seasons, and their sense of fit place in space and time. They felt belonging. Society wasn't perfect, individuals were probably no happier per se than they are now, but they had something: an essence, a sense of *grace* if you will, that post-agricultural people have lost, and as a result of which loss they are going crazy and destroying themselves and the planet they live on. Marriage is dissolving, the family is dissolving, all sense of belonging is dissolving.

Things fall apart; the centre cannot hold; mere anarchy is loosed upon the world. The blood-dimmed tide is loosed, and everywhere the ceremony of innocence is drowned.
   (W.B.Y., *The Second Coming*)

It's not so much that modern urban life is artificial and phony, and that subsistence agriculture is somehow more elevated and ennobling (which was e.g. Mao's and Pol Pot's view). Urban dwellers could live essentially the same lifestyle they are living now without making any major changes, and still connect to the cosmic currents that would give their lives a sense of meaning and purpose. That's what the techniques in the present series of books are for – to help people make those connections. It's not a matter of what people believe or even what they do every day; rather, it's a matter of becoming aware of who and what they really are; and where they belong.

Modern humans are not at all connected to what their true life's purpose is, since modern society tries to snip every connection to that purpose. Your roots, your ancestral lineage, your home and land, your place in the cosmos – all of these things are part and parcel of what your true life purpose is. Patriotism and religious beliefs are a pale, vacuous, intellectualized substitute for what a true sense of connection really is all about – a feeling of purpose. And if you lose touch with your true life purpose, as most people in modern society have done, then you are truly lost, lost, lost.

I think of the hunter's age and that which followed immediately as a time when man's waking consciousness had not reached its present complexity and stability. There was little fear of death, sometimes men lay down and died at will, the world of the gods could be explored easily whether through some orgiastic ceremony or in the trance of the ascetic. Apparitions came and went, bringing comfort in the midst of tragedy.

People today have no idea what it was like living in earlier times, just like they have no concept of what it would be like being a Mayan Indian living a subsistence lifestyle today. But the Maya are probably happier, on average, than Americans. They don't have all those phony expectations plumping up their unhappiness, their consciousness of everything they lack – which the media and advertisers keep harping on endlessly.

It's not only urban dwellers who have lost their connection to reality. Modern farmers are almost as disassociated from nature as are city-dwellers. Modern agriculture was in a crisis when Rudolf Steiner addressed himself to this problem a century ago; and the situation has worsened considerably in the interim. At least in the early 20th century farmers were still diversifying their crops, practicing what we now call organic management as a matter of course, and observing the rhythms of the seasons. But now, with the economic pressure towards monoculture and maximum profit, farmers have turned to highly technified, chemical management; greenhouse horticulture; and rapid transport of farm products by air from one part of the world to another, which has turned agriculture into another disconnected manufacturing process. And the resulting food, particularly after processing, is so much Soylent Green: denatured chemicals lacking any germ of life. Is it any wonder why people today feel so uprooted, lost, lacking something, something, something that they just can't define? As Steiner said back then, it's because of the crap they eat.

Modern society is completely off the track, at sea, wholly disconnected from reality. Everything that people are taught is desirable and good, is utterly phony. The whole American way of life is completely phony. Even the spiritual path is marketed as a commodity in America.

My instructors certainly expect neither a 'primitive state' nor a return to barbarism as primitivism and barbarism are ordinarily understood; antithetical *revelation is an intellectual influx neither from beyond mankind nor born of a virgin, but begotten from our spirit and our history.*

Magicians are not Luddites or romantics, trying to return to some primeval paradise lost. It is not that difficult for even us modern humans to make a connection, to feel that we are part of a living process, instead of isolated cogs in a heartless machine. The universe is not a heartless machine, and human beings are not interchangeable, dispensable objects. The universe is unfolding as it should, as it says in *Desiderata*. And each individual is part of this process of unfoldment. It's a joyous process – although there are pain and suffering wrapped up in it too. "Joy" doesn't imply giddy excitement every minute. But it does imply true purpose, true self-worth and self-esteem, true meaning. When you can start to feel compassion for yourself (get off your own case) is when you start to feel compassion for others.

True purpose is what Carlos Castaneda's teacher don Juan termed the "mood of a warrior": it's what makes you feel good (not smug); satisfied (not self-satisfied). True purpose feels like fulfilling your destiny (rather than scoring little points for yourself). This is what is meant by acting on your true feelings or intent; which in this book is referred to as being *in phase*. The whole purpose of magical training – going to the trees or nature spirits daily; sitting in nature and listening to sounds – is to imbue your life with a new mood, to replace your wonted customary moods of crabbed dissatisfaction inculcated by society. Little-by-little your true feelings kick in by the practice of just relaxing out in nature with nothing on your mind. This is where your true feelings take their point of departure: just *feeling* the world around you without reacting to it or acting on it.

For example, for most of William Butler Yeats' adult life he was hopelessly in love with a selfish, treacherous woman who led him on and trashed him emotionally; and he dabbled in numerous occult groups in the hope of making some important discovery and contributing something significant to mystical knowledge. In other words, for most of his life W.B.Y. acted *out of phase* – chasing after images and fantasies of what love and occult knowledge are really all about. Finally, after thirty years of the hopeless love affair, W.B.Y. finally decided to marry someone else (who was truly worthy); and a few days later his new wife began channeling the System which would become *A Vision*. In other words, he switched then from *out of phase* to *in phase*, and began to fulfill his true purpose in this lifetime.

It is pretty common, naturally, for people to act *out of phase* and blow their true purpose. In a recapitulation I did once I saw the moment when my father blew his true purpose in this lifetime. I was about nine or ten, and my family was gathered around the supper table laughing and having fun. Suddenly a gust of wind – not an actual wind, but like a chill or a deathly feeling – blew into the room and put a pall over everyone. It was from that moment that my father gradually lost it – cut himself off from us kids and withdrew into himself. I have no idea what that gust of wind or whatever was – what caused it; but I've since seen lots of examples of people whose souls were lost or blown away. Society itself is a crusher – to stay on course, to act *in phase* in our decadent and distracting present-day society, requires the utmost sobriety and discipline. To follow your own heart and find your true purpose in today's society requires you to ignore completely what everyone around you is thinking, believing, and doing (this is actually much easier to accomplish if you have been rejected by everyone around you, as most magicians have been).

The point is that if you keep hitting up against the same stone wall over and over, then maybe it's time to change direction. True life purpose, being *in phase*, doesn't lead you to fruitlessly batter your head against the same stone wall. True life purpose leads to an open road which you can travel easily, and lets you breathe freely. It's a matter of just relaxing and letting go (which is what magical techniques are designed to help you to do).

Memory is a living process. It has no beginning and it has no end; it's unfolding without going anywhere in particular; and every being and every moment is the sum of its parts. And those parts go all the way back to the first cell that emerged from primordial ooze and began to divide, through all of evolution, to the person you are this very minute, and onward into the infinite future. This is what you are; and if you lose your sense of connection to this process, then you bob around helplessly in torment. Modern society is turning this earth into a hell world, which is why W.B.Y. said that *A Vision* was *a last act of defense against the chaos of the world*.

A true life purpose is to *feel certain feelings*. That's all. Not to accomplish anything in particular in the world: not to be successful, or a failure, or mediocre and just get by; not to become enlightened, or to be saved and go to heaven; but just to *feel*. To feel triumphant, or defeated; or impoverished, or affluent; or cruel, or victimized; or helpless, or powerful; or fearful, or brave; or lustful, or repressed; etc. etc. Each life has a feeling of its own, which is like the sum total of all the feelings felt during that life. In different probable realities and lifetimes different facets of life purpose are felt. In lives in which you take the easy way out and follow socially-approved images and expectations without asking too many questions or reflecting upon meanings, you tend to get hung up on a low level of life purpose (which W.B.Y. termed *Will*); whereas in lives and probable realities where you make great personal sacrifices for other people's sake with no thought of reward, you get a little bit higher (the three higher *Faculties*). And in the lives in which you open your heart completely, you get a whole lot higher (reach the *Beatific Vision*).

The important thing to remember is that incredibly important decisions, which influence whether your subsequent life will be joyous or miserable, exultant or crushed into the mud, are often (usually, for most people) made in thoughtless moments ... "ha ha." Life purpose can and does change in a twinkling during any given lifetime or probable reality. For example consider Viktor Frankl's life purpose at Auschwitz, described in his book *Man's Search for Meaning*, which he understood very well meant to stop dwelling upon his own suffering and serve his patients as best he could. That was Frankl's life purpose only from the point when he was sent to Auschwitz. Prior to that his life purpose might have entailed escaping from Europe and avoiding all the pain and suffering he went through subsequently. He surely had probable realities of successful escape from the particular destiny which later unfolded: any chance thought he ever had of perhaps escaping before the Nazi *Anschluss* – had he actually acted on that impulse – would have led to a probable reality in which he avoided all that pain for himself. And, in those realities, his life purpose would have been very different in terms of the amount of suffering he had to undergo to learn his lesson (to serve his true purpose in that lifetime).

Just as true life's purpose can change in a twinkling, so too can it be blown in a twinkling. I apparently blew my true purpose for this lifetime by making a decision which seemed rather innocent – even virtuous and noble – when I made it; but which led in the fullness of time to my eventual divorce. My spirit guides' comments on this are: "Your purpose in this lifetime was to unite with (your wife). THAT'S what you incarnated for. And the pressure that drove you two apart was the pressure of all your previous lives of conflict and making war on each other bearing upon this lifetime. And now that pressure has increased because of you guys' failure in this lifetime. This doesn't mean that your life is a total failure – you always start from right where you are. But in terms of what you set out to do in this lifetime, yes, you have failed and there's nothing you can do to undo the damage now." Every time I reread these words it bums me out a bit, to say the least. But regret is cheap. All that really matters is taking note of the error and soldiering on. Most people blow their true purpose – that's quite normal in our society. People who are demon-possessed invariably blow their true purpose (unless they cast out their demons).

The extent to which people don't let themselves feel feelings – the extent to which they are repressing their true feelings (as society has taught them to do) – is the extent to which they are obstructing their life purpose (what W.B.Y. termed being *out of phase* rather than *in phase*). Yet this can also be called their life purpose: "they also serve who only stand and wait." The Willy Loman's and Warren Schmidt's of the world – those who feel timid and defeated – also have a life purpose; and that purpose is no less noble or ennobling than the life purpose of a Jesus or Buddha. Sometimes it is people's life purpose to suffer unspeakable pain, or boredom and "meaninglessness". When you run past life regressions you see that most of your own lives have been like that. It's all the same – there's no such thing as a wasted life or a wasted lesson, although certainly there are wasted opportunities. In my role as a priest of the Mayan gods I've been privileged to witness many other people's life lessons, which consist mainly of blown opportunities; and needless to say I've blown many, many opportunities myself. Only when you can truly feel that you've blown your true purpose (instead of covering your ass and blaming other people; or wallowing in self-pity) can you truly MOVE ON.

Light fibers are called that because that is the thought form they most resemble – they look like fibers of living light. But they can also be described as sounds, or rhythms. Yet none of this explains their real nature, because what they are about, is time. A light fiber is a feeling and it is attached to thought forms of time which our human cognition sorts into pasts and presents and futures.

Most of the time people operate on blocked light fibers – that's why their lives seem so sterile and empty and devoid of magic. Once in a great while they let themselves feel what is going on, as when they fall in love, or a baby is born. But most of the time people won't let themselves feel that much joy because they have too much (socially inculcated) self-hatred in the way.

Thought forms congeal change; they make it frozen and immobile. Thought forms from past lives are like a cancer – cells that have gone awry. Unlike thought forms created in this lifetime (which can be seen and talked to in Active Imagination, as described in my book *Thought Forms*), past life imprints make up the very fabric of your being. You can't brush them off or shake them out, but must rather love them in – accept them. It's the ultimate rebelliousness to accept and love who you are rebelling against. It's the final loving of yourself that you can accept the worst you have ever been. Only then can there be true and real change.

You never fulfill your true purpose by being a victim. You never fulfill your true purpose by self-pity. You only fulfill your true purpose by being a hero – by going beyond the bounds of the possible. This is why so few people succeed at it. That is how to make miracles happen – not by idly wishing or praying to God to save your ass; but by taking 100% of the responsibility for and control over your destiny. Frankl says the same thing – the real saints never made it out of the concentration camp. They accepted their true purpose.

It is sometimes asked, what is the true purpose of a life of unremitting pain and suffering? What is the purpose of a life of being caught up innocently in war, massacres, genocide, disease, grinding poverty, starvation? What is the purpose of suffering catastrophic fear and pain which you have done nothing to merit? The answer is that sometimes it is just a person's purpose to suffer. As Viktor Frankl put it:

"Dostoevski said once, 'There is only one thing that I dread: not to be worthy of my sufferings.' These words frequently came to my mind after I became acquainted with those martyrs whose behavior in camp, whose suffering and death, bore witness to the fact that the last inner freedom cannot be lost. It can be said that they were worthy of their sufferings; the way they bore their suffering was a genuine inner achievement. It is this spiritual freedom – which cannot be taken away – that makes life meaningful and purposeful.

"... It did not really matter what we expected from life, but rather what life expected from us. We needed to stop asking about the meaning of life, and instead to think of ourselves as those who were being questioned by life – daily and hourly. Our answer must consist, not in talk and meditation, but in right action and in right conduct.

"... When a man finds that it is his destiny to suffer, he will have to accept his suffering as his task; his single and unique task. He will have to acknowledge the fact that even in suffering he is unique and alone in the universe. No one can relieve him of his suffering or suffer in his place. His unique opportunity lies in the way in which he bears his burden."

*   *   *   *   *

Voices of the Ancestors

If we count back 10 generations, each of us has 1024 ancestors. Go back twenty generations, or about 500 years, and each of us has more than one million. In most cultures the "self" is understood to encompass, amongst other things, the sum total of one's ancestors. We have almost no concept of this in our modern society, just as we scarcely have a concept of our selves as being part of nature rather than antagonistic interlopers in a hostile environment. And just as much of our sense of disconnectedness, aloneness in the universe, and helplessness is due to our having severed our feeling of belonging to the earth, so to is our collective loss of soul due in large part to our having severed our connection to our forebears. In our modern world spirit guides have taken the place that ancestor spirits occupied in earlier societies – they advise us, ground us, and give us a sense of being part of an ongoing process. But modern spirit guides themselves consider that they are just a stop-gap: they're here temporarily to help humanity (or any individual) get back on the right track – that is to say, a track that doesn't lead to self-destruction; and they disappear again when they are no longer needed. And they are no longer needed when humanity (or any individual) is once again capable of listening to and understanding the messages of its ancestors.

Spirits do not tell a man what is true but create such conditions, such a crisis of fate, that the man is compelled to listen to his Daimon.

Just as talking, which is a crude, narrowly-focused mode of communication, replaced telepathy (direct knowing) at the time when agriculture was invented, so too did writing and books replace "channeling" ancestors (I put the word "channeling" in quotation marks since telepathy – what we now call channeling – was so much a part of the everyday reality of pre-agricultural peoples that it was like breathing: completely taken for granted). This is what so-called "ancestor worship" is all about in traditional spiritual societies, such as the Maya invoking all of their ancestors (in addition to their deities and holy places) by name at the beginning of their ceremonies.

When agriculture was invented, demons came in and taught humans smarts – cleverer ways of doing things. And as they became smarter and more demon-like, humans gradually lost touch with the voices of their ancestors, just as they learned to stifle their own hearts' messages. But where ancestors cared about humans and their future, the demons who presently run our society care about humans only as fodder. Just as we hybridize and genetically manipulate plants and animals to make them more palatable to us, demons teach us smarts to make us more delicious to them, since what they feed upon is our anger and fear. Demons don't care whether the human race self-destructs; to them that would be a great banquet. Our ancestors do care, but we can no longer hear their voices.

I must declare that those ancestors still live and that time and space would vanish if they closed their eyes.

General George Patton, who was a firm believer in reincarnation, also had a keen sense of the Voices of his ancestors: "Men of my blood ... have ever inspired me. Should I falter, I will have disgraced my blood." Once, during World War I, "I was trembling with fear when suddenly I thought of my progenitors and seemed to see them in a cloud over the German lines looking at me. I became calm at once, and saying aloud, 'It's time for another Patton to die,' called for volunteers and went forward to what I honestly believed was certain death."

Perhaps the easiest way to channel the Voices of your Ancestors is via automatic writing. This technique is described at length in my books *Magical Living* (for channeling spirit guides) and *Thought Forms* (as part of Active Imagination for channeling conceptual thought forms); so it will merely be outlined here. Go out to the cemetery where your parents or grandparents are buried. It's best to do this on November 1st, which is the day when the souls of the dead hover nearest to earth due to millennia of rituals by certain societies focused upon this intent; also it's best to do it during a lunar planetary hour. However, these special dates and times are just a help, not a necessity. If you can't get to the place where your ancestors are buried, just take their photos out to nature and sit under a large tree. Also take a notebook and pen. Sit down and try to clear your mind by listening to sounds, or paying attention to your breath. Writing down both your questions and the replies as they come in the form of a dialogue, ask your ancestors to talk to you. For example, you might start this way:

Me: "My ancestors, could you please come and talk to me? I am really trying to be open right now, and I want to hear what you have to say to me. I am trying to understand what my true purpose in life is; won't you please come and talk to me about it. Etc. etc."

This is just an example – you should ask your ancestors to talk to you using your own words and sentiments. Keep writing, keep on coaxing, until you begin to feel an answer forming in your mind, and then write it down. Just sit there, trying to keep your mind relaxed, and jot down anything that comes to mind. What happens next is between you and your ancestors: if nothing comes to mind, that's fine too, since lots of ancestral healings are nonverbal, like a massage or the smell of a rose are nonverbal. If you repeat this exercise regularly you'll start feeling a sense of grounding and guidance in your life – you'll just "know" it.

The trick to making this technique work is to not stop writing. That's the purpose of the writing – to focus your attention on the act of writing, like when you're taking notes in a classroom, so that there's less room for doubt, hesitation, fear, etc. Keep on writing, even if you're just writing the same plea over and over again. Do make it heartfelt – not just done mechanically – and eventually you'll start getting an answer. It really is so simple and straightforward you won't believe it.

Note that when a person does automatic writing for the first time, the answers tend to come out sort of inchoate and constipated. Don't worry – just push it right on out and don't worry about whether it makes sense or not. Usually in automatic writing a few words or phrases spring into your mind at a time, a little faster than you can write them down, though sometimes you might get whole blocks or paragraphs at once. You might also see memory pictures pop up before your mind's eye, or get flashes of dream-like scenes as you write. Record all of this because it's all relevant. Something might not make sense at the moment, but it will eventually if you keep a written record of it.

If nothing comes to mind in response to your entreaties; or if all that comes to mind is gibberish; then you are blocking. Your conscious mind might say, "This isn't working. I'm not doing it right." or "There must be some trick to this!" in its effort to subvert the process. Don't fall for that ploy! Keep trying, keep on writing, even if all you get is gibberish. Only trust can open you enough to write automatically; otherwise you tangle yourself with doubt. If you find yourself blocking, try switching to your non-dominant hand. Keep on writing, and at some moment your conscious mind will relax its grip and you'll start writing automatically. Then, simply write down what your ancestors tell you, asking any questions you like along the way. You might be surprised by the answers!

*   *   *   *   *

Past Life Regressions

Running past life regressions is a good way to start making a connection to your true life's purpose – the reason you were born and the reason you keep coming back. It's so simple to learn that you can easily master the basic method in less than an hour's time; yet it is so far-reaching in its ramifications that a few months of playing around with it for an hour or so every night can completely transform your life.

Most of us New Agers believe in the reality of past lives, even though we can't actually remember them. We embrace this doctrine because it seems logical: it explains the vicissitudes of our present existence as the patterns and choices we ourselves made in other lives. The ability to actually remember past lives seems to be the possession of a fortunate few, like Edgar Cayce, who are born with mysterious psychic powers far beyond our reach. But in fact, the ability to recall past lives can be easily learned by anybody – all that is required is an open mind. And there are incalculable insights (and surprises!) that await the adventurer willing to explore these byways of his or her own subconscious.

The entry technique given here is adapted from William Swygard's excellent booklets on *Awareness Techniques*. There's no need to memorize the following instructions: either have someone read them to you (you indicate to the reader when you have accomplished each task by saying "okay"); or else record the instructions for your own use, leaving a little time for yourself to complete each task.

Choose a time when you are calm, alert, and will not be disturbed. If you are an astrologer, you can use a lunar planetary hour; however this is merely a help, not a necessity. Have a notebook and pen (or tape recorder) at hand. Remove your shoes, loosen any restrictive clothing, and lie down on your bed. Take some deep breaths, and then put your attention on your toes and relax them with a deep breath. Move up to your feet and relax them with a breath; then relax your ankles, calves, knees, thighs, arms, hands, fingers and so on up to your head.

Take a deep breath and imagine that you are extending your length by stretching your legs until you are about a yard longer than your usual height. Then return to normal size. Take another deep breath and imagine that you are extending your length by stretching your neck until you are a yard taller than your usual height. Then return. With another breath imagine that you are extending your length by stretching your legs until they touch the wall. Then return. Take another breath and imagine you are stretching your neck until your head touches the wall behind you. Then return.

Then take a deep breath and imagine yourself swelling up like a balloon to twice your volume; then release the breath and imagine returning to normal size. After you've succeeded at this, take a breath and imagine yourself inflating and filling the entire room; then return. When you can do this, take a deep breath and imagine inflating yourself until you engulf the entire house; then return. Next, take a breath and swell up until you are bigger than the house; and let yourself float upwards into the sky. Look down as you rise and imagine you are seeing the house, the neighborhood, the surrounding countryside, as if from an ascending balloon. Allow yourself to float freely up, up, until you are in the clouds far above the earth.

Then command yourself to descend lightly back to earth in another lifetime. Look down at your feet; how are you shod? Look at your clothes; what are you wearing? Look around you; what kind of place are you in? Inside, outside? If inside, what is the building like? If outside, what are the surroundings like? Are there any other people around you? Who are they? What are they doing? What time or country does it seem to be? What are you doing in the scene? Why are you there? You concern yourself with these sorts of questions until you feel you're plugged into the past life; then you just let the thing flow and take you where it will. If someone has been helping you, you can describe the scene to them as it unfolds; if you are alone you can take notes (dividing your attention between the scene and the note-taking).

When you first come down the scene will be fuzzy at first. You look at your feet, then your clothing, then your environment, to put the pieces of the picture into place. You ask questions of the regression to connect yourself to it – to make that life vivid and bring it into focus. For someone like myself (who is not especially psychic), regressions are rather murky: I can't usually make out faces clearly, nor colors unless they're very bright. You see the regression with your mind's eye, but it's more felt than seen – more like a series of emotional tableaux than a movie. You usually only hit the high points of a given life; you don't see all the day-to-day routine. It's not unlike a daydream or fantasy, except you soon realize that something other than your conscious mind is running it, and that something is your feelings. The experience will be more or less vivid depending on how much you block it. Don't judge the experience (by thinking, for example, "This isn't real – this is just my imagination!"). Just let it happen; if you want to evaluate it, wait until after it's over. This is not an exercise for your conscious mind, so tell your conscious mind to butt out and keep its judgments to itself.

When you first start to use this sort of technique you don't know how it's supposed to feel (you can't believe it could be *this easy!*), so you may have doubts about whether you are doing it correctly. Don't worry – if anything at all is unfolding before your mind's eye, you're doing it right. If there is no flow or direction (you're stopped in one scene), it means you are purposely blocking it. You'll know quite well if you're doing this. To unblock yourself at any point, just ask more questions: What time of day or season is it? What kind of building / vegetation is around you? And so on.

In running past life regressions it is useful to have a notebook or recorder in hand to jot down the past life as it occurs. Since the content of a regression is largely emotional, it tends to fade quickly from conscious memory, and it's often useful to have a record of it for future reference. It's a simple matter to divide your attention between the past life and the notebook. Once you get the hang of the entry technique, you can dispense with the going up in the sky and coming down each time.

You might want to experiment with running past lives involving people you know from this life. Try this: when you're up in the clouds ask to see a past life involving someone you love in this life. Then ask to see a past life with someone you dislike in this life. Simply give the command: "I'd like to see a past life with so-and-so" at the time you command to view a past life. The powers that be will steer you to the right place.

Also, you can ask questions during the regression, such as: "Do I know that past-life person in this lifetime?" and you'll usually get an answer, which will come as either a conscious thought or a feeling. The theory is that you have an infinite number of lives with every being on earth, not to mention other places, but some are closer to your present life than others – more connected to it in terms of lessons to be learned in this life – and these are the lives that usually pop up in regressions.

The question naturally arises as to whether these past life regressions actually are past lives, or whether the whole thing is just an exercise in imagination. These regressions are not always factually accurate portrayals of other times and places (unless you're very psychic). You can certainly interpolate anachronisms into them if you want to. Moreover a life supposedly taking place in ancient Rome often looks suspiciously like something out of a Cecil B. DeMille movie. In other words, you obviously filter these regressions through your present-day concepts.

Also it is often difficult to relate to the "you" in a regression. He or she doesn't act or react the way you would, so it's hard to accept or understand in what sense that person is you; much less that you are personally responsible for all the mischief that person is doing.

Nonetheless there is an emotional truth in regressions that argues for their being taken seriously, no matter whether they are "real" (whatever that means) or merely figments. The real touch in a past life regression is with the feelings that the "you" in the regression is experiencing. There are emotional echoes – little pings of recognition – that you will know mean something to you personally, even if you are at a loss to put them into words. For example, you often recognize the people you know from this lifetime when you encounter them in regressions by the feeling you have for them. I first learned to feel the people around me (instead of merely react to them on a thought form level) by doing past life regressions: understanding how I felt about them in past lives helped me to get a grip on how I really feel about them in this life.

We all to some extent meet again and again the same people and certainly in some cases form a kind of family of two or three or more persons who come together life after life until all passionate relations are exhausted, the child of one life the husband, wife, brother, sister of the next. Sometimes, however, a single relationship will repeat itself, turning its revolving wheel again and again.

It is the emotional content of these regressions which is of primary importance, not whether they are conceptually real (although my spirit guides assure me that they are no more nor less real than the life you are living now). Nor is it important that you intellectually resolve the "meaning" of this or that life. You just try to be aware that such-and-such a person is hurting you in this lifetime because you asked him to, to atone for what you did to him in another life; or that your stirrings towards music, say, or agriculture reflect a valid part of your being – another life in which you were a musician or a farmer; or that your irrational anger, joy, fears, and hopes are often quite rational and logical after all.

The emotional recognition in a regression is due to an actual line which connects you to the "you" in the regression. Clairvoyants see these connections as fibers of living light, but most people sense them as feelings, emotional connections. The theory is that these fibers from other lives bind us to neurotic patterns of behavior in this one – we feel a compulsion to keep reliving our mistakes until we get them right. By running past lives it becomes possible to recognize these patterns, which immediately releases a lot of the energy that's tied up in them; i.e., it loosens the fibers between that life and this one, allowing the conscious mind to decide if it wants to do something about the patterns (instead of being dominated by them unawares).

After running a life, it often helps to jot down the impressions you have of it. What was the main thrust or purpose of that life? What lessons did you learn? How did you feel about it after you died? There's no need to become morbid or obsessed about past lives – just draw your conclusions and move on. After you have run a great many past lives, you will begin to notice certain trends or feelings that keep recurring over and over. For example, during a difficult time in my marriage my guides directed me and my wife to run scores of past lives that we had together, so that we would understand how it was that we were at the place we had gotten to. It turned out that in most of our past lives together one of us had murdered the other one. Beyond that there were many other recurrent themes throughout our lives together that were repeated in this present life.

The victim must, in the Shiftings, *live the act of cruelty, not as victim but as tyrant; whereas the tyrant must by a necessity of his or her nature become the victim. ...The souls of victim and tyrant are bound together and, unless there is a redemption through the intercommunication of the living and the dead, that bond may continue life after life.*

Because our viewpoint is necessarily couched in terms of linear time, it is inconceivable to us that everyone we have met in our lives – even strangers passing on the street whom we don't even nod to – get together on some level and agree to people each other's lives. It's very much like actors in a play getting together, rehearsing, having a performance, and disbanding at the end. The agreement takes place in what we consider to be dreamless sleep.

For most people the vast majority of past lives consist either of unremitting hardship and suffering, or else of selfishness and chicanery. I, personally, have had lots of lives as a scoundrel, and it's interesting how many bells these ring for me in my present life. It can humble you a little, or at least make you realize that in your own heart there is a killer, a drunkard, or a psychopath, no matter how pious and privileged you think you are; and they're not that far beneath the surface, either.

On the other hand, you'll find lives in which you were quite admirable – courageous, loving, and wise. These lives will also directly connect to your better side in this life, and confirm your sense of purpose and direction. It's this emotional recognition which is the gist of the thing. This is your own heart speaking to you, giving you messages of truth which you usually ignore or take for granted until they're somehow pointed out to you. Past life regressions bring a lot of subconscious flotsam and jetsam up to the conscious mind, which is necessary because everything originates in the conscious mind (what W.B.Y. termed *Will*), and can only be controlled or dispelled by the conscious mind; but first the conscious mind has to be made aware of it. Running past life regressions loosens our light fibers by tuning us into other moods ("life purposes") from other lives and realities.

An Example Past Life Regression

Because listening to other people's past life regressions is not unlike sitting through a slide show of their trip to Europe, I have deliberately chosen for this example the most bizarre, outré past life I've ever run. Notice how first I plug into the feelings of that lifetime, and only when that connection is made does the story unfold.

.... An old wooden shack. It looks like Appalachia, or maybe the pine barrens of south Jersey. I think it's the pine barrens. I hate my mother. I don't know if I really hate her, i.e. her treatment of me leaves me fuming; it's very unfair. She just happens to be a bitter, bitter woman who takes it all out on me. Father is dead? At least he's not present. It's just me and her. She uses me for her whipping boy, but although I *fume*, I bite my tongue and don't cross her. It's because I understand how unhappy she is, and that she doesn't feel she has any choice except to be the way she is. I tend to forgive her as we go along.

I seem to be more sensitive, understanding, and loving in this life than in most of my other lives (I think it's just an image). For example, I can talk to plants and animals. I try to spend as much of my time as possible off in the woods talking to my friends, the plants and animals. I run naked. I have animal vision and animal sense. I can tell when there are other humans around and I avoid them. With my mother I feel I am pretending to be a human being, but that actually I'm not. My humanness is a masquerade.

Actually, I'm kind of nuts, although I do have a lot of sixth sense intuition. It is true that I'm repressing a lot of feelings to maintain this façade of equanimity. I see now [from the vantage point of my present life] that a lot of my gentleness and communing with nature is an image, an escape from her, because I won't admit to myself how much I hate her. I pretend she doesn't affect me, that I'm not really human anyway. In other words, I'm not as gentle and spiritual as I think, that's just an image of myself that I have. I think I'm superior to human beings, that I'm on a level above them, but that's just a game I'm playing (although I *can* talk to plants and animals).

Anyway, I do hate my mother more than I'll let myself cop to. I try to pretend I'm above those sorts of emotions, and that she can heap all her poison on me and it doesn't affect me at all. I'm glad I'm there for her to do that to, I understand why she's doing it, it's not her fault, etc. etc.

Except one day I pop. Something in me just snaps, and I kill her. I hit her in the face with an iron bar. There's no thought behind it: she's carrying on like she always does and I'm taking it like I always do, and then the next minute I've killed her.

Then I sort of go into a state of shock. There's no precedent for this. My world heretofore wasn't that pleasant, but at least it was pat and figured out and everything had its place; and now my mother is dead and I've killed her. I'm totally at a loss; so what I do is go on as before. I pretend she's still alive. I prop her up in her chair and serve her food at meal times; we eat together; then at bedtime I carry her to her bed and tuck her in. In the morning I get her up and brush her hair, take her to the table for breakfast, etc. Even as the months go by and she starts rotting and falling apart I carry her back and forth from the table to her bed to her easy chair.

Of course, there's a part of me that knows this is a total fiction – that part is diabolical and is happy that the bitch is dead and I can mock her every day by pretending she's alive; it's like a sarcastic side of me. But the outward part – the image part – continues to pretend that nothing has changed. This is also calculated to make whoever discovers me think I'm nuts, so I won't be held accountable for killing her.

But it is the continuation of the masquerade I adopted when she was alive: "Oh yes, mother? Anything I can do for you, mother?" It's the continuation of my "nice guy", "spiritual guy" mask: that guy wouldn't have killed his mother, so of course I didn't kill my mother. The diabolical, sarcastic part of me is actually my anchor to sanity, and the nice guy mask is actually nuts. The two of them are in sort of a battle.

Probably, if I'd lived longer, the nice guy would have won and I've have gone completely nuts for good. But eventually a bunch of cops came in and shuffled me off, and everything after that is a blur of uniforms and cells – nothing that makes any sense. I guess I retreated into insanity to be able to handle it.

They must have executed me because I'm still young when I die. I meet my mother. She has not changed one iota. She is still, in the afterlife, playing all the same games she did on earth; and she was hanging around waiting for me to rejoin her and serve her. She doesn't blame me for killing her; she just wants me to take up the same role I played for her on earth; and I do it. There in the afterlife we create a perfect replica of the life we had together on earth: the same ramshackle house, furniture, etc., with her abusing me all day long and me sneaking off to be with the plants and animals. The only difference is that in the afterlife I no longer hate her. It's as if all my images finally came true – I'm truly indifferent to how she treats me, I know she's doing what she does because she can't help it, etc. I certainly don't love her, but neither am I repressing anger at her because I don't know what else to do.

We're still at it to this day – out there in the ozone somewhere she and I are still carrying on this pine barrens life as if nothing had happened.

In running past life regressions you have a safe and powerful technique for bringing useful information up from your subconscious, to help you get to your true purpose in incarnating, and to understand and accept who you really are. This is what W.B.Y. termed being *in phase* as opposed to being *out of phase* – i.e. being in tune with your true purpose in incarnating in this lifetime, as opposed to surrendering your free choice in life in order to conform to societal fiat (socially-approved images and expectations).

* * * * *

Probable Reality Progressions

The theory of probable realities is discussed at length in my book *Thought Forms* (which information is repeated below). The fundamental idea derives from Jane Roberts' Seth books and Carlos Castaneda's don Juan books; it is also the basis of the Many Worlds Interpretation of quantum physics. The idea of probable realities, if not the term itself, has become a common theme in popular culture in recent years. For example, the novel *The French Lieutenant's Woman* and the films *The Family Man*, *Deja Vu*, and *Sliding Doors* can be considered allegories for how events happen to the same protagonist in different probable realities.

Briefly stated, the idea is that every decision you make creates a complete reality of its own which is parallel to this one, but in which you decided the other way (this is a rather gross oversimplification, but sufficient for present purposes). Gary Zukov's book *The Dancing Wu Li Masters* summarizes the theory of probable realities as follows:

"The orthodox interpretation of quantum mechanics is that only one of the possibilities contained in the wave function of an observed system actualizes, and the rest vanish. The Everett-Wheeler-Graham ["Many Worlds"] theory says that they all actualize, but in different worlds that coexist with ours!

"According to the Everett-Wheeler-Graham theory, at the moment the wave function 'collapses,' the universe splits into two worlds. ... There are two distinct editions of me. Each one of them is doing something different, and each one of them is unaware of the other. Nor will their (our) paths ever cross since the two worlds into which the original one split are forever separate branches of reality."

It might be argued that even if probable realities do exist on a level of subatomic particles, that doesn't necessarily imply that they exist for humans – at least not in any consciously accessible or meaningful way. However, this is precisely what astrology – and W.B.Y.'s System – are all about. Astrology doesn't seek to examine and measure accomplished events (although sometimes it can do this) so much as tendencies and potentials.

Probable realities are not a question of the size of the particle involved. Rather, they are a question of the nature of time itself. Time is not how we perceive it to be in our normal, waking consciousness. Although human perception and cognition make sense to us humans, the universe itself doesn't make sense in a way that humans believe.

The existence of probable realities means that even physics and chemistry are not and can never be as mechanistic as materialistic scientists would like. We astrologers and magicians must not make the mistake of the materialists, falling for their incorrect assumptions about the nature of reality (in particular that time is linear – a complete, well-ordered field). We are not unitary beings who live our lives in linear sequence, but rather infinitely ramified "waves" who can only remember one single line of personal history at a time (although our memory can be expanded to include probable realities using the technique below).

Where materialistic science sees time as linear, W.B.Y.'s System sees time as rhythmic, as an emanation consisting of birth – death – rebirth. What we see as linear time is but one way of apprehending this emanation, which is useful for certain purposes but is a terrible distortion of what time really is. We apprehend time as linear because our thinking is linear, and we are constantly thinking-thinking-thinking from the moment we wake up in the morning until the moment we go to sleep at night. Animals and human babies don't apprehend time in this fashion, and neither did ancient human hunter-gatherers. Time is not linear, but to see this directly one has to stop thinking so much.

Materialistic science measures points and intervals along a well-ordered continuum, whereas W.B.Y.'s System measures cycles upon cycles. The moment of birth can be viewed as a point along a linear continuum, as it is in materialistic science; or, conversely, it can be viewed as a stage in the unfoldment of potentialities on various levels – i.e. as the intersection of many different interpenetrating cycles, as it is in the System.

A good intuitive description of what probable realities are all about is found in the *Seth* books by Jane Roberts:

"In your daily life at any given moment of your time, you have a multitudinous choice of actions, some trivial and some of utmost importance. ... It seems to you that reality is composed of those actions that you choose to take. Those that you choose to deny are ignored. ... If you wanted to be a doctor and are now in a different profession, then in some other probable reality you are a doctor. If you have abilities that you are not using here, they are being used elsewhere. ... These probable selves, however, are a portion of your identity or soul, and if you are out of contact with them it is only because you focus upon physical events and accept them as the criteria for reality."

Practically everyone has experienced bleed-throughs from other probable realities into this one at one time or another, without realizing what they were experiencing. Wistful longings; quasi-memories or presentiments; events which produce a déjà-vu-like sense of connectedness to another "you" in a similar but different reality; are often feeling connections with other probable realities. Once when I was deeply in love with a certain person, I went to a party expecting and hoping that she would be there. While she never came physically, I could feel her presence there beside me the whole time. My guidance later explained this sensation to me as follows:

"What keeps you glued into one track or lifetime is the sense of familiarity. To break that track is to feel all your lifetimes and probable realities at once, just like you felt C.'s presence at that party in another probable reality. That's an example of how you can have two different memories of the same event: going to the party with C., and going to the same party without her."

Me: "Did the same things happen at both parties?"

"Yes. Eduardo sang at both parties, but not the same songs. What do you think, stupid? Of course different things happened at both parties. That's not the point. The point is that life consists of feelings. You can only get to those feelings directly by getting past the screen of thought forms of importance and familiarity that hide them."

The Lightning Flash is therefore the man in emotional relation to his past, made present; & in intellectual relation to his future conceived as present. It is because of this that he is an individual & not merely a type of his phase. at every moment he chooses his entire past & his entire future, though he is not conscious of his choice till on the threshold of the <Beatific Vision> (W.B.Y., *Vision Papers* vm. 3)

According to the theory of probable realities, every single desire that you have or have ever had creates unto itself an entire probable reality. Every feeling is an entire universe. Everything you desire creates an entire world in which that desire is realized – i.e., every desire creates its own future. You don't desire something for the future, or in the future; but rather the future only exists as there is a light fiber of desire reaching out to it and creating it. And your mind chooses which possible future to go with, out of all the possible futures.

Similarly with memories. Every memory is a thought form record of an entire universe (a decision you have made). You believe that you have had a linear personal history – a series of events which began at birth and led up to where you are right now – and from here you will have a linear future. And there is one "you" who has had this personal history and who is going to have this personal future.

In fact, there are infinite number of "you's" who had an infinite number of probable pasts, and there are an infinite number of "you's" who will have an infinite number of possible futures. The action of mind is to select a path going backward and forward: it selects one particular set of memories going back, and one particular set of desires going forward, out of the culture and *Zeitgeist* (i.e., thought forms) it finds at hand.

All of the thought form material that's left over – all of the "could have beens" and "might have beens" and "should have beens" – are the probable realities for a given lifetime (and are in fact consciously accessible via the technique described below). Probable realities are parallel lifetimes which branch off from this one at each point where a decision, large or small, is made. That is why you must stand by your decisions; otherwise you are draining the energy you need in this lifetime to realize your true desires off into other probable realities. Probable realities are no more nor less real than this lifetime. There are always probable realities in which you get (or got) what you want (or wanted). Mind picks which probable reality to go with from the smorgasbord of possibilities.

Unlike average people, magicians stay fluid by grasping each moment anew. They ride the moment instead of being dragged through it by thought forms. Most of us have most of our light fibers tied to the people around us, the things in our environment, our memories of the past and desires for the future, etc. Magicians have all their light fibers free to seize the moment, to act fully in the moment, not tied up in personal history and future expectations. The only reason a thing has happened is because you believe it has happened.

For example, consider a person diagnosed as having some fatal disease (e.g. AIDS). The person chooses a moment in which a doctor says to him, "You have AIDS; you're going to die", and he makes that thought form of fear into an overwhelming belief when he could as easily – after the initial fear – just laugh it off and refuse *in his heart* to believe it. But instead, he makes the thought form into an overwhelming belief by assigning tremendous importance to it, and he then carries that belief through the rest of that probable reality.

At the moment the doctor said, "You have AIDS", another probable reality branched off in which the doctor said, "You don't have AIDS". These two probable realities interact on each other: in the AIDS branch, there is a wistful longing for the non-AIDS branch; and in the non-AIDS branch, a constant fear of the AIDS branch. The wistfulness of the AIDS branch may send messages to the non-AIDS branch like: "Enjoy your health! Appreciate what you have!" And the non-AIDS branch may send messages to the AIDS branch saying, "Cheer up! Life has its bright side too!"

If at any moment the AIDS patient realized that the AIDS is just a belief he could change – only a reality that he is creating by believing it every moment – then at that instant it would collapse and the person would be cured. But this becomes harder and harder to do as the person becomes "sicker and sicker"; i.e. believes more and more in his sickness, thus making it into an overwhelming reality (of course, this is a greatly oversimplified example; what is really going on out there in the universe is far more convoluted and infinitely ramified than anything the human mind could ever conceive of).

Which probable reality you find yourself in at any given moment is largely a function of what conscious choices you are making for yourself, or else what thought forms you are letting live your life for you. Consider, for example, a desire for joy. Suppose your mind has attached to that desire the thought form of "getting a raise". Since most people have thought forms working at cross purposes, there are various probable realities in which that basic "getting a raise" thought form could be physically realized. If you truly feel in your heart that you deserve the raise because you've done a good job and you want your world to reflect your joy in accomplishment, then you'll take a probable reality branch in which you receive the raise and are joyous about it. However, if in your heart you know you don't deserve the raise but are only desiring it for your own glory, then you can either take a probable reality branch in which you get the raise and feel false joy about it, or else you don't get the raise and feel disappointed about it. In the latter two cases your true feelings are trying to steer you to true joy by making you feel shame (false joy or disappointment). Just because you block the natural action of the feeling with your thought forms doesn't mean that the feeling isn't still operative and calling all the shots; all it means is that you experience the joyous impulse as shame rather than joy.

In the above example, all three probable realities are equally "real". Which one you choose for this lifetime (this personal history) is a function of which choice of the three you decide to make for this lifetime: one choice you make by going along with your true feelings, and the other two you make by going along with your glory thought forms, at the moment when the universe pops the possibility of getting a raise up before your eyes.

But in another lifetime, to that very same light fiber of joy to which in this set of probable realities you attached the thought form of "getting a raise", you could have attached any number of other thought forms depending upon the circumstances of that life. For example, in other lifetimes that same joy fiber could mean "successfully hunting that mammoth" or "becoming emperor of Rome" or "receiving many alms"; and in each of those lives you can choose different probable realities based on whether you got what you wanted or not.

A child's anger at a deceased parent for having abandoned him; a woman's feeling of guilt for having been raped; a parent's self-recrimination for an unavoidable accident suffered by her child; are all valid feelings because those probable realities were indeed chosen in preference to happier ones. For example, the parent whose child died in an accident, who spends weeks thereafter ruminating on "If I hadn't done this ... " and "If I'd only done that ..." is actually reviewing all her decisions (branching points into other probable realities) which led up to this reality.

Some psychologists believe that it is infantile for a child to blame himself when his parents divorce; yet the child is absolutely correct: he chose that probable reality. This is what is meant by "taking responsibility for your already-made decisions" or "taking responsibility for the situation in which you find yourself" because that is what you have chosen for yourself: that is your intent – the place you have to start from. In Viktor Frankl's book about his experiences in Auschwitz, *Man's Search for Meaning*, he described the various opportunities he had to leave the concentration camp or to obtain advantages which, had he accepted any one of them, would have led to his death. And the chain of events – the miracle – which led to his ultimate survival was the decision he made at each branch point to consider the needs of his patients above his own needs.

Different probable realities are always impinging emotionally upon one another: for example, déjà vu, and inexplicable emotional reactions generally, are often bleed-throughs from other probable realities. Feelings of longing are often the beckonings of other probable realities. When you feel that you would have been better off had you married someone other than your present spouse, or had you selected some other career, you are sending and receiving messages from the realities in which the decisions went the other way. People always want to believe that the grass is greener in another probable reality; but in fact when you actually run probable reality progressions, you usually find that while in some ways the alternative probable realities may be happier than this one, they're nonetheless somehow out of joint – they don't square with who you are now, for having made the decision which put you in this one in the first place.

The probable realities which branch off from this lifetime can be viewed using the same entry method as is used for running past lives. Probable reality progressions are actually a much more interesting application of the basic regressions technique: if you have ever idly wondered how your life would have turned out if you'd done things differently, now you can find out.

To run a given probable reality branch, inflate yourself like a balloon and rise up into the air as usual in running a past life regression; but instead of willing to come down to earth in a past life, instead command to come down into the other probable reality. Or, if you have no specific probable reality in mind, you can ask to come down into a probable reality which sheds light upon your present situation in this life. You should have your notebook (or recorder) at hand to take notes and jot down your impressions as the other probable reality unfolds.

You should run probable reality branches out to the very end, even if that takes several sessions. Otherwise the tendency is to stop once you've garnered sufficient evidence that you *are* happier in that other reality, i.e., confirmed yourself in the illusion that your happiness derives from your circumstances, rather than from who you are. Take 'em out to the bitter end – you'll see that as long as you're still you, you've got the same problems no matter what reality you find yourself in.

A number of years ago I fell madly in love with a young woman who was the epitome of all my images of what I wanted in a wife. This was at a time when my marriage was in an unhappy and frustrating place; and since the other woman was also strongly attracted to me and made no attempt to conceal it, I found myself torn apart in the classic struggle of Temptation vs. Duty.

My first child was then three years old, and I couldn't justify to myself the idea of abandoning him, no matter how I felt about my wife. So I avoided the other woman, since it got to a point where I couldn't stand being in her presence – it was too painful to have to dissemble and squelch all these feelings which were screaming to be let out.

Eventually the other woman moved away. Over the next few years my marriage went downhill; my second child was born, binding me even more tightly to the marriage; and I began to spend more and more of my time in a fantasy world in which I was married to the other woman. It reached a point where most of my waking thoughts were captivated by this other probable reality in which I was blissfully happy and all my expectations were fulfilled. I hated myself for having let that opportunity slip by me, and I made various unsuccessful attempts to trace the woman.

There came a point where a crisis was reached, and my wife and I began discussing divorce. The consequences of divorce shocked both of us sufficiently to jar us into seeking some sort of rapprochement, and for the first time we actually began to work on rebuilding our marriage (that's when we started doing the past life regressions). But my heart wasn't fully in it – I was still clinging defensively to the probable reality with the other woman.

So I traced it out. Using the regression technique, I followed out the probable reality in which I ditched my wife and went with the other woman. Except for the sadness of leaving my son, it was as wonderful as I'd always thought it would be – we were deliriously in love with each other, and we had some exciting adventures together. But then, about six years into the relationship, at about the time when in this life my wife and I were talking divorce, my true love fell in love with another man.

Now the probable reality branched again. In one branch she dumped me for the other guy, and I was completely shattered. I had built my entire life around her, made her the centerpiece of my existence, and now I was left with nothing. In the other branch she chose me over the other man; but then I started having affairs, and she had more affairs, and over time we gradually drifted apart.

In the weeks after I traced out this probable reality with the other woman, I found myself thinking about her less and less; and after a month or so I stopped thinking about her altogether. The obsession which had consumed me for years just died on the vine.

Running out probable reality branches is a necessary exercise, because so many people have their energy tied up in fancies and speculations of how much better off they would have been *if only* .... And this tying down of your light fibers in other probable realities gives you fewer fibers to use successfully in this one: it drains you in both probable realities, since you're neither here nor there. You must be able to go wholeheartedly with any decision you have made, to give yourself wholeheartedly to the probable reality in which you find yourself, since this is the only reality you can work with. To succeed in this life – to follow your true purpose – you need to get back the energy you have tied up in other ones. You have to consciously make that same decision again; and running probable reality branches is an easy way to do this.

The probable reality technique can also be run off into the future. This is actually one of the most useful applications of all these regressions techniques. If you have a major decision facing you; or want to see how your future relationship with a certain person will go; use the regressions entry technique and ask to see each possible branch, and then decide which one you like better (which one feels right).

Will the human race be able to save itself in the coming century, let alone prosper? Or will it self-destruct and drag the planet down with it? There are probable realities which go either way. Which one of these you find yourself in – or place your children in – depends upon which one you choose for yourself.

You call the outer circumstances of your life – the situations and relationships in which you find yourself – for some reason; and you can also change that reason if only you don't lose sight of (feeling for) the ultimate goal. This means reaching out to probable realities in which there is joy, no matter how improbable they may seem at the moment, rather than to ones which will only reinforce your self-pity and self-hatred. Hope is the fuel that propels desire lines forward. This means faith not in ultimate success, but in ultimate self-worth.

*   *   *   *   *

Recapitulation

When the past life entry technique is applied to actual memories from this present lifetime, it is called *recapitulation*. The technique of recapitulation is very similar to other shamanistic and psychotherapeutic techniques for treating soul loss or post-traumatic stress, respectively (which are two ways of viewing the same phenomenon). For example, among the K'ekchi Maya of

Guatemala, loss of soul (*xmuhel*) is usually caused by a sudden fright which shocks the person into lassitude, illness, or muteness. The affected person must return to the spot where the fright occurred and call their name three times to bring their soul back. In some Behaviorist psychotherapies, the traumatized person visually follows the therapist's moving finger while recollecting the traumatic memory, to thereby discharge pent-up feelings attached to that memory. In other words, recapitulation in one form or another is a well-known healing technique in both shamanism and western psychotherapy.

It is the nature of waking consciousness to experience suffering, as the Buddhists say. The suffering arises from a moment-to-moment self-pinching mechanism by which you hypnotize yourself into believing in, and clinging to, the illusion of a separated self. This mechanism is the basis of your ability to focus your attention when you are awake (as compared to the wooziness and lack of continuity of dreaming); and this is what we term "importance". Importance is the feeling that you have that there is something which is more important to pay attention to than what is happening in the now moment. At the same time, importance provides you with your ability to think, since thinking pre-empts the now moment – it is concerned with either the past or the future (except for e.g. problem-solving, which does take place in the now. But how much of your moment-to-moment thinking is of the now, as opposed to dwelling in the past or future)?

Importance is a clenching up because you are suffering so much: it is a moment-to-moment decision to be unhappy, which enables you to focus your moment-to-moment attention when you are awake. It is your importance which you surrender when you go to sleep and dream, which is why dreaming is lighter, less encumbered, and usually more enjoyable than being awake. As compared to being awake, dreaming is more vivid and alive; it lacks that inexorability which makes being awake, i.e. everyday life in modern society, such a drag. Waking consciousness is by itself, by its very nature, a drag for all sentient beings since it requires constant self-pinching to stay awake (where humans stay awake by constant thinking, most animals pinch themselves awake with other thought forms such as "constant vigilance for a predator or prey").

Importance is the basis of the principle of mind – it's what mind is "made of" – and it is symbolized in astrology by the synodic cycle of Mercury in the same way that the principle of memory is symbolized by the synodic cycle of the moon. Importance is your self-consciousness: the moment-to-moment sense (or feeling) you have that you are watching yourself as you act (and commenting upon it: feeling shame over your looks or feelings, or shame over the things that you've done in the past and are hiding from other people; and at other times feeling glory in comparing yourself to other people in your fantasies of the future). Ultimately the only way of eradicating importance is through recapitulation. Only recapitulation can truly free you; enable you to lighten up and let go; and give you back your joy.

Recapitulation is far and away the most important of the three regressions techniques discussed in this book; and a serious magician will recapitulate his or her entire inventory of life memories before death (everyone recapitulates their entire inventory of life memories at the moment of death – what W.B.Y. termed *Return* or *dreaming back* and Raymond Moody termed "The Review"). You start out with the usual past life regression entry technique; but when you are up in the clouds you command to come down in a specific memory from this lifetime (or, you can go into the recapitulation just asking to be shown a memory which relates to your current life situation).

Recapitulation memories are often quite different from normal, conscious memories of the same event. Conscious memory is a highly selective faculty, especially when the memory carries an emotional charge. How many times have you been in an argument with someone, and neither of you could agree on what was said just a moment before? Well, individual conscious memory is just as prejudiced, particularly when there are years of reliving it to prove something at stake. In recapitulation, you can not only feel what you were actually feeling at that time; but you can also feel the feelings of everyone else in the scene.

Recapitulation is often more difficult than running past life regressions because you tend to block it more. After all, past lives are terra incognita, and may not even be "real". But your memories of this life are not only real, they are the sacred repository of everything you cherish and fear. To recapitulate them is to expose the webs of self-justification and self-pity which you have woven around them to the light of sober reason. Very often, after recapitulating an emotionally charged memory, you realize that your conscious memory of it is totally false: that *isn't* what really happened; that *isn't* how you actually felt at that time. Thus even a shallow recapitulation can be quite therapeutic in that it releases blocked feelings about specific memories, even if it doesn't completely free the light fibers which connect to them.

To free up the light fibers connected to a specific memory, enter the past life regressions technique requesting that memory. To make this work well your impression should be quite vivid: you should be as much or more "there" as "here". The less vivid the experience is, the more you are blocking it. To unblock yourself, just run a little bit of it at a time; i.e., don't force yourself.

Once you are back in the memory and feeling the feelings that you felt at that time, you are ready to proceed. Whenever you get to a strong emotion, take a short, sharp indrawn breath into your solar plexus, and at the same time feel that you are sucking the light fiber attached to that emotion back into your navel. If you are clairvoyant you'll actually see the fiber, but most people have to imagine that there is a light fiber there that you are pulling back into your navel, "feeling" it go in with the indrawn breath. Then, with a firm chopping motion of your hand in front of your navel, cut out the light fibers which any other people in the scene may have stuck in you. Don't worry about whether or not you are doing it right; if you're doing it in good faith, you're doing it right. Trust yourself.

You may not feel any immediate difference after recapitulating a memory; however, over the next few days you should feel lighter and more joyous in some indefinable part of your being. This is because you've made yourself younger. Pinning our light fibers down in old memories is what weakens us and makes us grow old. If you could recapitulate all your emotional memories and pull back all of those light fibers, you wouldn't grow old at all (anyway, that's what I've been told).

The theory of light fibers, briefly stated, is that you are connected to everything else in the universe by feelings. To a clairvoyant, feelings appear as fibers of living light through which energy flows back and forth. When there is an unblocked flow of energy, then you feel good – your environment has validated you, made you feel like you're worth something in the cosmic scheme of things.

But when the energy flow is blocked, either because you are refusing the energy from that fiber (for whatever reason); or because you are withholding your energy which should go through that fiber; then there are problems, frustration, suffering. Clairvoyants see these as fibers interfering with one another, and you sense them as contradictory feelings – how you *really* feel struggling against how you're *supposed to* feel (what your parents and society have taught you), with how you're supposed to feel usually winning out.

The only way to untangle these contradictory feelings is to bring them up to conscious mind, because all these hidden agendas were, at one time or another, conscious. There are no real surprises in any of this – you'll recognize all of it, because it was you who consciously decided to stick all that stuff down there in the subconscious in the first place.

When you find yourself caught up in non-fulfilling or self-defeating situations and behavior patterns, you can be sure that you, yourself, are the one who asked for it all. At some point or other you decided, for what at that time seemed good and sufficient reasons, to choose that situation or behavior pattern. You shot out a light fiber to it; perhaps created a thought form to manage it; and then put it on automatic pilot and never thought about it again. And it's been running your life ever since.

"Recapitulation reveals to us a crucial facet of our being: the fact that for an instant, just before we plunge into any act, we are capable of accurately assessing its outcome, our chances, motives and expectations. This knowledge is never to our convenience or satisfaction, so we immediately suppress it."
– Taisha Abelar, *The Sorcerers' Crossing*

The purpose of recapitulation, and all of these regressions techniques, is to free up psychological energy that is pinned down in light fibers which are no longer serving a constructive purpose. In a recapitulation you consciously return to the memory point where a crossing light fiber was activated. You look at the situation; you feel what you felt then; and you understand why you felt the way you did. You sympathize with yourself, even though in retrospect you may feel as if you were pretty stupid.

For example, people often make promises or vows during their lives, and these promises remain active long after the need for them has passed. Then they can become hang-ups. When I was about nine, I once brought an especially good report card home to my parents. I was really happy about it, and I burst into the house in the joyous expectation of receiving their hearty congratulations. This was at a time when it had seemed to me that nothing I did was good enough for them; and now I was convinced that their long-withheld approval would finally descend upon me.

I came into the room where they were talking together and ran up to them expectantly; but they resented my intrusion and wouldn't even look at the card. They said they were busy and told me to go away. I ran up to my room and cried and cried. I tore at my hair, and I wanted to tear up the report card, but I was afraid of the possible consequences of that so I just crumpled the edges a little. But I swore an oath that from then on I would never, ever do anything good or praiseworthy for them again, if that's how they were going to treat me. And, as a result, I never did as well in school as I could have; I never graduated from college as I was expected to; and I dropped out of society and never became a worldly success as they had hoped. I got my revenge – even thirty years later, when their friends at the country club would recount how much their offspring were pulling down as corporation lawyers or cardiac specialists, my parents had to hem and haw.

In retrospect, of course, the whole thing seems rather asinine – a self-defeating life born of a lousy little promise. But I didn't even realize I had made such a promise. I don't have any conscious memory of it; I first found it in recapitulation. But ever since I connected with that little boy crying on that bed, and pulled the line carrying that angry promise back into my navel, I've been more successful in life.

It's easiest to recapitulate memories (there is less tendency to block) when you are on the same physical spot where the memory occurred originally. Try this: go back to the place where you grew up, or any other place you've lived or worked in that is associated with powerful memories. Gain admittance to the building, if possible; but if it isn't, just stand outside the building looking at it. You're just somebody with a notebook looking at a house. Try to bring back some of the feelings associated with that place, and then enter the regression technique asking for a specific memory; and then pull your lines out of that place. If it was a place of pain or sadness for you, cut off the feelings of unhappiness which still cling to you with a sharp cutting motion of your hand in front of your navel. Then turn around and leave, and don't look back. If it was a place of heaviness for you, you should feel immediate relief and release. If you don't feel any difference, don't worry about it; just try again some other time. It's best to do these kinds of things during a lunar planetary hour (but this is merely a help, not a necessity).

Notice that you only pull back your light fibers from memories of this life; you don't pull light fibers out of past or probable lives. This is because those "you's" are not sufficiently "you" to justify your pulling their fibers also – it would be like interfering in someone else's life. In any case, I have been warned not to do it, so I suggest you don't do it either.

An Example Recapitulation

This example recapitulation is also rather atypical. Several years ago, during a dark period in my life, my spirit guide Sandra directed me to recapitulate memories of times in my life when I had been joyous and light. The following is a transcription of one such recapitulation:

I'm about five or six years old. I'm with a young man. He is blonde and roughly dressed. He does yard work for my mother. He has to get a load of something and he takes me along with him in his old pickup truck. We are driving along joking – I'm really happy with him. I have a huge smile on my face and I'm laughing all the way.

"Bob, you are a toad stool!"

"I am NOT a toad stool!"

Gales of laughter. He stops the car at a highway overpass and we get out.

"Come over here and look down."

I went to the edge of the overpass and looked down at the cars zipping by below.

"Which car would you like?"

"I don't know," I said. "All of 'em."

We stood looking down at the cars.

"You are a special boy." he said.

"Why?"

"Because you can fly."

"How can I fly?"

"Just stand on the overpass and jump."

So I stood on the overpass and flapped my wings and pretended to fly.

"See, I'm flying!"

"So you are. Now fly up to that cloud." He pointed at a cloud.

I flapped my arms and felt like I was really flying up and up. He was flapping his arms and flying right next to me.

"Now look down." he said

I looked down and the cars looked smaller and smaller, as if we were getting higher and higher in the sky. We frightened some birds, and I laughed at the expression on their faces as they flew off in a bustle.

We went higher and higher. You could see the cars on the highway below like little moving dots. We came up to the cloud and landed on top of it.

"Here we are." he said.

"What do we do here?" I asked.

"We're waiting for the rainbow to come out."

We waited for a long time, but no rainbow came.

"The rainbow is the bridge to the other world." he said.

"What other world?"

"The world of the angels. Look – there's one!"

I looked and saw a bright light in the sky in the distance. But no rainbow.

"No rainbow today. More's the pity. I guess we'll just have to fly back home. Come on."

He held my hand and we jumped off the cloud. We didn't fall fast, but floated down like two feathers. We landed on the road near the pickup truck. I rolled on the ground laughing, I was so happy. I was so happy that I started to cry.

Me: Was this a dream I had once?

Sandra: It was like a dream, but you were awake. The man was your friend you "invented". But he was actually as real as you, or as real as me. You went with him in his truck a lot and had lots of adventures with him. You loved each other. He was your love friend.

Memorable Events

In *The Active Side of Infinity* Carlos Castaneda describes how his teacher don Juan had him make a list of memorable events in his life as an important tool (or better said: map) for spiritual growth. By "memorable events" is meant those poignant moments when the Spirit intervened directly in your life to show you a lesson – you were a witness; and what you saw illuminated your path from then on. Only rarely are these memorable events about you (involve you as the central figure). As don Juan said, "The stories of a warrior's album are not personal ... about you as the center of everything. ... The memorable events we are after have the dark touch of the impersonal. That touch permeates them." Where what most people consider the signal events in their lives are part of what W.B.Y. termed *Will*, the true memorable events originate in *Faculties* higher than *Will* – and they imperceptibly color and shape your subsequent life in undefinable ways forevermore.

The memorable events are to be recapitulated; but the primary purpose of making the list is to provide a different touchstone – an alternative inventory of events which define who you think you are – than your usual inner dialogue of the events which plump up your self-importance (your image of yourself as triumphant or a victim). Those events – your self-exculpating memories of your moments of greatest glory and greatest shame – merely exacerbate your customary moods of self-pity. What's bringing you down in life is not stuff that's going on outside of you / happening to you; rather, the stuff that is happening to you is being drawn to you by your customary moods. The constant repetition in your mind of thought forms which arise from (and reflect back) your self-importance in an endless, squirrel-on-a-treadmill loop – the constant saga of YOU – must be replaced by a catalogue of wholly impersonal memorable events in order to dethrone the importance of your wonted customary moods of heaviness, and feel light and joyous instead.

As Castaneda put it (quoted in Armando Torres' *Encounters With the Nagual*):

"'One of the tasks of sorcerers is to constantly analyze the insinuations of the spirit. For this purpose, they often use a book of memorable events, a map of those occasions when the spirit intervened in their lives, forcing them to make decisions – voluntarily or involuntarily.' He explained that the advantage of this technique is that when we write, we detach ourselves from things and events, at least to a minimal extent, and thus we are able to focus on them with more objectivity. 'It is not about describing our daily routines, but of being attentive to the strange moments when intent is manifested. Those are magical junctures, because they produce changes and they put us face to face with the meaning of existence.' ... 'Although signs of the spirit are a personal matter, there are ordinary events that in general mark people's life, like being born, choosing a career, intertwining your destiny with another person, or having children. Also illnesses and serious accidents, because they establish a nexus with death. For those who have the fortune of finding a conduit of spirit in the shape of a *nagual*, this is, certainly, the most memorable event of all. The interventions of intent are precursors, very significant memories for a warrior, and they can be used as reference points of where to start when one is exploring episodes of personal history. It requires speed and clarity to select them and to synthesize them, extracting the personal stuff and leaving the magical essence. When properly done, they become what the new seers call abstract centers of perception, a matrix of intent, which a warrior has the duty of deciphering.'"

II. The Four Memories of the *Daimon*, or Ultimate Self of Man

*What marks upon the yielding clay? Two
   marks
Made by my feet, two by my daimon's feet
But all confused because my marks and his
Are on the selfsame spot, his toes
Where my heels fell, for he and I
Pausing a moment in our headlong flight
Face opposite ways, my future being his past.*

(W.B.Y., *Images* [unpublished])

Just as it is sometimes useful to personify death as an actual entity, so too is it convenient at times to regard dreamless sleep as an entity, which we term the *Daimon*. The *Daimon* can be likened to a one-man band whose foot on the drum beats out the monotonous rhythm Stasis, Change, Stasis, Change; whilst the tuba oompas out the same old melody Focus, Awareness, Focus, Awareness.

In W.B.Y's nomenclature, the term "*Daimon*" means something similar to what Jane Roberts referred to as "Oversoul"; and what Carlos Castaneda called the "Totality of Oneself." In brief, the *Daimon* may be thought of as the sum total of a person's human memories. That is to say, the *Daimon* consists of all of a person's memories from all of his or her past and future lives, as well as all of the probable realities from all those lives (but keep in mind that this is a gross oversimplification – what is really going on is far more intricate than anything which the human mind could possibly comprehend). The point is that a person's experience each passing moment – and the decisions made in each passing moment – are being shaped by the pressure of all this memory.

Memory is a series of judgments and such judgments imply a reference to something that is not memory; that something is the Daimon, *which contains within it, co-existing in its eternal moment, all the events of our life* [*Will*], *all the we have known of other lives* [*Mask*], *or that it can discover within itself of other* Daimons [*Creative Mind* and *Body of Fate*].

W.B.Y.'s notes on the *Daimon* read as follows:

All that can be said of the daimon *in this place can be put into a few sentences It is a self creating power none is like another, what in a man personally is unique is from the* daimon *and this* daimon *seeks to unite itself now with one now with another* daimon *but can only do so through the human mind* [n.b., what we term "thought forms"], *for without the human mind it has neither reflection nor memory. We represent it thus because it does not perceive, as does the human mind of man, object following object in a narrow stream, but all at once & because it <does not> perceive objects <as separated in time & space>, but arranged alone as it were in the order of their kinship with itself, those most akin the nearest & not as they are in time & space. Though it enters into memory & reflects in the human mind, it is not contained within that mind nor can that mind see the whole object as it is present before the* daimon. *though sometimes, it knows of it, through its own increasing excitement* [Critical Moments – i.e. spiritual epiphanies] *& sometimes it shows some perception of the* daimon *in such a way, that the perception seems miraculous by seeing it separated from the general framework of its thought, as in prevision, & clairvoyance* [& regressions techniques] *& those affinities of the personality which are so swift that different personalities seem to coexist within our mind. Though for the purposes of exposition we shall separate* daimon *& man & give to man a different symbol, they are one continuous <consciousness> perception.*

(W.B.Y., leather notebook ca. 1927*)*

Something of the *Daimonic* point of view was expressed by Delancey Kapleau in describing her post-enlightenment experience (in *Three Pillars of Zen*) as follows:

"1) The world as apprehended by the senses is the least true (in the sense of complete), the least dynamic (in the sense of the eternal movement), and the least important in a vast 'geometry of existence' of unspeakable profundity, whose rate of vibration, whose intensity and subtlety are beyond verbal description.

"2) Words are cumbersome and primitive – almost useless in trying to suggest the true multidimensional workings of an indescribably vast complex of dynamic force, to contact which one must abandon one's normal level of consciousness.

"3) The least act, such as eating or scratching an arm, is not at all simple. It is merely a visible moment in a network of causes and effects reaching forward into Unknowingness and back into an infinity of Silence, where individual consciousness cannot even enter. There is truly nothing to know, nothing that can be known.

"4) The physical world is an infinity of movement, of Time-Existence. But simultaneously it is an infinity of Silence and Voidness. Each object is thus transparent. Everything has its own special inner character, its own karma or 'life in time', but at the same time there is no place where there is emptiness; where one object does not flow into another.

"5) The least expression of weather variation, a soft rain or a gentle breeze, touches me as a – what can I say? – miracle of unmatched wonder, beauty, and goodness. There is nothing to do: just to be is a supremely total act.

"6) Looking into faces, I see something of the long chain of their past existence, and sometimes something of the future. The past ones recede behind the outer face like ever-finer tissues, yet are at the same time impregnated on it.

"7) When I am in solitude I can hear a 'song' coming forth from everything. Each and every thing has its own song; even moods, thoughts, and feelings have their finer songs. Yet beneath the variety they intermingle in one inexpressibly vast unity.

"8) I feel a love which, without object, is best called lovingness. But my old emotional reactions still coarsely interfere with the expressions of this supremely gentle and effortless lovingness.

"9) I feel a consciousness which is neither myself nor not myself, which is protecting or leading me into directions helpful to my proper growth and maturity, and propelling me away from that which is against that growth. It is like a stream into which I have flowed and, joyously, is carrying me beyond myself."

What "space and time are unreal" in Proposition 2 means is that instead of modeling so-called "reality" in terms of space and time, it can be more fruitful to view it as a tetrapolar magnet whose poles undulate:

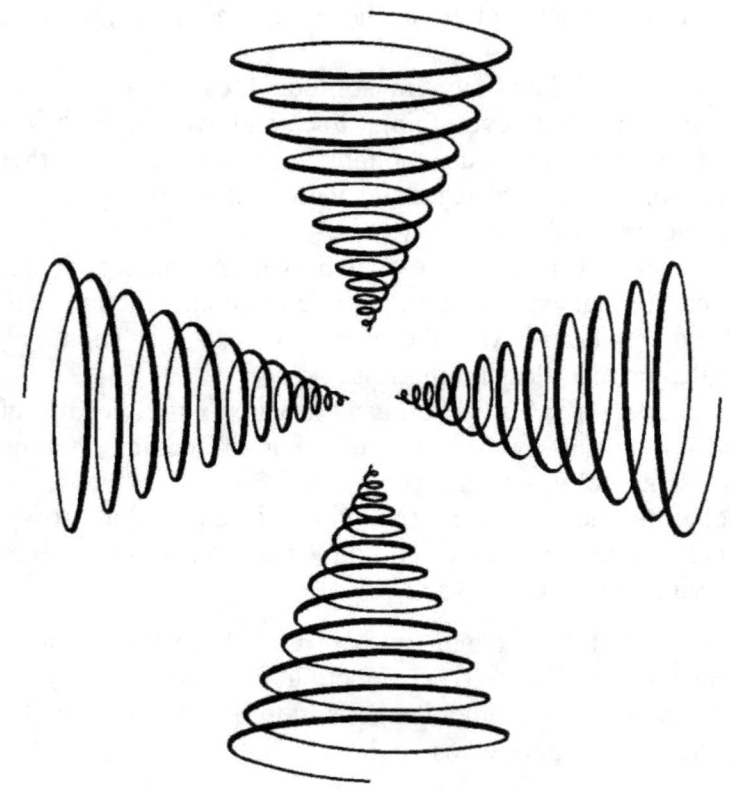

The vertical gyres (helical spirals or cones) represent dream consciousness, and the horizontal gyres represent waking consciousness. In this diagram the four gyres are shown as separated, for the sake of clarity; however they should be conceived of as interpenetrating so that the vertex of each gyre lies on the base of its opposite; moreover what is being represented is a pulsating movement from one gyre to the other so that they "turn into" each other: as one diminishes, its opposite increases. Moreover, they are portrayed here as being of finite extent, where it would be more accurate to conceive of them as infinite.

The vertical gyres represent the motion from Stasis to Change; and the horizontal gyres represent the motion from Focus to Awareness:

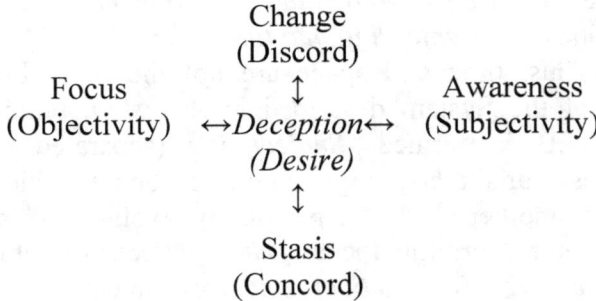

- the poles of Stasis <=> Change (increasing <=> decreasing familiarity) give rise to the subjective experience of spatial orientation (ground of the *Principles*); and

- the poles of Focus <=> Awareness (increasing <=> decreasing importance) give rise to the subjective experience of temporal orientation (ground of the *Faculties*).

The vertical axis of this system is memory (familiarity / space) and the horizontal axis is mind (importance / time); and the motive energy which keeps the whole thing pulsating is desire (death – without death keeping things separated, it all collapses into nothingness).

In this System time and space are understood to be cognitive devices or techniques by which sentient beings perceive and organize their experience, in much the same way that the senses are ways in which animals (but not plants) perceive and organize their experience; or like language and thinking are ways in which humans (but not animals) perceive and organize their experience. Time and space are not features of an external "reality" (which would have some sort of objective existence outside of the beings perceiving and organizing it): *Timeless individuality*

[Daimon] *contains archetypes of all possible existences whether of man or brute, and as it traverses its cycle of allotted lives, now one, now another, prevails. We may fail to express an archetype, or alter it by reason, but all done from nature is its unfolding into time.*

Thus, time and space are not the basic building blocks of the System described in *A Vision*, but instead what W.B.Y. termed *Subjectivity* (separatedness or awareness) and *Objectivity* (union or focus), which turn into one another. N.b.: I, personally, would reverse this nomenclature, terming focus (*primary tincture*) subjective and awareness (*antithetical tincture*) objective. It all depends on how you want to look at it.*

** That's the largesse of duality – you can always reverse the nomenclature and come to a correct conclusion. In the words of Wolfgang Köhler (in *Gestalt Psychology*), "But how can I say that a chair, for example, is an objective experience, if I must admit that it depends upon certain processes in my organism? Does not the chair become subjective on this ground? It does and it does not. At this very moment we have changed the meaning of the terms 'subjective' and 'objective.' In a preceding paragraph 'objective' denoted a characteristic which some parts of my experience, in contrast to others, possess as such (exactly as they have size, color, hardness, and so forth). But as the term 'subjective' has been used just now it refers to the genetic dependence of all experience upon my physical organism. In this latter meaning, subjectivity is not itself an experienced attribute; rather, it is a relationship which we ascribe to *all*, and therefore also to objective, experiences once we have learned to regard them as results of organic processes. Quite often the two denotations of the term are confused in the most deplorable manner, as though what is genetically subjective ought also to appear as subjective in experience. Some Introspectionists [such as Bob Makransky], for instance, seem to think that, properly speaking, the chair before me must be a subjective phenomenon, which appears before me only as a consequence of learning or interpretation. On the other hand, since no such subjective chair

W.B.Y. represents what he terms *Objectivity* and *Subjectivity* not with lines, as space and time are represented in materialistic science, but rather as two interlocking, pulsating, rotating helical spirals or *gyres*; and sometimes with interlocking cones:

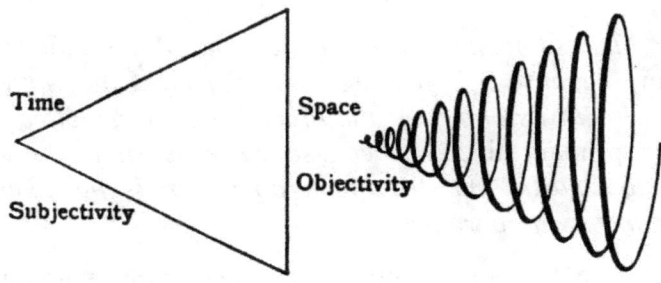

A line is a movement without extension, and so symbolical of time – subjectivity ... and a plane cutting it at right angles is symbolical of space or objectivity. Line and plane are combined in a gyre which must expand or contract according to whether mind grows in objectivity [focus] *or subjectivity* [awareness].

---

can be discovered, the Behaviorist derides the Introspectionist for dwelling in a world of imaginary ghosts. The simple truth is that some of the experiences which depend upon processes in my organism have the character of objectivity, whereas others which depend upon different processes in the same organism have the character of being subjective. This contrast has nothing to do with the genetic subjectivity of both types of experience, i.e., with the fact that both depend upon events within the organism [Oh? – B.M.]. After this, I hope, misunderstandings of the term "objective experience" will no longer be possible [!]. When I talk about a chair, I mean the chair of my everyday life and not some subjective phenomenon." [*Excusez-moi* ... so your everyday life is not a subjective phenomenon? In any event, in this discourse we will adhere to W.B.Y.'s use of the terms "subjectivity" and "objectivity"– B.M.]

Subjectivity and Objectivity are intersecting states struggling one against the other. This is also called *Deception*, or striving. We term it the principle of *Desire* (province of the planet Venus, just as memory is the province of the moon); and it is the force which keeps the Great Wheel of reincarnation turning.

The subjective cone is called that of the antithetical tincture *because it is achieved and defended by continual conflict with its opposite; the objective cone is called that of the* primary tincture *because whereas subjectivity ... tends to separate man from man, objectivity brings us back to the mass where we began.*

The movement from objective (*primary* = union) to subjective (*antithetical* = separatedness) and back again is represented in organic life by the quotidian movement from dreamless sleep through dreaming to waking, and thence to lucid dreaming; and it is represented in human life in particular by the movement from unself-consciousness (symbolized by the new moon = complete plasticity) to self-consciousness (symbolized by the full moon = complete beauty) and ultimately to selflessness (the *Beatific Vision*).

All meaning in astrological geometry derives from Pythagorean number symbolism (as Dr. Marc Edmund Jones pointed out in his lessons in *Pythagorean Astrology*). In Pythagorean number symbolism 1 is a symbol for Focus (*primary tincture*); 2 is a symbol for Awareness (*antithetical tincture*); 3 is a symbol for Stasis, and 4 is a symbol for Change. Thus, for example, the conjunction is the aspect of Focus, the opposition is the aspect of Awareness (and also two of something – e.g. two Fans or two T-Squares – are always more aware – self-conscious – than one of that thing), the trine is the aspect of Stasis (stability), and the square is the aspect of Change (conflict).

In terns of cognition, Focus and Awareness are opposites: one increases as the other decreases. For example, psychedelic drugs enhance awareness at the expense of focus. If we take a shower while tripping, we can feel (are consciously aware of) every individual drop of water as it hits our skin as a discrete event. On the other hand we can't balance a checkbook while tripping because we can't focus that much attention – there's too much going on to be able to focus. Focus is a screen of inattention, a criterion for selecting just one of the innumerable possibilities of where attention will be placed at any given moment (by "forgetting" or ignoring everything else) in order to bring just one piece of the overall picture into high relief.

Infants, perforce, experience the world as pure awareness since they are as yet incapable of focus. Adults take it completely for granted that they only see a single image with their two eyes; but they had to learn how to do this. A newborn sees two images, and it takes some time for babies to learn how to ignore (screen out) this fact, so as to blend the two images into one. Usually a baby accomplishes this tour de force at about two months of age, when he or she begins smiling at people. Before that time the infant had to integrate two, less-focused visual images of the person. And, as the photograph gazing exercise in my book *Magical Living* shows, it is not readily apparent to an infant that the two images which he or she is seeing reference the same person, inasmuch as the two images can appear quite different, and have very different feelings to them. So it takes the infant a while to realize that there is only one person there that he or she is seeing; and that there is only one witness (self) there seeing that person (rather than two).

It is in fact our socially-conditioned ability to create just one visual scene out of two which props up our sense of there being a single, unified ego (a "me" to whom things are happening) in the center of things. To newborns there are two distinct sights being seen with each eye and sounds being heard with each ear, not one; thus there are apparently two selves there, not one; and as a result newborns have little sense of possessing a self at center – of there being a singular "me" there in the midst of things.

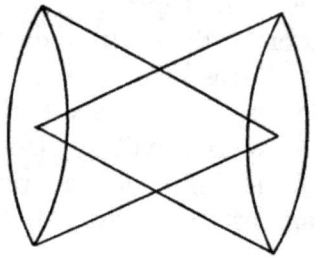 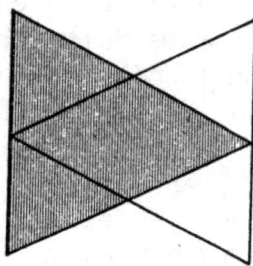

By the antithetical *cone, which is left unshaded in my diagram, we express more and more, as it broadens, our inner world of desire and imagination, whereas by the* primary, *the shaded cone, we express more and more, as it broadens, that objectivity of mind which, in the words of Murray's* Dictionary, *lays 'stress upon that which is external to the mind' or treats 'of outward things and events rather than of inward thought' or seeks ' to exhibit the actual facts, not coloured by the opinions or feelings'. The* antithetical tincture *is emotional and aesthetic whereas the* primary tincture *is reasonable and moral. Within these cones move what are called the* Four Faculties: Will *and* Mask, Creative Mind *and* Body of Fate.

CONE OF THE FOUR FACULTIES
(each level includes the ones below it)

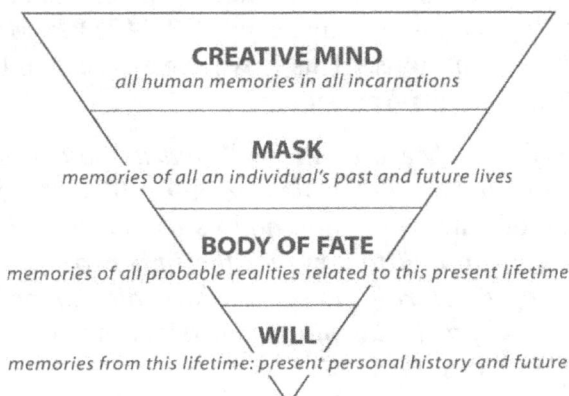

The field of activity of the *Daimon* is symbolized by the *Four Faculties*:

The stage-manager, or Daimon, *offers his actor an inherited scenario, the* Body of Fate, *and a* Mask *or role as unlike as possible to his natural ego or* Will, *and leaves him to improvise through his* Creative Mind *the dialogue and details of the plot.*

The scheme of the *Four Faculties* is an arbitrary way of describing four types of memories, four different aspects of the principle of memory:

Memories from this present lifetime (i.e. the thought forms of this present personal history) make up **WILL**. This is what we access in recapitulation.

Will together with the memories of all probable realities related to this lifetime make up **BODY OF FATE**. This is what we access in probable reality progressions.

Body of Fate together with memories of all of an individual's past and future lives make up **MASK**. This is what we access in past life regressions.

Mask together with memories of all human beings in all their incarnations make up **CREATIVE MIND**, or collective unconscious. This is what we access in listening to the Voices of our Ancestors.

Will *and* Mask *as the will and its object, or the Is and the Ought (or that which should be),* Creative Mind *and* Body of Fate *as thought and its object, or the Knower and the Known, and to say that the first two are lunar or antithetical or natural, the second two solar or primary or reasonable. A particular man is classified according to the place of* Will, *or choice.*

or in other words,

Will *and* Mask [are] *the will and its object, or the Is and the Ought (or that which should be,)* [i.e., *Will* is the lower self operating on automatic, mindless conditioning; whereas *Mask* is the person's ideal or higher self, apparent only in moments of great clarity and heroism]; Creative Mind *and* Body of Fate [are] *thought and its object, or the Knower and the Known,* [*Creative Mind* and *Body of Fate* refer to how the person relates to other people – *Creative Mind* is the person's social conditioning and also ancestral karma derived from his or her race, tribe, clan, and family – the taken-for-granted cultural assumptions which shape the person's thinking and sense of place in the world; whereas *Body of Fate* indicates how the person adapts to and fits him or herself into the everyday social milieu] *and to say that the first two are lunar or antithetical or natural, the second two solar or primary or reasonable* [the first two – *Will* and *Mask* – are individualized, particular to the person – the "natural man"; whereas the second two – *Creative Mind* and *Body of Fate* – are shaped by other people – the culture or immediate social context in which the individual finds him or herself "being reasonable" by playing the rules of the game]. *A particular man is classified according to the place of* Will, *or choice*. [*Will* is what we mean by character and it can be classified according to the phase of the moon which obtained at the moment of the person's birth].

By the word "memories" here is meant memory traces: moods or predispositions or predilections – or better said, grooves. These are coded in our very molecules. Imprints from other lives and realities exist in every cell, nay, in every molecule of our bodies. Geneticists are only now beginning to even scratch the surface of all the coding contained in a single cell – how far away they are from decoding the molecules! Materialistic scientists think that all molecules are the same – but in fact, there are no two water molecules alike – they are all as different and individual as human beings are, although still all H_2O. Our physical bodies really are a microcosm: they contain not only all the memories of this lifetime imprinted on every cell in our bodies, but all the memories of other lifetimes. What we call our memories are merely certain feelings (light fibers) which we associate with events (thought forms). Our bodies are made up of infinite imprints, of which we are consciously aware of very few.

The *Four Faculties* symbolize four levels of motivation in everyday life – four levels from which a person may act in making everyday decisions. Decisions made in one lifetime affect all lifetimes. Every decision impinges on the totality; and the totality impinges on every decision. Every decision ever made affects and is affected by an infinitude of lifetimes in an eternal Now moment: *All things are present as an eternal instant to our* Daimon ... *but that instant is of necessity unintelligible to all bound to the antimonies* [Faculties].

When not affected by the other Faculties [Will] *has neither emotion, morality, nor intellectual interest, but knows how things are done, how windows open and shut, how roads are crossed, everything that we call utility. It seeks its own continuance.*

Body of Fate, *the series of events forced upon him from without, is shaped out of the* Daimon*'s memory of the events of his past incarnations; his* Mask *or object of desire or idea of the good, out of its memory of the moments of exaltation in his past lives; his* Will *or normal ego out of its memory of all the events of his present life, whether consciously remembered or not; his* Creative Mind *from its memory of ideas – or universals – displayed by actual men in past lives, or their spirits between lives.*

Will is the socially-conditioned person who is awakened by the alarm clock and goes to the bathroom and showers and dresses and has breakfast and goes to work etc. etc. every day: *when Will acts alone all is abstract utility, economics, a mechanism to prolong existence.* Will is the robot which is wholly governed by routines and knee-jerk responses; which has given up personal feelings and choices to do what is expected by society and to submit to the daily grind. *Will* is the *Daimon*'s level of social conditioning: the "good citizen" who will go to heaven when he or she dies. It's both our "goodness" or our "phoniness", depending on how you want to look at it.

Naturally, most people live their lives almost entirely on a level of *Will* – they have sold out their true hearts' desires, and they are completely obsessed with hiding shame from other people and seeking glory in their eyes. In most people's lives the higher *Faculties* only come into play every once in a while; and usually only for a brief instant. Most people miss these poignant, *Critical Moments* completely – they just brush past them because they are in a hurry; or overlook them because they are completely focused upon their mindless routines and expectations; or turn aside from them in fear. Unfortunately the REAL decisions – the major branching points which determine how things will go in the person's life from then on – are made in these poignant moments. Thus, most people's lives are a catalogue of blown opportunities which they don't even realize consciously that they've blown (this is why recapitulation is such an eye-opener; you get to see all your screw-ups and how you have nobody to blame for them but little old you).

The 28 lunar phase types in the astrological horoscope refer specifically to *Will*: the socialized person, the one who has asked no questions but has bought into society's ready-made solutions willy-nilly. Your lunar phase shows where the world makes way for YOU. *Will* is the decision-making level of everyday life, the now moment (symbolized by the cone vertex in the figure); but it is being impacted upon by the higher *Faculties*. When *in phase*, *Will* is true feelings, listening to what your heart is saying, and acting on intent rather than social conditioning. This means putting *Will* – moment-to-moment decision – at the service of the higher *Faculties*; putting yourself in a position to be alert to, and to grab, those cubic centimeters of chance when they happen (this is the purpose of magical training).

The difference between *Will out of phase* and *in phase* is the difference between intention and intent: intention consists of words and concepts, whereas intent is feelings. Intention is image, phoniness, denial; whereas intent addresses what is really going on. When *Will* is *out of phase* it manifests its lunar phase type in the most superficial, game-playing manner possible; i.e. it is a description of the person's intention – the role they play to impress the gallery and applaud themselves (or weep in self-pity). Whereas when *Will* is *in phase*, the lunar phase type describes the person's intent – what they are really commanding of the Spirit.

When *out of phase, Will* manifests through a conviction of rectitude and taking umbrage; hence it is completely self-centered and self-important. Usually, decisions made on the level of *Will* do not take into account other people's viewpoints; or much sense of responsibility for ultimate consequences. *Out of phase, Will* is animated principally by hiding shame (slinking from an embarrassing past) and seeking personal glory (striving for a fantasized future).

Body of Fate is the part of the *Daimon* which gazes outside the classroom window on a spring day – it's the person's wistful longings, ideals, and romance; his or her daydreams and fantasies. It is on a level of *Body of Fate* that we connect to others – *the visible world is the sum of the* Bodies of Fate *of all living things* – whereas on a level of *Will* other people are just there to serve or impede the purposes of the lower self. *Body of Fate* relates to other people in both negative (expectations) and positive (affection and unselfishness) ways: it's the level of approval and approbation, of what we see when we primp ourselves in front of the mirror; of our imagined reflection in the eyes of other people; the internal representation of *the physical and mental environment, the changing human body, the stream of Phenomena as this affects a particular individual, all that is forced upon us from without, Time as it affects sensation.*

Body of Fate refers to openness to new experience, willingness to take into consideration hunches and intuitive guidance – echoes from other probable realities – and also other people's points of view. When *Body of Fate* predominates over *Will* people are willing to take risks and to fly with their impulses; and also to take other people's feelings into account.

Body of Fate is the mood of a particular lifetime in all its probable realities. It's the level of our empowerment in our own right, apart from what other people think about us. The more we let our choices be made for us by others, the more our *Will* dominates our *Body of Fate*. The more we follow our own hearts, the more our *Body of Fate* – or sense of individuality and concomitant respect for the individuality of other people – will dominate our *Will*. When we act from our *Body of Fate* level is when we are the most daring, resourceful, intuitive, and romantic.

When we act from our *Will* level, we take everything that happens to us very personally – as a personal triumph or affront. On a *Body of Fate* level, by contrast, we take note of our triumphs (of what has worked) instead of vaunting them; and we try to trouble-shoot our defeats instead of exculpating ourselves. We analyze objectively where we went wrong; and we learn from our mistakes (instead of repeating them endlessly, as we do when acting from our *Will* level). We mentally inquire into the meanings of things, rather than react with the mindless, knee-jerk thought forms we picked up from our parents and society (as we do when acting from our *Will* level). As a result, when we act from our *Body of Fate* level, we create opportunities for ourselves in the future – we create probable realities which will bring us our true heart's desire (rather than trap ourselves in an endless loop of self-pity thought forms, which is what the *Will* level is all about).

The *Body of Fate* is what is shown by the astrological horoscope: the horoscope reveals the *Daimon*'s highest (and lowest) potentials in a given lifetime. Attempts to use the natal horoscope to describe *Will* – the precise sequence of thought form decisions which make up our personal history in this present lifetime – often lead to incorrect predictions. The birth horoscope of the *Daimon* is valid for all of his or her probable realities rather than for any particular one of them. The birth horoscope shows tendencies, propensities, possibilities; but not facts (although sometimes these can be intuited by a psychic astrologer by directly accessing this information in the Akashic Records). All probable realities for a particular lifetime start from the same birth moment: they are all variations on a theme begun at the same moment in time. Both *Will* and *Body of Fate* begin from this same birth moment (although they have different "times" or scenarios of death. Physical death can occur at any instant; and there are always probable realities in which you die right NOW!). In contrast to both *Will* and *Body of Fate*, *Mask* has neither beginning nor end, but is deathless. It's the *Daimon*'s level of eternality.

Mask is our sense of personal significance: whatever dreams, hopes, ambitions, and duties we hold in our inmost heart of hearts. Where *Body of Fate* operates on a level of mind (thinking things through), *Mask* operates more on a level of feeling (intuition or direct knowing). *Mask* includes our dedication, competence, and responsibility, which we give voluntarily out of our own heartfelt sense of connectedness and obligation to nature and for the well-being of future generations. *Mask* is not a level of fantasies but of purpose: it seeks to understand "what is worth living for and what is worth dying for" – *the image of what we wish to become, or of that to which we give our reverence.* This is a weightier part of the *Daimon* than *Will* or *Body of Fate*. *Mask* refers to a morality, an economy, a sense not so much of social responsibility (*Creative Mind*) as of responsibility to truth, to our own heart's *object of desire or idea of the good*. *Mask* is what leads people to stand up for what they know is right in the face of certain rejection or death. Where *Will* is what we have termed "lower self", *Mask* is "higher self"; and *Body of Fate* is like an intermediary between these two. *Mask* is the ultimate individualized part of the *Daimon* (memory above this level

– *Creative Mind* – is no longer individualized but shared amongst all humans). *Mask* is what we discover when we run a lot of past life regressions and come to know the feel of who "we" are in our totality; of what we keep coming back in human form to accomplish; the overall mood which informs the totality of our past and future lives.

Among subjective men (in all those, that is, who must spin a web out of their own bowels) the victory is an intellectual daily re-creation of all that exterior fate snatches away, and so that fate's antithesis; while what I have called 'the Mask' is an emotional antithesis to all that comes out of their internal nature. We begin to live when we have conceived life as tragedy [or comedy]."

(W.B.Y., *Autobiographies*)

Mask is our individual ideals, talents, etc. All that we are capable of from all of our possible lifetimes: all the peaks and valleys; not just exalted moments, but also moments of greatest depravity, suffering, etc. When we act from our *Mask* level is when we feel the most centered, self-certain, and competent. It is our sense of craftsmanship and artistry; our sense of fitness and correctness – of doing a job well for its own sake. In other words, we operate from our *Mask* level when we act with no thought of personal reward.

When we act from our *Mask* level, we intuit that everything which happens to us is a lesson, and has an ultimate purpose: we reach for understanding rather than personal advantage (as we do on our *Will* and *B.F.* levels). Because our *Mask* level – in contrast to our *Will* and *Body of Fate* levels – transcends individual lifetimes, we operate from our *Mask* level when we act with no fear of death because we know that there is something more important happening than our individual death; e.g. the cornfield at Antietam. Our *Mask* level is our touch with the eternal: when we act from this level, we are ultimately selfless and courageous. The *Mask* level is our level of irony; of seeking meaning and ultimate self-acceptance (in contrast to primarily seeking security or applause, which is the motivating engine of the *Will* and *Body of Fate* levels).

Creative Mind is the part of the *Daimon* which is capable of awe and wonder. It is the most humble and self-effacing aspect of our *Daimon*: our feeling for the sacred and holy, whether we consider this a matter of religious devotion or philosophical belief. *Creative Mind* is what we have termed the Voices of the Ancestors – our role in the panorama of human evolution and history. *Creative Mind* has nothing to do with us as individuals, but has everything to do with our true purpose in incarnating on this earth at this time; *The* Creative Mind *contains all the universals.* It is – as *Desiderata* put it – our right to be here. It is our feeling of connection to an ongoing process that unites us to our basic humanity (whatever that means to us). *Creative Mind* is our sense of solidarity with the human race: *All* Daimons *were of course one on a final analysis, & yet they were each unique & each perfect.* (W.B.Y. leather notebook ca. 1927). Charlie Chaplin's humor is a good example of *Creative Mind* at work: it is universal amongst all humans (cutting across all cultures, equally funny for Eskimos or Chinese or Samoans; and just as hilarious now – a century after it was created – as it was then; and likely to be just as funny a century or a millennium from now).

Although we modern humans have almost completely lost our ability to communicate with each other on a *Creative Mind* level, this was in fact the main wavelength of communication of ancient humans, facilitated by the Voices of the Ancestors. In other words, the *Four Faculties* are also "levels" or "wavelengths" of communication between individuals (and between individuals and spirits). For example, the *Body of Fate* level is the one on which lovers and would-be lovers signal to one another; it's also the level of children's (and improvisational actors') communications. Although we modern humans have almost lost our ability to communicate with each other on a *Creative Mind* level, in fact this was the main level of communication of ancient humans – and the corresponding *C.M.* level for each animal species is the wavelength upon which animals communicate with each other.

Geneticists believe that e.g. inherited physical or psychological disorders can (or will someday) be described in genetic terms; however, that is but one point of view. Magicians hold that this materialistic viewpoint is indeed one way of approaching / looking at this phenomenon; but while these conditions do indeed derive from ancestors, it is more as a karmic condition than anything which can be described in terms of molecules and equations; and this karmic condition is what W.B.Y. termed *Creative Mind*.

Creative Mind is like a wind that blows across the earth and orients all people this way or that. It's like the mood of the times – the *Zeitgeist* – the unfolding of human experience as directed by the spirits of our ancestors; and also each individual's personal adaptation to this *Gestalt*. It is precisely because our society has lost its ability to listen to the Voices of the Ancestors that it no longer cares about future generations or our mother, the earth; and is giddily destroying both in its insatiable greed and stupidity. When we act from the level of our *Creative Mind* we feel obligated to put something back for the good of the planet or other people. We understand that it's not about us; not at all.

Will *and* Mask ... *are lunar or* antithetical *or natural*, [i.e. descriptive of the individual] ... Creative Mind *and* Body of Fate ... *are solar or* primary *or reasonable* [i.e. descriptive of the individual's relations with others].

The point is that our moment-to-moment decisions in any lifetime are being made on one or the other of these four levels. For most people, 99.99% of decisions are made on the basis of *Will*, or socially-conditioned actions and reactions. But every now and then everyone has affecting moments – moments of consciousness or conscience or conscientiousness – when we sense that probable realities are branching off this way or that; or we can feel echoes from other lifetimes and realities; or we obey voices from deep inside us. At these poignant moments – what W.B.Y. termed *Critical* or *Initiatory Moments* or "*IM*'s" – we feel connected to something deeper than our usual, everyday routines and habits; and that something is our true purpose in this lifetime:

All IM's reveal weakness in the self (in subjective man in its realisation of the objective world). They give a shock to the belief in self & bring the man under the influence of an image, they increase 'lure' to cure inaction & abstract dreaming. ... All IM's change the mind. The 'lure' is caused by an external event (P.F.) [Body of Fate – spontaneous impulse] *& this is produced by the* daimon *& the IM forces up into conscious some emotion that compels realisation of its contrary ... The* daimon *drives us from the self made prison.* (W.B.Y., *Vision Papers* vm. 3)

The *Four Faculties* are four stages in the evolution of human consciousness. Ancient humans were principally acting on a level of *Creative Mind*. Ancient people were far less individuated than we modern humans are. The descent into individuation (what we term "separatedness") through *Mask, Body of Fate*, and finally *Will* is a process of increasing isolation, disconnectedness, and alienation (this is what the first half of the cycle of 28 lunar phases – from

Phase 1 to Phase 15 – describes). The descent from a sense of belonging to something greater than one's lower self (Objective or *Primary tincture*), towards individuation and concomitant isolation / imprisonment / anguish within a separated lower self (Subjective or *Antithetical tincture*); and the evolution back again; are rather similar to William Blake's innocence – experience – super-innocence: *After Phase 22 and before Phase 1 there is a struggle to accept the fate-imposed unity, from Phase 1 to Phase 8 to escape it.* This cycle is the theme of the progressive symbolism of the 28 lunar phases; and at the same time, it can also be construed as an allegory for the progression from infancy to adulthood and back again (as old people lose their grip / interest in worldly achievement and seek something meaningful – or an anodyne – instead).

Life purpose – which is what is shown by the symbolism of the 28 phases of the moon, i.e., the struggle towards (from Phase 1 to Phase 15) and back (from Phase 15 to Phase 1) from individuation-separatedness-isolation – is ultimately forged (or lost) on the level of *Will*. That's the focus, the level on which each individual, moment-to-moment, day-to-day decision is made. That's why *Will* is placed at the apex of the inverted cone diagram – it represents the now moment. It's the fulcrum point, the place of conscious awareness in most beings. *Will* is everyday life – what most people consider "reality".

The point of magical training, such as listening to the Voices of the Ancestors (*Creative Mind*); running past lives (*Mask*), probable realities (*Body of Fate*), and recapitulation (*Will*), is to expand our conscious awareness to include our three higher *Faculties* by connecting us to the *feelings* of these thought forms, to help us recognize and respond from deeper levels of motivation than the obsessively hypnotizing thought form circus of the *Will* level.

Recapitulation is the technique used to dethrone the hypnotic power of the *Will* level. Most people are consciously aware in their daily lives only of *Will*: they make their daily choices based wholly upon the thought forms of a particular life history (their social training and adaptation to same – what decisions have worked in the past and thus make them feel the most secure, no matter how self-defeating – when viewed objectively – those decisions may be). Most people don't understand that thought forms – the things which happen to them – are beside the point, and actually don't matter in the least. Events are merely symbols for feelings. If we can feel the feelings directly then we can activate our higher *Faculties* in the now moment. When the higher *Faculties* can be brought to bear on the now moment, then it is possible to make more intelligent decisions in the now moment than can be made using the *Faculty* of *Will* alone. *Will* is a definition of self which involves very little reflection or intelligence – it's a level of knee-jerk reactivity.

Actually, each *Faculty* – each level – is a more and more expanded view of the now moment. The now moment is a *feeling* – that's all it is. And that feeling is the product of infinite interactions on infinite levels. Just as on a level of quotidian life we arbitrarily divide our consciousness into three parts – waking, dreaming, and dreamless sleep – so too on a more encompassing level of our being we divide our consciousness into four parts: personal life history, sum total of probable realities for a lifetime, sum total of past and future lives, and sum total of human experience.

This is all merely a manner of speaking, of making sense out of the senseless. There aren't any *"Faculties"* out there in the real world, because there isn't any "real world" – this is just a way of speaking about the unspeakable, of dividing chaos into four arbitrary categories.

Nor are there really three levels of quotidian consciousness; it can't be divided up as neatly as we are accustomed to thinking. We are accustomed to believing that there is a big difference between waking and dreaming, but from a light fiber point of view – i.e. seen from the point of view of the feelings involved – we are only really awake when we are thinking. If we are not thinking, we are actually dreaming, whether our bodies are nominally awake or not.

The point is that there are no hard and fast division lines between waking, dreaming, and dreamless sleep: they shade into one another. It's merely our prejudice that seems to keep them distinct – our prejudice to believe that what we experience when we are awake is "real" (i.e., important); and what we experience when we are dreaming is "unreal". And it is also just our prejudice which screens from our conscious awareness the three higher *Faculties* impinging upon our everyday, humdrum existence (except now and again during *Initiatory Moments*).

As we are able to activate our higher *Faculties* in our quotidian lives more and more – which means feeling the underlying feelings of everyday life instead of reacting to the thought form events (as society has taught us to do) – then our daily life becomes more dreamlike and ineffable. Our belief that there is such a thing as an outside reality impinging upon an abiding "ME" is what's unreal – it's a distortion or obfuscation of the feelings which we are actually feeling (and which are calling up that "reality").

What separates the *Four Faculties* is forgetfulness or disconnectedness. Forgetfulness (and with it, focus and control) increases as the descent is made down the cone from its base to its apex, from *Creative Mind* to *Will*:

Will forgets everything but this immediate, conscious line of personal history;

Body of Fate forgets everything but this particular incarnation (in its manifold variations);

Mask forgets everything but the individual self.

Creative Mind is what some have called *Gestalt* or Collective Unconscious – all the racial memories shared with other humans, our common sense, which we can draw upon simply by virtue of our being human. Note that in this System we are not interested in superhuman memories – e.g. *Anima* and *Animus*, which all animals share; nor e.g. primate – mammal – vertebrate – animal – multicellular – unicellular memories; but only thought forms which all humans share. That is the *Daimon* – the human part of the Akashic Records.

Mask is our past and future lives, *Body of Fate* is our probable realities, and *Will* is our particular personal history. The point is that all four of these different types of memory interact on each other. All of these types of memory bear upon the present moment and help to create it. Different types of people specialize in one or another combination of these *Four Faculties*, which are symbolized by the phase of the moon at the moment they were born.

Just as the division between waking, dreaming, and dreamless sleep is not as distinct as we usually imagine, neither is the division between the *Faculties* as hard and fast as shown above. For example, the difference between probable realities in this lifetime (*BF*) and other lifetimes (*Mask*) is not as distinct as we may think. The same opportunities / relationships appear in life after life, offering similar choices (in slightly different guises). Master magicians lose their sense of separation between this lifetime (*Will*), other probable realities (*BF*), other lifetimes (*Mask*), and other people (*CM*). This is because they can feel the light fibers directly (the light fibers to which these particular thought forms are attached). They can feel those feelings directly, so they don't get hung up in the individual thought forms by reacting to them with their lower selves – by taking personally the things that happen to them rather than just accepting them detachedly.

Grabbing onto a particular thought form is what keeps us centered in a particular moment of time. To plunge into time is to let go of all sense of control – to feel as though we are hurtling through a void every moment in which nothing is real (important) or familiar; yet without losing our marbles about it.

Our mind – our sense of order and stability – and our sense of the flow of time arise together. This is a symbolic view of what our waking consciousness does: it imposes a flow of linear temporality on ineffable feeling in order to make some sort of sense out of the dream – to make it seem "real" – just as dream consciousness imposes an orientation in space on unbounded chaos in order to make it seem familiar. But things making sense (being important), or seeming familiar, are not innate features of the universe – they're a blip. Things *don't* make sense; and *nothing* is ever the same. Things making sense or seeming familiar – reified as time and space – are a matter of *Will* alone.

So, if we are going to act from our three higher *Faculties*, we have to come to a point in our daily lives in which we don't care so much about whether or not things make any sense – whether or not there is any rhyme or reason for anything. We have to feel comfortable feeling disoriented – not worry so much whether things are under control or not. We have to let go and relax, even in the midst of a maelstrom (which is what everyday life becomes like once we lose the self-pity which keeps our *Will* level glued together; and what everyday life will be like when society collapses and the earth turns against us humans). We have to cultivate intuition and intent in place of beliefs and blind obedience to what we have been taught. We must act fearlessly and faithfully, and find our own means of tuning out the incessant yada-yada static emanating from society which traps us on our *Will* level. To enter a state of timelessness we have to make a conscious effort to slow ourselves down on all fronts in our daily lives, to release the obsessive fixation of the concerns of everyday society. This will be especially necessary when everyday society is collapsing and everything is spinning out of control (dissolving back into the dream willy-nilly).

When we activate our higher *Faculties*, we feel that our daily lives are more or less okay as is; that things are tolerable; and that they are unfolding as they should at this particular moment; moreover, there's nothing we can do about anything anyway. When we act *in phase*, we feel that we can handle the things which happen to us without pother; that life does indeed have a purpose because we can feel that purpose from moment-to-moment. In other words, we can easily recognize when we are following our true life's purpose by how skillfully or unskillfully we deal with our everyday lives and relationships – by how much attention we pay to something other than our own petty concerns and expectations (comfort and security).

What we have been conditioned to consider the passage of "time" is actually not a linear process at all, but rather an interplay between these four levels of memory. Giving one or another level precedence, or importance, is what we consider the movement of time; but it has nothing to do with sequence, as we suppose. Rather, it has to do with seek – once. As long as something is being sought, as long as there is striving, then there will be a movement of attention which we perceive as time – entrapment in one furrow of attention. When striving ceases, so too does linear "time".

This is symbolized in *A Vision* by the interplay of the *Faculties*: *Will* and *Mask* are considered to be *antithetical* since they are specific instances of the general *primary Body of Fate* and *Creative Mind*, respectively. *The first two are lunar or* antithetical *or natural, the second two* solar *or* primary *or reasonable. ... The* Will *has a natural desire for the* Mask *and the* Creative Mind *a natural perception of the* Body of Fate; *in one the dog bays at the Moon, in the other the eagle stares on the Sun by natural right.*

That is to say, a person's present history and future (*Will*) is but one probable reality branch off of this lifetime (*Body of Fate*); and a person's cycle of incarnations (*Mask*) is but one individual's experience of the totality all human incarnations (*Creative Mind*). Because *Mask* is a generalization of *Will* (in the sense that both relate to a particular individual), *Will* and *Mask* are considered to be contrasts or opposites: *describe* Will *and* Mask *as the will and its object, or the Is and the Ought (or that which should be).* Similarly, *Creative Mind* is a generalization of *Body of Fate* (in the sense that both relate to the individual's relations with the people who surround him or her); thus *Creative Mind* and *Body of Fate* are considered to be contrasts or opposites: *thought and its object, or the Knower and the Known.*

The other pairings – *Will* with *Creative Mind*, and *Mask* with *Body of Fate*, are considered to be discords (since in each pair the first is *antithetical* and the second *primary*). Thus it is said that *in* primary *phases the* Mask *and* Will *are enforced, the* Creative Mind *and* Body of Fate *free. In* antithetical *phases the* Creative Mind *and* Body of Fate *are enforced and the* Mask *and* Will *free.* To summarize W.B.Y.'s System (very) briefly: as a person goes about his or her *Will*ful way, he or she is being tugged this way and that by the call of other probable realities, incarnations, and the human *Gestalt*. Only at Phases 1 and 15 is there a knife point of equilibrium (stasis), and instantaneous flash (*Initiatory Moment*) of recognition (termed "*interchange of the tinctures*").

Will is the thought form material we have readily at hand. *Body of Fate* is all our "could be's" and "could have beens". *Mask* is all our dreams and hopes. *Creative Mind* is all the ideals and spiritual possibilities available to humans. And in any given moment, all four of these levels are interacting, manifesting, driving us relentlessly forward through "time". Who "we" are is a conjunction of tendencies (memories, habits) in a moment of time; that is to say, an ongoing process. And that's what time is: a conjunction of memories bearing upon a specific moment which we consider to be "ME".

However, human life is part and parcel of thought forms, and thus this distinction of four types of thought forms, which correspond to four types of memories, is a useful way of categorizing the strivings of different people. It is *striving* which keeps the Great Wheel of death and rebirth turning; when striving ceases, human life ends (and divine life – the *Beatific Vision* – begins). The point is that struggle is what keeps life going, and when struggle ceases, so does all distinction between e.g. this lifetime and some other, or this person and that one. All struggle is a struggle towards separatedness (which W.B.Y. terms the *Antithetical tincture*): when struggle ceases, so too does separatedness – i.e. individual consciousness. This is what the 28 phases of the moon show: the cycle of development of the emergence, the growth, and the surrender of separatedness.

IV. The Phases of the Moon

The Lunar Rhythm

All early calendars were lunar, and have now been replaced by a solar calendar. This is highly symbolic. The fact is that the human race in its infancy was matriarchal – the female principle always precedes the male. When the human race invented agriculture and began to stabilize waking consciousness, it also passed its baton to the males. Heretofore the males hadn't done much of the work of keeping society glued together. What little "thinking" was being done was being done by the women. The culture – in the sense of religion, science, technology, crafts, literature, etc. – was in the hands of the women, who handed it all over to the men at the time agriculture was invented.

The calendar was originally invented by the women. The women made it lunar because it was precisely the ebb and flow of lunar rhythms that they were trying to track. You only need a solar calendar when you're doing agriculture because the work you do revolves around the seasons. And although hunting and gathering were also seasonal (depending on what game and plants were available in what season), this wasn't so much a part of primitive peoples' existence. They were vaguely aware of the yearly cycle, but didn't think in those terms much because they had no need to plan much of anything.

So why have a calendar at all, you might ask, much less a lunar one? The reason for this is because in those days, when women still ran the show, the human race was tuned in to certain vibrations, or laws of nature, which ebbed and flowed with the lunar cycle, just as agriculture revolves around the yearly cycle. That is, there are certain wavelengths of knowledge, or techniques for accomplishing things such as healing, music-making, hunting, fishing, gathering, weaving, love-making, etc. which oscillate on a lunar rhythm. Humankind has almost completely lost all of this knowledge; it survives in schemes of planting, etc. by the moon. All of these schemes are valid even if they apparently contradict, such as Europeans planting on a waxing moon near full, and the Maya planting just past new moon. It doesn't matter. The important thing is that the moon's phase be taken into account consistently, to hook onto the body of memory that exists "out there".

Indeed, to live your life according to the moon, using the rules in any astrological rule book (good times to set eggs, make jellies, cut hair, prune trees, etc. etc.) would put you in touch with some of the profoundest rhythms underlying human existence. This is why the Hasidic Jews find so much joy in what seems to most people a sterile, repetitive existence: they are tuning into that feminine rhythm of joy in repetition, in dancing to the beat of the cosmos. The reason why the Hasids find the sabbath so joyous isn't because they get a respite from their labors, but because they then tune in to the lunar rhythm of the universe. The Hasids use a lunar calendar, as do the Muslims, and that is why they are so vigorous (which their effete, solar-calendar critics see as "fanatical").

The reason weekends are fun is because they tie people into their deepest memories of joy, from way back when humankind was still in its infancy. It isn't that people have more fun on weekends because they're free to do what they choose; rather, the cyclic nature of the weekend, based as it is upon the lunar cycle, is intrinsically a hearkening back to the primordial joy which is humankind's true estate, when it was still attached to the rhythms of the moon. Just tuning into the lunar cycle of the week guarantees some joy. Mondays exist for the same reason – if you're going to have an up, you have to have a down – that's the inherent nature of cycles.

The lunar calendar developed at different times and in different places. Depending upon the sophistication of the particular society, it may only have consisted of a 28 or 29 day calendar (i.e. 29 day names) repeated endlessly; or it may have been tied to the solar calendar with intercalary days. It began to be noticed that certain feelings or intents repeated (or better said, could be made to repeat) at certain predictable intervals according to the moon's phase; or in other words, that you could know what to do at a given time by observing the moon's phase in the sky, rather than just feel what to do directly using your own intuition. You could use the moon's phase as a shorthand record or mnemonic device for the feeling or intent. It isn't really an inductive process – it isn't that they observed that seeds planted on the waxing moon outperformed seeds planted on the waning moon; rather, they identified the intent of "successful plants" with the waxing moon; they glued that feeling (of wishing their seeds the best of success) to the thought form of planting on the waxing moon, just as Americans glue feelings of loyalty, gratitude, and patriotism to the thought form of the flag. What makes planting by the moon "come true" is the fastening of the intent to the power of the lunar rhythm, and it doesn't matter how this is done – you could as easily determine to plant on the waning moon, as the Maya do. What is important is the intent, the symbolic act. It doesn't even matter if the plants die, or if a rainstorm washes out all the seeds the day after they're planted. That has nothing to do with it. The goal of planting by the moon – and of all acting by the moon – is *joy*, not maximum production.

So the lunar calendar is primordial – it existed in hunting times in differing degrees of sophistication. It was the invention of agriculture which brought about the solar calendar. This symbolic act made humankind a waking or thinking species, which acted on mind and reason rather than on intuition and feeling. The trouble is that in switching calendars (modes of operating) the male civilization also lost a lot of the sheer joy which had undergirded the female civilization which preceded it. It was a very joyous thing, which the males had to repress in order to stay awake and working all day long. And it is most definitely and literally tied to the lunar calendar. So, if you want to get back to feeling as joyous as ancient people did – as light and in tune with your environment as primordial humans were – and take a short-cut to living out your true purpose in life, then you should quit using the solar calendar and start using a lunar calendar (not that there aren't other ways of doing this; but switching calendars is one way).

Just start by using a lunar calendar, whether Jewish or Muslim or Chinese or whatever. Observe a seven-day weekly cycle of activity within a 28-day month. The week as a unit of measure is a survival from this early Goddess religion calendar. Seven and four are the two basic lunar numbers. Do the same things on the same days each week. Plan monthly activities by lunar phase and daily activities by Planetary Hour (which system is based upon the week symbolism). Schedule activities for e.g. the "second Tuesday" each month. You'll see a real difference in your feelings about yourself and the world, in particular your sense of belonging to the universe – your sense that the universe is nourishing and sustaining you – if you plan your activities around the moon's phase and sign. Women should plan their lives around their menstrual cycle and ritualize the time of menstruation (as the Hasids do). This is just a way of making a feeling or intuitive connection with a different channel of energy – a line of memory which is prior to the present waking line of memory – a truly joyous way of living your life.

The idea is to go wherever there is joy, and to do whatever is joyous. We're not trying to recapture the feeling of the last few thousand years of hunting (just prior to the invention of agriculture), because that period was a bummer. We are not going back to a primeval state of humanity just because it was a primeval state of humanity; but because there was *joy* there. By living your life according to the moon, you'll automatically recapture a lot of this joy in your everyday life. You can make what to other people would seem a sterile, boring routine into a fulfilling life of joy, just by tying all your activities to the moon.

There are certain activities which are intrinsically lunar: e.g. travel, sickness, prayer, lunacy. Anything which means a vacation from, or a hiatus in, the routine, workaday world (*Will*) is intrinsically a lunar activity. These activities especially should be regulated by the moon. New projects and travel should commence on a new, waxing moon, during a moon Planetary Hour. Sickness should be treated by the moon by observing which treatments should be carried out under which phases and signs of the moon (which you can learn from books on medical astrology). Sickness is indeed the only respite that some people allow themselves from the driving urgency of everyday life – the only way they allow themselves to tune in to the lunar rhythm. But there are more joyous ways of doing it than that; and in fact if it isn't being done joyously, then there's no point in doing it at all.

The best way to plan daily activities is by using the Planetary Hours (see my book *Planetary Hours* for tables and instructions on how to use Planetary Hours).

Life is difficult enough in the best of times; Planetary Hours give you a way of using the lunar rhythm to plan your daily activities and make the best use of every day. For example, it's best to wait until a Jupiter hour to call or contact people who owe you money; make romantic plans during Venus hours; do rituals or healings during moon hours; and so on.

The way to tune in to the joyous lunar rhythm in your astrology is to add lunar elements to your charts, even if you continue to use a solar-based horoscope. The Hindus do this with their twenty-seven lunar mansions, but western astrologers can do it any way you like, e.g. with William Butler Yeats' *Great Wheel*, Ronald Davison's Draconic Zodiac, lunar mansions, nodes, critical degrees (see Appendix II) or the Part of Fortune. It doesn't even matter how you compute these things – whether you use tropical or sidereal lunar mansions, or which of the various possible formulas you use to compute the Part of Fortune. All systems are valid as long as you do things the same way consistently. What you are trying to do is to use the lunar technique to hook up to an intent; and I assure you, that intent will bring you joy.

*   *   *   *   *

The Power of Symbolism

All repetition is a manifestation of the principle of memory, symbolized by the moon. When you use repetition in prayer, or incantations, or advertising, you are calling upon the power of memory to accomplish something in the world "out there". Symbolism is a way of tuning into a feeling, of grabbing onto a certain *intent*. Memory (familiarity) is at the basis of all this – i.e., it provides you with a way of making something which happened once happen again.

As Dr. Marc Edmund Jones said, symbolism is more powerful than reality. It is more powerful because it is closer to the truth, and the truth is that what you consider *reality* is only a symbol. This is the basis of many magical acts, such as e.g. cutting other people's light fibers out of your body during recapitulation with a chopping motion of your hand in front of your navel. Magical acts are merely symbolic acts; but what they symbolize is the calling forth of irrevocable intent. The logic of magic – of tuning in to the fundamental rhythms of the universe – is very different from the logic of everyday society.

What magicians are out for is *power*. That's what they're getting with all their weird incantations and rituals. That doesn't mean worldly power. Magicians don't want anything that the "real" world offers, since they know it's all phony. What magicians want is power, which is obtained by putting as much feeling, energy, and importance behind something which is purely abstract and symbolical, as most people put behind their quest for money, or glory in the world, or love from the opposite sex.

The power of symbolism doesn't depend upon the particular symbolism being used. Consider the power of the moon. To time the affairs of your life according to the moon is to hook yourself into the lunar rhythm. Whether you plant on the waxing or waning moon; or whether you go by tropical or sidereal signs, is of no importance. It doesn't matter which system you use, as long as you use one system consistently. This is what makes the materialistic astrologers tear their hair out: they cannot reconcile these "blatant contradictions" – that two competing systems could both be correct. This is because they are only looking at superficial appearances.

Similarly, the attempts to show statistically that plants sown at different times respond in such-and-such a fashion, are doomed to failure. You don't plant by the moon to grow a bigger, or heavier, or even more nutritious (in the sense of what you'd find by analyzing the ash) plant. You plant by the moon to grow a more *joyous* plant. Gardens that are planted by the moon are more joyous, more vigorous, more alive than gardens which aren't planted by the moon; and that vigor is communicated to the people who eat those plants. You don't even have to garden organically: it isn't the chemicals which make supermarket produce unfit to eat; it's the disrespect with which those plants were treated (though the farmer who is respectful of his plants is very circumspect in the kind and amount of chemicals he uses).

To treat a plant with respect means to consider what it would like. It likes a little nitrogen now and then, for example, which all farmers know. But they don't all know that it would also like to be planted with a consciousness of the rhythms of the moon. The farmer, by observing the rhythms of the moon, communicates a certain joy to his plants which they give back to him when he eats them. He hooks his plants up to a feeling (intent) of joy, even if he's only doing the astrology thing mechanically. Agriculture is an intrinsically joyous occupation, which is why attunement to the lunar rhythm has survived there longer than elsewhere in our culture. Practically all farmers farm for the love of it (or did before agribusiness reduced them to slavery), and they are attuned to the lunar rhythm of joy even if they're not consciously planting by the moon. The rest of us are living off that love. That's why modern society has been able to persevere in spite of all the denatured dreck people today eat.

Ancient people were intuitively attuned to the moon. They didn't need ephemerides to tell them when to do things: they could just feel it. For example, a hunter could just sense that tonight would be a good night to fish, or to hunt a particular type of game, or to visit other people and sing, or to just lay around. Modern people haven't completely lost this facility to sense what they really feel like doing at any moment, but they tend to cut themselves off from this sense with their schedules and busyness and "important" things which take precedence in their minds over their feelings. We moderns are too far away from our true feelings to be able to follow them now. We're more comfortable getting information out of books than through our own feelings. That's okay – that works too.

All life on earth is attuned to the lunar rhythm, and the extent to which people are or aren't in tune with this rhythm is the extent to which they are or aren't in tune with their true purpose and feeling of connectedness to the world around them. For example, the easiest way to head off the impending environmental crisis would be to get everyone in the world to switch back from a solar to a lunar calendar.

Notice that by "the moon" we do not refer to the physical object in the sky subject to measurement. The physical moon doesn't have anything to do with anything. There are no "rays" or a materialistic causality involved. The physical moon is just a symbol for rhythm, just as the sun is a symbol for spirit. But both of these symbols are primordial – i.e. they meant what they mean long before there were humans on the earth; or before there were a sun and moon in the sky. All memory is impressed upon, or manifests through, the moon, just as intent manifests through the sun.

The moon symbolizes one aspect of the Spirit, namely memory – repetition. Repetition, or rhythm, is eternality. This is just one aspect of the Spirit: you can consider that the Spirit is made of light fibers, in which case you are considering its solar aspect; or you can consider that it is made up of vibrations or sounds, and that is its rhythmic or lunar aspect. The lunar aspect is the joyous aspect – indeed, joy is rhythm, and rhythm is joy.

In traditional astrological symbolism the sun is male and the moon is female, but this is a false symbol. This a later accretion or interpolation. Actually, the sun is asexual (or better said, purely sexual); the moon is female; and Mercury is male. This corresponds to the three levels of dreamless sleep, dreaming, and waking. It was the human males who, at the time of the invention of agriculture, when they took over the reins of power from the females, shifted the symbolism around to justify their repression of the females. This was in turn a symbol for their repression of their own female sides – their feelings – in order to put as much energy as possible behind the development of their reason – their minds. Actually, every culture on earth developed differently, and the foregoing description is just a general trend in the development of European culture. The men ripped off the females' energy to do things like build computers. On the other hand, it is unlikely that the females would have built computers if left to their own devices. Female energy is innately joyous, but it's not much of a whiz at gadgetry.

In any case, the men shifted the symbolism around. It was then that the zodiac was invented, which glorified the sun. Actually the zodiac *is* valid, the sun *is* a very powerful symbol, but it doesn't mean what the men think it means. Mercury is depicted in the common system of symbolism as being sterile, sexless, androgynous, youthful. And that is quite correct: that is a valid description of male energy. The point is that humankind has been putting most of its energy for the past ten thousand years into developing mind (Mercury principle) at the expense of intuition (lunar principle). It has been developing reason at the expense of joy. And one way of getting back to the original feeling of joy is to tune into the moon once again. How precisely you do this is irrelevant, so long as you are putting energy into the project and are serious in your efforts to live your life by the lunar rhythm.

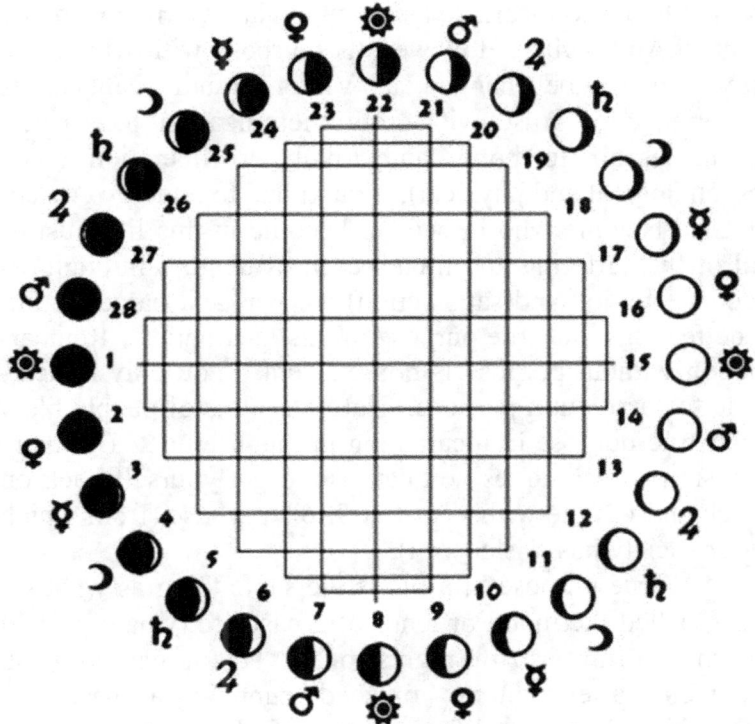

The Phases of the Moon

This wheel is every completed movement of thought or life, twenty-eight incarnations, a single incarnation, a single judgment or act of thought. ... Every phase is in itself a wheel ... Man seeks his opposite or the opposite of his condition, attains his object so far as it is attainable, at phase 15 and returns to Phase 1 again.

The Great Wheel of 28 lunar phase types is another technique for making a connection, a feeling connection, to your true purpose in this life. Everyone is born with a true purpose, which is different in every lifetime but which can be thought of as the intersection of sets of tendencies (memories). Now, a true life purpose can be changed. For example, the true purpose may have been to suffer; so the person chose to incarnate as a Jew in Nazi Germany and be sent to Auschwitz. However, the purpose with which you are born can be changed, as Viktor Frankl changed his experience of Auschwitz from victimization to service, from despair to hope, and finally to liberation (both psychological and physical). Frankl had to undergo Auschwitz to become who he was to become in this life; just as all of the suffering and travail each of us goes through (as well as the joy and satisfaction) are part and parcel of our true feelings, our true purpose in this incarnation. Reincarnation without purpose is non-existent. You only reincarnate to carry out a purpose. Naturally, lots of people blow their true purpose in incarnating in this lifetime. But there are simple techniques you can use to get yourself back on track and in tune with your true life's purpose (from which your society has misled you).

True purpose in a life is the same thing as what we have called the mood or tenor of a past life (what you feel when you run past life regressions). This is why you ask yourself, after you've finished running a past life regression, how that life made you feel. That's what its purpose was. It is not true that the purposes of all lives are to evolve spiritually. Sometimes the purpose is to relax and enjoy. In other lives the purpose is to struggle; or to face catastrophic fear; or to be totally crazy. Your true purpose is to fulfill your destiny, whatever that is. And that's what the 28 lunar phase types show: what different types of people's destinies are; and how they can cooperate with or hinder the fulfillment of their true life's purpose.

Moreover, it isn't really possible to consider the 28 lunar phase types in isolation, but rather as interconnected to all the other types. There are numerical interconnections between phases and correspondences with the *Four Faculties*, which will be described presently. Another mnemonic for suggesting phase interpretations, based upon the Chaldean order of the planets, will be described below.

When you are following your true purpose in this lifetime – the reason why you were born – then you are said to be acting *in phase*. Conversely, when you are being self-indulgent or self-pitying and are wasting this incarnation, then you are said to be acting *out of phase*. *Pity is primary, whereas desire is* antithetical: *When pity is separated from wisdom we have the False* Mask, *a pity like that of a drunken man, self-pity, whether offered in seeming to another or only to oneself: pity corrupted by desire.*

When an *antithetical* man is *out of phase*, he reproduces the *primary* condition, but with an emotional inversion – and vice versa. *Antithetical* virtue is *calling that good which a man can contemplate himself as doing always and no other doing at all* & primary *virtue comparing itself to a standard—am I as good as that saint, as that man/standard that tradition and society reveres as good.*

Out of phase means behaving like the opposite of the natal lunar phase (e.g. Phase 19 is *out of phase* when acting like Phase 5). When natives of the *primary* phases (23 to 7) try to go their own way independently, they are acting are *out of phase* (since following one's dream is the prerogative of the *antithetical* phases): *In* primary *phases man must cease ... from self-expression, and substitute a motive of service for that of self-expression.* Similarly, when natives of the *antithetical* phases (9 to 21) try to fit in and belong (seek approval and validation), then they are acting *out of phase* (since adaptation to outer constraints is the hallmark of the *primary*). For example, W.B.Y. was born into Phase 19, an *antithetical* phase; and all of his efforts to fit in and belong to various occult groups such as Golden Dawn and the Theosophical Society led to nothing but disputes with their leaders; similarly, his bending himself completely out of shape for thirty years to try to win the favor of a completely selfish woman who rejected and rejected and rejected him led to nothing but despair. It was only when he stopped trying to fit in and belong and instead struck out on his own that he switched to *in phase*. Conversely, *primary* phase natives do better by reining in their own egos and tuning in to what is going on around them. In this book the characteristics of natives acting *out of phase* will often be indicated by parentheses.

Natives of the *primary* phases are following their true purpose when they forgo "doing their own thing" and instead let themselves be led. The point is, that from an astrological viewpoint the very first thing to consider when asking yourself the question of how to live your true life's purpose, is to consider whether you are of a *primary* phase (in which case you should do your best to listen and to serve); or whether you are of an *antithetical* phase (in which case you should follow your own star – your inner voice and intuition).

The first two quarters, from new to full moon (Phases 1 through 14) represent the descent of spirit into matter (*towards Nature*): the natives become more and more disconnected as the cycle progresses (with an increasing sense of isolation and anguish). The last two quarters, from full moon to new moon (Phases 15 through 28) represent the ascent of spirit to source (*towards God*): the natives lose individuality as the cycle progresses (with an increasing sense of dissolution into selflessness). What increases and decreases moving from Phase 1 to Phase 15 and back again is separatedness. The early phases are simple and ingenuous; which little-by-little becomes a stronger sense of self-consciousness. As Phase 15 is approached there is an increasing rage, or struggle to be free of all social restraint: *The being of* antithetical *man is described as full of rage before Phase 12, against all in the world that hinders its expression* [i.e. in rebellion against society], *after Phase 12, but before Phase 15, the rage is a knife turned against itself* [rebellion against one's own internal dialogue, or as it is called here, *Automatonism*] since the natives are now sophisticated enough to understand that these chains are within themselves; and they despise their own weakness (dependence upon other people's validation for self-definition).

In this book we tend to associate the *primary tincture* with social conditioning because that's what it means on a level of *Will*. But on the levels of the higher *Faculties* it means obeying a more abstract power. Similarly, the descent into matter and ascent to union is but another way of saying movement toward self-centeredness becoming movement towards selflessness.

As Phase 15 is passed, the hard-won freedom of the separated self is surrendered (or expunged) little-by-little, until by Phase 28 the life is pretty much devoted to service (or bondage). It is reborn in unself-consciousness at Phase 1. In the first half of the cycle the person struggles harder and harder to free him or herself from the compulsion of social conditioning; and in the second half he or she is increasingly compelled to yield to karmic restraint. Phase 15 is the moment of greatest independence; and Phases 28 and 1 are the moments of greatest conformity (to the laws of God or Man).

In the words of commentator Neil Mann:

"The System thus posits a relatively conventional esoteric view of the soul's progress, which involves being sent out from Godhead to gain experience through many lifetimes with the ultimate purpose of return to Godhead, as expounded by theosophic interpretations of Buddhism and the Cabbala. ... The pattern of the life varies according to the stage on the Wheel and in the Cycles, but fundamentally requires the individual to find self-fulfillment and acceptance of its life. On a larger level the various stages upon the Wheel involve a growth away from God as Nature towards independence and self-realisation and a return to God as Spirit. On the level beyond this, the soul evolves further with each Cycle; two souls may both be at the same

Phase, where the disposition of the *Faculties* will entail a basic congruence between the natures of their lives, but if they are in different Cycles their level of development will be different." – (Neil Mann, *Yeats's* A Vision: *Ideas of Man and God*)

This is an important point: the lunar phase is not an indication of how "advanced" a soul is (whether a new or old soul); but merely what that soul's true purpose (karmic role-to-be-played) is in this lifetime. In the words of Dr. Michael Newton (in *Journey of Souls*):

"Making hasty judgments on a soul's maturity based solely on behavioral traits has its pitfalls. The design plan of souls could include holding parts of their energy in reserve in some lives. Sometimes a negative trait is selected by an otherwise developed soul for special attention in a certain body. ... Do souls choose bodies whose intellectual capabilities match their own development? For instance, are advanced souls drawn to human brains with high intelligence? In looking at the scholastic and academic achievement of my clients, I find there is no more correlation here than with an immature soul being inclined to bodies with lower intellectual aptitudes. ... A person may be highly intelligent and yet have a closed attitude about adjusting to new situations, with little curiosity about the world. This indicates a beginner soul to me. If I see someone with an evenness of mood, whose interests and abilities are solidly in focus and directed towards helping human progress, I suspect an advanced soul at work. These are souls who seek personal truths beyond the demands of ego."

One of the things which is being symbolized here is the evolution of consciousness from inorganic life (*primary* = dreamless sleep) through one-celled life (dream consciousness) to multicellular life (*antithetical* = waking consciousness) and back again to the *primary* (= lucid dreaming, which is the next stage in the evolution of human consciousness after waking; i.e., everyday life in future human society will consist of what we today term "lucid dreaming").

As *Proposition V* states: *Human life is either the struggle of a destiny against all other destinies* [i.e. *antithetical*], *or a transformation of the character defined in the horoscope into timeless and spaceless existence.* [i.e. *primary*]. In summary, death is *primary* and life *antithetical*, and the two twirl around each other like yin and yang:

Antithetical = Subjective = emotional and aesthetic => aristocratic – tends to separate man from man => expresses our inner world of desire and imagination.

Primary = Objective = reasonable and moral => democratic – brings us back to the mass where we began => expresses that objectivity of mind which treats of outward things and events rather than of inward thought.

Personality, no matter how habitual, is a constantly renewed choice, varying from an individual charm, in the more antithetical phases, to a hard objective dramatisation; but when the primary phases begin man is moulded more and more from without ... The primary is that which serves, the antithetical is that which creates.

In the words of Neil Mann, "The *primary* person follows the patterns established by custom and society. The fully *antithetical* man is one who lives at great tension, whose life is one of 'constantly renewed choice', as opposed to the *primary* person who conforms to a code, and needs merely to apply it to a situation like a stencil."

Primary phases possess a herd mentality, whereas *antithetical* phases are solipsistic. This is not a matter of individualism per se, since Phase 1 (for example) can be quite individualistic in its blithe free-spiritedness; yet it always casts a glance about to see what other people are doing or how they are reacting – it measures itself against others. The antithetical phases (especially Phase 15), by contrast, are unconcerned and indifferent to what other people are doing or thinking (or perhaps view others as obstacles to be overcome, rather than a jigsaw puzzle within which the self must somehow be made to fit). At the same time, *seen by different analysis the individual phases are alternately antithetical and primary.*

One thing the moon's cycle symbolizes is the process of socialization – how a newborn becomes an adult. The different phases show different people's adaptations to their social conditioning. Unless you have had the experience of extended intimate contact with a foreign culture, it is difficult to imagine just how much the *degree* of socialization varies from one society to another. The very basic cognitive assumptions – to give a simple example, the visual details that people from different cultures focus on and pay attention to when viewing the same scene – can vary considerably from one society to another.

The Great Wheel of 28 lunar phases is designed to be a universal symbol – an algebra, if you will – with certain built-in properties which can be applied to different models. In similar fashion to the way in which the concepts of group, field, and vector space can be applied to different facets of the universe, the Great Wheel can be interpreted in different ways and applied to different cycles. One thing that the cycle of 28 phases models is birth – maturity – decline – death – rebirth; and this can be interpreted in different ways. Indeed, W.B.Y.'s interpretation of the Great Wheel and Busteed-Tiffany-Wergin's interpretation of it differ somewhat between themselves; and both are somewhat different from the System of interpretation given in this volume (although all are valid in different contexts).

The number 4 symbolizes material manifestation, and particularly the physical world of four directions – i.e., space. The number 7 is a symbol for karma, kismet, destiny – i.e. time. Thus four and seven together symbolize the everyday world of space and time. We sentient beings on this earth apprehend this world as existing in a matrix of space and time; true memory, on the other hand, apprehends the sum total of who we are in all our incarnations; hence it – our *Daimon*, or total human awareness – exists outside the limits of space and time. The so-called "universe" is just a projection of thought forms of space and time, which in W.B.Y.'s System is symbolized by 4 x 7 or 28. The number 28 is used in preference to the more accurate 29 (since the moon's synodic cycle is actually closer to 29 days than to 28) because 28 is more abstract – a perfect number (the sum of its divisors) – hence more symbolical (powerful). To repeat Dr. Marc Edmund Jones' dictum, symbolism is more powerful than reality (because what we consider to be "reality" – waking consciousness – is just a highly evolved, specialized, and embellished form of dreaming; in the same way that e.g. banking is a highly evolved, specialized, and embellished form of bartering).

Seven and four are the two lunar numbers; and any symbolic system based upon four and seven must be considered to be basically lunar (*antithetical*). The days of the week are thus a lunar symbol; and the Planetary Hours are also a lunar symbol (since they are calculated from the days of the week, and employ the Chaldean Order of the seven planets). As another example, the system which was channeled through *Messages from Michael* is congruent numerically with W.B.Y.'s System (i.e., is lunar). The system given in *Messages from Michael* resembles W.B.Y.'s System in some ways, but is quite different from it in other ways (for one thing, the personality types cannot be calculated but rather must be deduced from sets of seven archetypal types).

By contrast, three, four and twelve are solar symbols; and any symbolic system – such as the zodiac and circle of astrological houses – which is based on 3, 4 and 12 is solar (*Primary*).

Note that the moon's synodic cycle can be analyzed in a variety of ways, and these different measures all show different things about the native. For example, considered from the point of view of soli-lunar aspects, phases 10 and 19 correspond to moon trine sun and phases 5 and 24 correspond to their sextile; and, therefore, these phases might be supposed to bring opportunities and relationships which foster the childlike simplicity, ingenuousness, and self-delight (blithe free-spiritedness) which characterize the harmonious aspects between the sun and the moon. However, this point of view is not particularly fruitful in unraveling the meanings of phases 10, 19, 5, and 24 (and indeed can be somewhat misleading). In like fashion, it might be thought that phase 15 is favorable for marriage since in this phase the Part of Fortune falls in the 7th house of partnership; but indeed phase 15 means something very different from what this line of analysis would lead one to expect (since phase 15 is actually the most isolated and solitary of the phases). This is not to say that alternate ways of interpreting the moon's synodic cycle are invalid; rather, they indicate different things, and just happen to use the angular relationship between the sun and the moon as their common measuring stick.

And, as mentioned previously, the cycle of 28 phases can be analyzed in a great many ways. The systems given by W.B.Y. and Busteed-Tiffany-Wergin view the Great Wheel of 28 phases superimposed on a zodiac of 12 signs (although the two versions have different attributions of phases to signs). There is no, one, single correct way to interpret a symbol; but rather, lots of different and seemingly contradictory ways can be equally correct (just as the Maya use a different scheme of planting by the moon than do Europeans; but their systems are nonetheless equally valid). The important point is not which interpretation of the System is correct; but rather to use the symbols to fasten onto the power of the lunar rhythm as a tool for self-understanding. For example, one method is: *According to this astrologic system the ascendant of a horoscope is always placed before it & judged directly under the middle point of the phase of the native, & all the aspects & planets are studied in relation to the phases at which they are placed.* (W.B.Y., *The Discoveries of Michael Robartes, Vision Papers* vm.4)

However, there are aesthetic (amongst other) reasons to avoid mixing different systems of astrological symbolism – in this case, imposing a solar symbol (the zodiac and the circle of houses) over what should basically be a lunar symbol: *the relation between the wheel of twenty-eight Phases and that of twelve months has turned out as insoluble to the symbolist as was that between the solar and lunar year to the ancient astronomers.* In the present book, the 28 phases will be analyzed in terms of four groups of seven, in which the four groups correspond to the four lunar quarters and the seven correspond to the seven traditional planets taken in Chaldean order. The point is that the Great Wheel is a universal symbol; it yields to many different interpretations and analyses; it is a matrix or framework with many different examples and applications. Other examples of interpretations of the Great Wheel of 28 phases include the 28 lunar mansions (delimited by fixed stars, as in *Picatrix*); and also the critical degrees of the zodiac (a traditional division of the zodiac into 28 parts. See the Appendix for details of this system).

In this book the background astrological system against which the 28 lunar phases are analyzed is the Chaldean order of the planets: sun – Venus – Mercury – moon – Saturn – Jupiter – Mars. That is to say, starting with Phase 1 (which is ruled by the sun), each succeeding phase is ruled by the succeeding planet in Chaldean order. Thus the Chaldean cycle repeats four times through the 28 phases. This approach was suggested by the spirits who channeled this work; who also are of the opinion that the System is flexible and can be interpreted in different ways, and that all interpretations – the present one; W.B.Y.'s System; and Busteed, Tiffany and Wergin's; are all valid techniques for tuning into the power of the lunar rhythm.

Each lunar quarter is a full Chaldean cycle, from the sun to Mars. The sun and Mars are similar principles (have a similar meaning astrologically); but Mars phases are phases of struggle against death and solar phases are phases of rebirth. The solar phase beginning each quarter arises out of the ashes of the preceding Mars phase (this can be especially true when considering the progressed lunar cycle, wherein progressed Phase 28 often consists of defeat or exhaustion; and the succeeding Phase 1 consists of renewal and rebirth of hope).

The disjunction points in the Chaldean cycle (between moon-ruled phases and Saturn-ruled phases – i.e., between phases 4 & 5, 11 & 12, 18 & 19, and 25 & 26) are the points where the *tinctures* are said to close and open: these are points of inflection where the movement towards *primary* reverses and begins moving towards *antithetical*, or vice versa. The present exposition takes a somewhat different view of the closing and opening of the *tinctures* than that presented in *A Vision* – a view based upon the experience of interpreting actual horoscopes.

To interpret the meaning of a phase it is necessary to see how it arises from the preceding phase(s) and dissolves into the following one(s), as well as its phase and rectangle rulers and the other three phases belonging to the same rectangle. In other words, to use this System as a spiritual tool, the thing should be viewed as a cycle (rather than just looking up the interpretation for your particular phase).

One way of looking at the planet which rules your phase is to consider it to be similar in meaning to having that planet conjunct the Ascendant of your birth horoscope. The symbolism of that planet is a description of your outer personality (*Will*), your self-image – how you conceive of yourself and present yourself to others. The difference between planets on the Ascendant and Great Wheel phase rulers is that not everybody has a planet conjunct the Ascendant; and some people have several. But everyone has one and only one planetary ruler of their lunar phase. Besides, different things are being shown. Planets conjunct the Ascendant are rather superficial strategies ("come-ons") for manipulating the social milieu for one's own benefit. Planetary rulers are *moods*, deeper descriptions (or better said: descriptive of a deeper part of the person) than are planets conjunct the Ascendant. Planets conjunct the Ascendant often reveal parental training (à la Gauquelin); but phase rulers show something the person came into this life with, before he or she was born.

The cycle of 28 lunar phases in its entirety symbolizes reincarnation – the cycle of birth-death-rebirth – the descent of spirit into matter (of soul into flesh); and its subsequent ascent (return to source) – whether this takes place over a myriad of lifetimes; or just one lifetime; or just one instant. This is why W.B.Y. described it as *every completed movement of thought or life, twenty-eight incarnations, a single incarnation, a single judgment or act of thought.* It always leads to rebirth, which is why traditionally phase 1 is listed or repeated after phase 28 (though for heuristic reasons this is not done in the present volume).

This evolution in consciousness is symbolized by the moon's monthly synodic cycle of 28 phases: Phase 1 begins at the new moon; Phase 8 at first quarter; Phase 15 at the full moon; and Phase 22 at last quarter. To calculate the lunar phase in your own horoscope:

    1) Subtract the longitude of the sun from the longitude of the moon (adding 360° to longitude moon first if it is less than longitude sun). Example: Longitude moon = 19° AQ 47' and Longitude sun = 22° GE 51': Arc = 319.783 − 82.85 = 236.933.

    2) Multiply this Arc by 28 and divide by 360. Example: 236.933 x 28 / 360 = 18.428.

    3) Take the integer part (drop the decimal) and add one. Example: 18 + 1 = Phase 19.

It is not altogether clear from *A Vision* itself that the phases of the moon should be calculated in the obvious way as 1 + INT{28 * (Longitude Moon − Longitude Sun) / 360} − and in fact W.B.Y. himself is equivocal on this point. For example, he assigned Phase 16 to his unattainable beloved Maud Gonne at times; but in *A Vision* the symbolism for Phase 14 − her actual astrological phase − obviously refers to her when it speaks of Helen of Troy drawing *perpetually upon glass with a diamond*; and also when he says of the phase that *here are women carried off by robbers and ravished by clowns* (W.B.Y. was utterly distraught when Maud married Irish revolutionary John MacBride, whom he termed a "clown" in a poem addressed to her which expostulated on the folly of the match: *thou art mated with a clown. And the grossness of his nature will have weight to drag thee down*). W.B.Y. assigned himself to Phase 17 rather than 19 (the actual value); yet his description of Phase 19 contains a rueful comment upon his own hopeless love for the treacherous Maud Gonne: *Here one finds men and women who love those who rob them or beat them, as though the soul were intoxicated by its discovery of human nature, or found even a secret delight in the shattering of the image of its desire*. The commentator Neil Mann states that "although the symbolism of the System gives it an astrological appearance, it is not based upon the movements of the heavens, and that an individual's Phase cannot therefore be assigned by calculation or any other independent method." Indeed, Busteed, Tiffany, and Wergin give alternate methods for calculating natives' phases astrologically.

In the present book we will calculate the lunar phases in the obvious way for the simple reason that it was channeled to do so in this fashion; moreover, it works just fine. There's nothing wrong with doing it this way; and this technique yields clear insights into different people's personalities and karma. Indeed, as Neil Mann says, "Yeats acknowledges ... that the System could have been presented quite differently." In fact, looking at the progressed lunar cycle can also be most illuminating: for example, W.B.Y. won the Nobel Prize for literature when his natal lunar phase repeated (progressed Phase 19 = June 28, 1923 to June 9, 1924); and he switched from *out of phase* to *in phase* when the *tinctures* opened (at the end of progressed Phase 12 of his 2nd progressed lunar cycle (September 27, 1916 to October 4, 1917).

Of the *Four Faculties*, the 28 lunar phases refer principally to the native's *Will*: *A particular man is classified according to the place of* Will, *or choice* [the fulcrum of the cone of the *Four Faculties*]. *A man of, say, Phase 13 is a man whose* Will *is at that phase ... describes his character and destiny.*

Your lunar phase shows how you fit yourself into your immediate social group: what superficial role you play, how you make yourself comfortable amongst your fellows. It shows your self-presentation, the way you introduce yourself (so to speak) in casual, tête-à-tête relationships (and particularly when meeting someone for the first time). Your lunar phase shows how you put your best foot forward, how you convince others (or better said: use others to convince yourself), which usually works better on casual acquaintances than with intimates. This is why it can be likened to the ruling planet conjunct the Ascendant (which in astrology reveals the person's self-projection in casual relationships) – but here it's more of a customary mood than it is a sales pitch or superficial image.

In W.B.Y.'s System, *all phases from Phase 8 to Phase 22 are* antithetical, *taken as a whole, and all phases from Phase 22 to Phase 8 are* primary. That is, the *antithetical* phases are those in which the moon's light predominates over its darkness; and the *primary* phases are those in which the moon's darkness predominates over its light. Phase 1 (new moon) is considered the extreme *primary* self-expression and Phase 15 (full moon) the extreme *antithetical* self-expression.

The synodic cycles of the inferior planets Mercury and Venus (their cycles of revolution around the sun as seen from the earth – i.e., their cycles of phases) also exhibit the *primary / antithetical* distinction. As is also the case with the moon's cycle, conjunction with the sun is *primary* (socially conditioned or constrained) and elongation from the sun is *antithetical* (individualistic). The Mercury cycle shows how natives know that they are *right*: Mercury conjunction sun natives (*primary*) know that they are right because they faithfully and unquestioningly uphold what their parents and society have inculcated into them; Mercury elongation natives (*antithetical*) know that they are right precisely because they haven't bought into what they were taught, but rather have figured out all the angles for themselves. The Venus cycle shows what natives believe that they *deserve*: Venus conjunction sun natives (*primary*) believe they are undeserving (unworthy) unless they can be or do more than is humanly possible; whereas Venus elongation natives (*antithetical*) believe they deserve whatever they can grab.

The lunar synodic cycle, by contrast, shows how natives *define* themselves; where the natives feel that they *belong*; how they fit themselves into their social group (*primary*) or emphasize their distinctiveness (*antithetical*). For example, Phase 1 belongs everywhere, is at home everywhere; Phase 15 belongs nowhere, is out-of-place everywhere; and Phases 8 and 22 aren't sure where they belong (and never will be). A person's lunar phase indicates the social role that makes him or her feel comfortable: that is to say, their customary mood, which they put on when they wake up in the morning, and with which they greet life and other people throughout the day (and themselves when looking in the mirror). Their phase shows what they bring to their social milieu: their true purpose (in the ideal case); the justification for their existence.

As mentioned in the Preface, if there were no memory then every transaction would be pure and free and aboveboard, with no hidden agendas or unacknowledged motives. Everything would happen spontaneously. This is the bouncy mood of Phase 1. Whereas the mood of Phase 15 – overburdened as it is with memory – is somber and melancholic. The differences between natives of these extreme types – Phase 1 (complete objectivity) and Phase 15 (complete subjectivity) – can be summarized as follows:

Phase 1:	Phase 15:
(born day after new moon)	(born day after full moon)
Complete Plasticity (able to adapt to any social environment)	*Complete Beauty* (always stands out and stands alone)
IRREPRESSSIBLE	ANGUISHED
Enthusiastic, puppy-like	Knowing, pensive, abstracted
Personal, self-assured	Impersonal, cool, distant
Unself-conscious	Utterly self-conscious
Impulsive	Impassive
Fresh, innovative	Reflective
Sassy maverick	Self-possessed and politic
Must prove self	Nothing to prove to anyone
Enjoys many and varied relationships	Few or no close relationships
Friendly, outgoing, personable	Reserved, brooding, self-absorbed
Reaches out to experience and master a broad range of skills and activities	Cultivates one or a few particular areas of expertise or competence where definitely shines

It is said that Phase 1 (being complete plasticity: adapting chameleon-like to any social environment) and Phase 15 (being complete beauty: just being themselves in any social environment) are not human phases, but this is not correct: they are human, all right; but although they walk among us, they are not of us – they are on their own wavelengths. Phase 1 natives are utterly *primary* (focused upon themselves, in the same way that an infant is focused completely upon itself and has no inkling of being separated from its mother – and when a bit older cries in despair at this realization); whereas Phase 15 natives are utterly *antithetical* (unfocused upon anything, taking everything in indiscriminately, and have no inkling of belonging but rather feel as though they are plummeting through a void). Phase 1 natives question nothing – they take everything for granted; whereas Phase 15 natives exist in a state of heightened vigilance verging on paranoia and can take nothing whatsoever for granted.

The four lunar quarters can be considered to symbolize the four ages of mankind – childhood, adolescence, maturity, and old age – so as the cycle progresses there is a greater depth of feeling and enlarged sensitivity to, and appreciation for, meaning rather than stimulation. The moods of the quarters representing adulthood (2nd and 3rd) are *antithetical* (self-ish) whereas the moods of the quarters representing childhood and old age (1st and 4th) are *primary* (thrall and surrender, respectively).

The Four Ages of Man

He with body waged a fight,
But body won; it walks upright.
Then he struggled with the heart;
Innocence and peace depart.
Then he struggled with the mind;
His proud heart he left behind.
Now his wars on God begin;
At stroke of midnight God shall win.

(W.B.Y., *Supernatural Songs IX*)

In the wheel of the Faculties, Will *predominates during the first quarter,* Mask *during the second,* Creative Mind *during the third,* Body of Fate *during the fourth.*

The rulerships of the four lunar quarters by the *Four Faculties* is not a sharp distinction but rather a progression of dominance which culminates at the end of each quarter: From Phases 1 through 7 *Mask* slowly predominates over *Will*; from Phases 8 through 14 *Creative Mind* slowly predominates over *Mask*; from Phases 15 through 21 *Body of*

Fate slowly predominates over *Creative Mind*; and from Phases 22 through 28 *Will* slowly predominates over *Body of Fate*.

The cycle of the Quarters moves from individual history and incarnation (*Will* => *Mask*) to greater abstraction (*Mask* => *C.M.*); and then brings it all back home to mundane existence (*C.M.* => *B.F.*) – but now the emphasis is on other people rather than the self. In a sense the progression of the Quarters resembles the symbolism of the Zen oxherding pictures, in which the final picture in the series portrays a return to everyday life after the aspirant has achieved enlightenment.

The Four Quarters

	<= Primary =>	<== Antithetical ====>		<= Primary =>
	1st Quarter	2nd Quarter	3rd Quarter	4th Quarter
Strongest Faculty	Will	Mask	C.M.	B.F.
Elemental Attributions	Earth	Water	Air	Fire
Automatonism*	Instinctive	Imitative	Creative	Obedient
4 Conditions of *Will*	Instinctive: Body should win	Emotional: Heart should win	Intellectual: Mind should win	Moral: Soul should win
4 Conditions of *Mask*	Intensity	Tolerance	Convention / systemization	Self-analysis
Defects**	Sentimentality	Brutality	Hatred	Insensitiveness

* *Automatonism* is the tendency of the momentary attention to run hither and thither (described as Instinctive in the 1st Quarter, Imitative in the 2nd Quarter, etc.)

** Defects of False *Creative Mind* [sense of STATUS vis à vis other people] which bring the *False Mask* [DENIAL of one's true purpose]

First Quarter (*Will* – phases 1 through 7): These phases are INSTINCTIVE, spontaneous, uninhibited, and light of spirit. Their candid naturalness lends them a winning charm – they are unabashedly themselves at all times – and their unself-conscious artlessness leavens any group of which they are a part. They are fresh and playful, with a vigorous, youthful energy and a carefree (heedless) joie de vivre. *All men, from Phase 2 to Phase 7 inclusive, are intellectually simple.* First quarter natives are endearing (and frustrating) in their naïveté: for them, everything is clear-cut, black and white, open and shut. There are no subtleties or vast karmic meanings to be grasped and digested. Everything is simple. Their youthful solipsism and knee-jerk reactivity make them rather self-interested and self-aggrandizing: they seem concerned with others only insofar as they can somehow be put to use; or they consider people a standard against which to judge how well they are doing. As the quarter progresses there develops a larger awareness that life is in fact a weighty business which requires a greater earnestness and deliberation (2nd Quarter).

Second Quarter (*Mask* – phases 8 through 14): These phases are EMOTIONAL, reflective, self-conscious, and aware. They are guarded, less forthright than First Quarter natives: their spur to action is not impulse but rather intuition. They are cautious and calculating, always taking the possible consequences of their decisions and other people's reactions to them into account. They have a greater depth of responsiveness than the First Quarter types, and they can be overly sensitive (quick to take offense). They feel things deeply and find it difficult to just let go and move on. Their preoccupied indwelling and fixation on themselves give rise, as the quarter progresses, to a felt need for less personal involvement and a more objective overview (3rd Quarter).

Third Quarter (*Creative Mind* – phases 15 through 21): These phases are INTELLECTUAL, concerned with principles and abstract considerations (woolly, distracted). They march to the beat of a distant drum and have an air of sublime confidence, as if they are on the inside track in life (superior, patronizing). They primarily seek concord and harmony; they possess a broad, philosophical, long-range point of view; and they try not to take things too personally (as the first two quarters do). They are fair-minded, impartial, aloof, and disinterested (vague); and they don't allow themselves to become too involved or compromised (unreachable). Their blithe independence shies from constraints, which as the quarter progresses calls up a need for a deeper sense of understanding and meaning in life (Last Quarter).

Last Quarter (*Body of Fate* – phases 22 through 28): These phases are serious, conscientious, and reserved, with a strong sense of MORAL imperative. Their choices and actions are constrained by strict standards of honor and decency, and they feel a compelling obligation to do their best and give their all (self-righteous). It is interesting how the Last Quarter phases tend to reverse the usual planetary symbolism: Phase 23 is rather morbid and gloomy for a Venus phase; Phase 25 is feisty and combative for a lunar phase; Phase 26 is brazen and daring for a Saturn phase; Phase 28 is subdued and wary for a Mars phase. It is here that the relentless striving of the previous phases exhausts itself; thus Last Quarter natives are perhaps the only ones who live in peace with themselves and their world (or at least have that potential). They are resolute and immoveable (obstinate); thoroughly dedicated to the service of their ideals (unrealistic, off on their own tangents); and schooled in self-restraint, self-denial, and endurance. As a result, these natives carry an air or sense of onus or burden (world-weariness), tinged with a resigned, shrug-of-shoulders, gallows humor. Thus, as the Quarter progresses the overwhelming mood of ponderous incumbency turns little-by-little into disinterest, indifference, and finally levity (1st Quarter).

Excluding the four phases of crisis (Phases 8, 22, 15, 1), each quarter consists of six phases, or of two sets of three. In every case the first phase of each set [Venus & Saturn phases] *can be described as a manifestation of power, the second* [Mercury & Jupiter phases] *of a code or arrangement of powers, and the third* [moon & Mars phases] *of a belief, the belief being an appreciation of, or submission to some quality which becomes power in the next phase. The reason of this is that each set of three is itself a wheel, and has the same character as the Great Wheel.*

Just as each of the four quarters can be thought of as symbolizing a stage of human life (childhood, adolescence, adulthood, old age), so too can the seven phases within each quarter be thought of as symbolizing stages of human life. In this scheme, each quarter can be considered to consist of an initial phase of stasis or equilibrium (or, in the cases of Phases 8 and 22, seesaw disequilibrium), followed by two sets of three phases each – the first one a phase of empowerment; the second a phase of learning / organization; and the third a phase of submission.

We can think of the first hemi-quarter (Venus => Mercury => moon) as being *primary*, symbolic of infancy and childhood, and moving towards *antithetical*; and the second hemi-quarter (Saturn => Jupiter => Mars) as being *antithetical*, symbolizing adulthood (after sexual awakening), and moving back towards *primary*. Of course, in normal human life these two periods – childhood and adulthood – are of vastly different lengths, with childhood lasting much, much longer than adulthood. Isn't it true that childhood is eternal: it lasts forever, you never seem to grow up. Whereas with the onset of adolescence everything speeds up – everything comes at you so fast; and then before you know it, it's over (and you never accomplished all that you had striven to). A materialist might explain this by saying that a child's sense of the passage of time has not yet developed; whereas a magician would say that the transition from childhood to adulthood is when people lose their sense of timelessness and don the straitjacket of unremitting (sexual) urgency.

The point is that our sense of the passage of time is nothing more nor less than striving. In childhood we don't strive (except momentarily, in response to this or that immediate exigency). But we don't have goals or plans (unless adults foist them upon us willy-nilly). But with the onset of sexual desire, everything changes and the urgency of life seems to speed up the passage of what we take to be "time". It's like Freud said – it's all about sex.

The inner planets can be likened to the Buddhist *skandhas*: the sun can be thought of as *vinnana* (awareness, intent); Venus *vedana* (desire, expectation); Mercury *sankhara* (mind, importance); and moon *sanna* (mood, familiarity). Consider, for example, the "life cycle" of a sensation: first there is pure awareness (sun = light fibers) – the background or canvas upon which the sensation is painted. Then comes empowerment (Venus = the sensory thought form) – the initial phase of the sensation, e.g. the first pulse of an orgasm or smell of a rose or spoonful of tiramisu, which is exquisitely intense. Subsequent pulses or smells or tastes lose that initial purity and immediacy as the "=>**I**<= **am experiencing this sensation**" (Mercury = the conceptual thought form) takes over, and consequently the feeling dulls, becomes more remote, more separated from the true (original) sensation. In the final phase (moon) the sensation becomes routine, familiar, a memory. Actually, each individual sensation – pulse, smell, taste, whatever – goes through all of these phases (or *skandhas*);

it's just that it's easier to see the progression it if you consider several happening in a row.

A hemi-quarter is analogous to the development of separatedness in the way a newborn learns to deal with the world. In the beginning he is completely ga-ga – aware, but not aware of what he is aware of – just pure moment-to-moment feeling (sun). Sun phases are in thrall; in these phases striving is minimal because there's no one there to go anywhere; and nowhere to go.

The first phase in each hemi-quarter is ruled by Venus (empowerment) which turns into Mercury (learning / organization) and then moon (submission). One way of thinking about this is that a newborn has no sense of a self-at-center; but he quickly becomes aware of others (Venus). In the ideal case, others are smiling and cooing at the infant and providing him with whatever he might desire (so he doesn't cry). In the less-than-ideal case, where Venus in the natal horoscope is afflicted or combust, the infant becomes aware of others in a negative, dysfunctional way. But, the infant soon understands that there are others out there who respond to him in one way or another, who empower him (it's not all just an exercise in cosmic indifference).

The next stage is when the infant begins to develop a mind of his own (Mercury). This is very much tied up with his discovering his body and learning its potentials and limits (e.g. coordinating eyes and hands to reach out to touch and grab things): that there's a "ME" to whom things are happening – a separatedness or duality between experience and experiencer. The infant didn't comprehend this point (or, better said, delude himself into believing this illusion) previously. It is during this stage that the infant realizes that he is separated from the smiley (or grumpy) faces out there. This is basically accomplished when he can successfully "blend" the two scenes which his two eyes are perceiving into one seamless whole; and he interprets this as signifying that there is just one "ME" in the middle of everything (instead of two "ME's", as he had heretofore perceived). In the Mercury stage he realizes he has a self-at-center, and this self can do things in the world "out there".

In the next stage, that which was fully conscious during the earlier stages becomes taken-for-granted, assumed, part of a pattern. Mercury symbolizes conscious thought, the moon symbolizes habit. Life becomes a routine, the years roll by, everything is reduced to familiarity. What ties life together – what ties one day to the next – is an underlying mood (seriousness, frivolity, dreaminess, rancor, creativity, rebelliousness, whatever). In a sense, this mood is what the 28 phases of the Great Wheel purport to describe – one's customary moods; one's touch point in life; the underlying feeling which assures us that we are ourselves (and not somebody else); which is what we have termed *Will* (since it is a matter of making moment-to-moment choices which reinforce a wonted mood). It is our customary moods with which we "choose our own realities". The mechanism by which life seems to keep relentlessly coming at us – repeating the same situations and relationships over and over – is our *Will*, which becomes "set" in the moon phases.

It is at this point in the cycle, just when everything seems to be down pat, that everything gets shaken up. Sexuality rears its ugly head; and the rules of the game are completely changed. In the System this is described as the *tinctures* closing and opening at the disjunction points where the Chaldean order breaks – where the moon phases (4-11-18-25) turn into Saturn phases (5-12-19-26). In our model this is the transition from childhood to adulthood at sexual awakening. W.B.Y. said (with reference to the Second Quarter – which particularly represents adolescence):

At Phases 11 and 12 occurs what is called the opening of the tinctures, *at Phase 11 the* antithetical *opens, at Phase 12 the* primary [this is because the odd phases are considered antithetical and the even phases primary. This is a different conception of the closing and opening than we will use in this book]. ... *The opening means the reflection inward of the Four Faculties: all are as it were mirrored in personality, Unity of Being becomes possible. Hitherto we have been part of something else, but now discover everything within our own nature. Sexual love becomes the most important event in life, for the opposite sex is nature chosen and fated. Personality seeks personality. Every emotion begins to be related to every other as musical notes are related. It is as though we touched a musical string that set other strings vibrating.*

The points in the cycle where the *tinctures* close and open are points where a reversion occurs in the movement from *primary* to *antithetical*, or vice versa. In the *antithetical* quarters, a note of *primary* is introduced; and in the *primary* quarters, an awareness of the *antithetical*. In the hemi-quarter model, the first hemi-quarter (Venus => Mercury => moon) has been a move from *primary* towards *antithetical*. The second hemi-quarter (Saturn => Jupiter => Mars) is a move from *antithetical* back towards *primary*. In the Chaldean model described in this book, this "switch in direction" occurs at the disjunction points between moon and Saturn phases. In W.B.Y.'s model: *One may regard the subjective phases as forming a separate wheel, its Phase 8 between Phases 11 and 12 of the larger wheel, its Phase 22 between Phases 19 and 20* [sic – he means between Phases 18 and 19]; *the objective phases as another separate wheel, its Phase 8 between Phases 25 and 26, its Phase 22 between Phases 4 and 5.*

The empowerment of sexual awakening is symbolized by Saturn because in most cases this is the point in life in which people are challenged to make things happen for themselves. Up until then (usually) everything the child needed was provided by others; and even in those *primary* societies in which the marriage partner is chosen by others, it is marriage – or at least the fulfillment of sexual striving – which requires people to take responsibility for themselves, voluntarily assume and discharge obligations, define their limits (what they are capable of and what they will stand for). This is what Saturn is all about. When Saturn is afflicted in the natal horoscope, people may not be particularly successful at applying themselves to achieve these goals (to make an independent life for themselves); but in one way or another they are forced to do so – even if this means being a homeless lunatic wandering the streets and picking through the garbage dump for sustenance.

The organization / codification stage of adulthood is symbolized by Jupiter, which symbolizes detachment, acceptance, taking a broad overview (in the ideal case). This is what adulthood – as opposed to childhood – teaches (or should teach): that it's not about *you*; but rather about what you can offer. Thus the cycle is moving back towards the *primary* again.

The final stage, submission, is symbolized by Mars because these phases are phases of struggle: struggle against death, struggle to the death; trying to hold it together in the face of immensity (feeling overwhelmed). It is in Mars phases that the person discovers that – just when it seems that everything is under control – "nothing is lost (Phase 7); nothing is won (Phase 14); nothing defended (Phase 21); and nothing undone (Phase 28)."

The Seven Chaldean Planets

The seven Chaldean planets symbolize different personality traits (what used to be termed "humors"). In *primary* phases they describe how people blend in or fit themselves into their social milieu; in *antithetical* phases they indicate how people distinguish themselves or hold themselves apart from their social milieu. *Primary* phases compromise; *antithetical* phases rebel or blissfully do their own thing; and the planetary ruler shows how they do this. What is shown is how the person adapts that planetary impulse to either separating self from or integrating self into his or her social milieu.

Sun: ☉ The sun phases represent rebirth: death in one realm implies rebirth in some other realm. That is to say, there is less striving in these four phases (a greater self-adequacy than the other phases), hence these natives' lives have less sense of an orderly progression – less "time glue" binding them to everyday existence (Phase 1 is completely centered in the now moment; Phase 15 is completely burnt-out; and Phases 8 and 22 don't know whether they are coming or going). Sun phase natives tend to be self-centered and solipsistic. They don't really fit in anywhere. In one way or another they hold themselves above / outside of their social milieu: Phase 1 is utterly unself-conscious and amused by it all; Phase 15 utterly self-conscious and bemused by it all; Phase 8 is at pains to stand out and shine; and Phase 22 is at pains to fit and trim. They possess an untrammeled sense of PURPOSE: they just *are* – not out to prove or accomplish anything in particular. These natives are self-contained, self-assured (smug, self-satisfied), footloose, and free-spirited. Sun phases are independent and self-reliant, with considerable personal flair and panache and a cocky noblesse oblige (condescending). Their disinterest and intrepidity make them natural-born leaders (this is their true purpose, their true role in life); and in one way or another they tend to dominate any social group of which they are a part, even while holding themselves emotionally aloof. In *antithetical* Phase 15 they shine when they boldly stick to their guns in the face of doubt and confusion; in *primary* Phase 1 their vivacious enthusiasm and positivity are an inspiration for everyone. Underlying the solar phases is a mood of alienation / indifference which gives rise to a felt need for caring (Venus).

In **Venus** ♀ phases issues of self-worth and self-esteem become paramount – what makes a person feel good. The aim in these phases is ENJOYMENT – of themselves and other people. They are adept at taking life as it comes and making the best of things, and bringing out the best in others. They are by no means as effusive and brash as sun natives, but rather are self-effacing, gentle and low-key, with a soft exterior that others find relaxing and inviting. In contrast to natives of the standoffish sun phases, Venus natives are sociable, gracious, accommodating, and courteous, with an open and intimate manner. They are quick to extend a helping hand and to indulge others (and they can be rather self-indulgent themselves). They are sincere, are good listeners, and are patient and upbeat; so they make good teachers and counselors. Their true purpose is to find harmony, common ground, modi vivendi. In *antithetical* phases their sprightly, saucy charm and wry good humor help keep things in perspective; in *primary* phases their calm, quiet authority is a reassuring influence. Underlying the Venus phases is a mood of bland acquiescence and susceptibility which gives rise to a felt need for detachment, impartiality, and self-definition (Mercury).

In **Mercury** ☿ phases the emphasis moves from self-worth to self-sufficiency; from group belonging to individual dexterity. Mercury phase natives emphasize their MENTALITY: they think for themselves and reach their own conclusions rather than unquestioningly accept the prevailing mores. Their cool, aloof manner contrasts sharply with the welcoming familiarity of Venus phase natives, and their insights are shrewd rather than caring. They are glib talkers rather than receptive listeners, and their conversation is clever, humorous, ironic, and outspoken (brusque, sharp-tongued). They analyze and question; are fond of learning and experimenting; and they take pride in exhibiting their virtuosity and acuteness (on the negative side they can be intolerant and judgmental of others, and always ready with an excuse for themselves). Their true purpose is to communicate. They are political animals; in disputes not of their own making they tend not to choose sides, but rather play the objective umpire or referee (rather than lend a sympathetic ear as the Venus types do). In *antithetical* phases their unique perspective is delightfully refreshing; in *primary* phases they love to preach and lecture. The blithe matter-of-factness and flippancy of Mercury can produce a feeling of being left out or passed by, with a concomitant longing for a deeper and more meaningful sense of conviction (moon).

Moon ☽ phase natives seek ASSURANCE and rootedness in life – an anchor rather than a sail; faith and conviction rather than ingenuity and prowess. They tend to be cautious rather than exuberant, and they seek harmony and peace rather than agreement with their own ideas. They are patient, gentle and yielding. It may happen that a moon native has suffered a harsh, dysfunctional childhood (which will be indicated by afflictions elsewhere in the natal horoscope) and feigns a gruff, bristly exterior as a protection to hide his or her vulnerability (particularly in Phase 25). However, beneath the surface these natives take everything very much to heart; and the people who know them well realize that they are basically soft Teddy bears. Their true purpose is to be tender, delicate, and act on conscience: the hallmark of *antithetical* lunar phases is a fearless obedience to the dictums of their own hearts; in *primary* phases they are sympathetic, solicitous, and considerate – quick to assist and support others. Their easy-going indefiniteness and susceptibility to being imposed upon calls for a greater firmness, strengthening of personal limits, and willingness to confront rather than withdraw (Saturn).

Here the cycle breaks (the heretofore prevailing *tincture* closes, and with the following phase the opposite *tincture* opens): if the natives have been too *primary* (seeing themselves as reflections in other people's eyes) they now become more *antithetical* (standing on their own two feet). And if they have been too *antithetical* (self-centered) they now feel an incumbency for the *primary* (greater self-limitation and discipline).

Saturn: ♄ Where moon natives tend to be irresolute and laissez faire, with a tendency to let things slide rather than make a stand, the mood of Saturn (by contrast) is one of taking complete RESPONSIBILITY for oneself and making one's own way in life. These natives are dignified, unyielding, stern, and determined; and they play their cards very close to their chest. They tend to be suspicious and refuse to rely upon other people or the common assumptions which everyone else is taking for granted. Unless Saturn in the natal chart is debilitated or afflicted, these natives are hard-working and hard-driving, imposing and intractable, with a no-nonsense, dominating presence (curt, rude). Their true purpose is to be hard, practical, and utterly fearless: they do not hesitate to roll up their sleeves and get down to what they feel must be done with a minimum of reservations, fuss, or argument. In *antithetical* phases the focus is on the path beneath their feet; in *primary* phases it is on whatever they conceive their duties and obligations to be. But they cannot be budged an inch from their own aims and ends, in pursuit of which they can be deaf to entreaties and maddeningly indifferent to social norms and niceties, or even common logic. Their self-containment, ornery stubbornness, and tendency to brush people aside calls for lightening up and taking a broader view (Jupiter).

Jupiter: ♃ Where Saturn phase natives tend to be stern, forbidding, and completely focused on themselves and their objectives, Jupiter phase natives exhibit a lightness of spirit and a benevolent UNDERSTANDING of both other people and their own limitations. They have a philosophical outlook on life and are sociable, broad-minded, and humanitarian. Like the Saturn types they are reserved rather than effusive, but they make boon companions with their amused bonhomie, interest in other people, and tolerance for divergent points of view. They are not necessarily humorous, but rather good-humored. Their true purpose is to weigh and balance: in *antithetical* phases they take on the role of doyen or disinterested moderator of any social group in which they find themselves; in *primary* phases their dedication and concern are a reliance for everyone. They hold themselves above contention (reserved, vague) and turn aside from unpleasantness, referring their behavior to abstract standards of civility and fair play. Their detachment and tendency to temporize make them shy from conflict and commitment, which highlights a need for greater decisiveness: a willingness to plunge ahead and devil-take-the-hindmost (Mars).

Mars: ♂ Where Jupiter people manifest benign and well-meaning disinterest, Mars phase natives are passionate, bold, and brash, whose mainspring to action is pride in ACCOMPLISHMENT. Like the Jupiter phases they don't allow themselves to get too involved; but their brisk and breezy impersonality and enterprise contrasts sharply with the neutral affability of the Jupiter types. These natives are audacious, cheeky, and scrappy; they speak their minds (tactless) and let the chips fall where they may. They are concentrated, intense, and quite willing to go to any extreme to make a point; or just for the sake of going to an extreme. There is a constant awareness of death in Mars phases – of death breathing down one's neck or speeding time up. Their true purpose is to spice life up with a spirit of dash and daring: their unflinching moral courage is either a model of rugged independence for other people; or else a gnarly thorn in their sides. In *antithetical* phases Mars people intrepidly strike out on their own; in *primary* phases they tirelessly devote their lives to defending / upholding a higher ideal, or readily sacrifice themselves for others. The insistent pickiness and quick-trigger combativeness of Mars shows up a need for impersonality and insouciance (sun).

Note that the foregoing model is just that – a model. There is no eternal truth in it – it's just a way of getting a handle on the meaning of the Great Wheel. The point is to be able to view the cycle of the Great Wheel as a progression in which each individual phase is but a stage leading to the next phase; i.e., the phases should be viewed in terms of becoming rather than completion. In this sense the System is similar to the *I Ching*, which is a different scheme, based upon a different numerical symbolism, but with a similar purpose: tracking change. Instead of applying the model to the way in which a newborn adapts himself to his world, it could be applied to the stages new employees go through when they join a business enterprise: at the beginning everything is pretty overwhelming (sun) and the person is watching everything; then others train and guide the new employees (Venus) until they learn to do the job themselves (Mercury) and turn it into routine (moon). They then enter a new phase of accepting (or declining) responsibility for making decisions (Saturn); find themselves organizing work priorities / directing others (Jupiter); and struggle to advance in the enterprise or perhaps strike out on their own; or get fired (Mars). Or, the model could be used to describe the stages couples go through when entering into a love relationship. The model can be applied to anything which is born, dies, and is reborn.

The purpose of any model is to obtain an understanding (by analogy) of a more complex system. In this book, the more complex system is grasping your true purpose, which is obscured by the multi-layered nature of your existence in worlds upon worlds and lifetimes upon lifetimes. It's not possible to understand your true life's purpose just by referring to the particular line of probable realities which make up your present history (and future). There is too much other stuff going on "out there" which is impinging upon this process. This will be described in the following section on the influence of the *Faculties* upon the phases. As mentioned previously, when my marriage was disintegrating our spirit guides had my wife and myself run scores of past lives we had had together in order to see how we had gotten to where we were at in this life. The point is, that if you want to find your true life's purpose you must consider that it has ramifications which did not just begin when you were born; nor will they end when you die.

The model of the System given in this book is – like W.B.Y.'s scheme – designed to cobble together keyword interpretations for the 28 different phases. It's merely a mnemonic; there's no deep truth in any of it, although W.B.Y.'s version was designed to illustrate how the interactions between the *Four Faculties* produce the illusion of linear time. I, personally, find W.B.Y.'s schematics rather obscure, in contrast to the Chaldean view (but that could be because I am already familiar with the astrological symbolism which underlies it). But it doesn't really matter how the Great Wheel of 28 phases is simplified so long as it makes clear the fact that each phase leads to / fades into the next; that the cycle is a progression; and that it can be viewed on many different levels as wheels upon wheels, and wheels within wheels. This is the important point vis-à-vis using the following scheme in astrological delineation: you can't just read the interpretations for a phase, in cookbook fashion, and expect to understand where that person is coming from and whither he or she is going. Rather, the person must be seen as a process of becoming (a wave) rather than as a completed entity (a particle).

The Rectangles

The present approach to interpreting the individual lunar phases considers them as belonging to groups of four: the Cross of Crisis (Phases 1 and 15 = new and full moon; and Phases 8 and 22 = first and last quarter); and six rectangles each ruled by a Chaldean planet:

Table of Rectangles:

Interchange of *tinctures* →	☉	1	15		
	♂	2	14	16	28
	♃	3	13	17	27
closing / opening	☽	4	12	18	26
of *tinctures* →	♄	5	11	19	25
	☿	6	10	20	24
	♀	7	9	21	23
Inversion of *tinctures* →	☉		8	22	

The Rectangle rulerships run in reverse Chaldean order and provide an "undertow" or "backwash" effect beneath the seesaw / sinusoidal "flow" of the *tinctures* which culminates at points of inflection where the Chaldean cycle breaks – between the moon and Saturn phases (4-5, 11-12, 18-19, and 25-26) – at which points the reverse Chaldean order reverses again (so that the moon and Saturn rectangles do a "flip-flop" out of the expected order). After the moon phases the overlying *tincture* of that quarter is said to close, and at the commencement of the Saturn phases the opposite *tincture* is said to open. From the point of view of interpretation, what this means is that in the center of each quarter the opposite *tincture* makes an unexpected appearance, like the dot of yang in the midst of yin and vice versa (similar to the interchange of the *tinctures* at Phases 1 and 15 and the inversion of the *tinctures* at Phases 8 and 22).

When the rectangle ruler is the complement of (rather than the same as) the primary phase ruler, it puts a "substrate" of self-awareness under this phase ruler. For example, Venus phases in Mars rectangles are peppier, with more pizzazz and panache than are the low-key double Venus phases; and Mars phases in Venus rectangles are more subdued and attuned to other people's feelings than are the intense and driven double Mars phases. Similarly, Mercury phases in Jupiter rectangles are more sober and conscientious than are the simplistic and matter-of-fact double Mercury phases who see everything as black or white; and Jupiter phases in Mercury rectangles try harder to understand than do the rather smug and complacent double Jupiter phases. Saturn phases in moon rectangles are more sensitive and aware than are the hard-edge double Saturn phases; and moon phases in Saturn rectangles are more conflicted or defensive than are the easy-going, "let-it-be" double moon phases.

The Influence of the *Faculties* Upon the Phases

The following section is an explanation of how the Table of Keywords for the Influence of the *Faculties* Upon the Phases was constructed. Knowledge of this information is not necessary in order to use the Table of Keywords or the interpretations for individual phases which are based on it; and indeed it is suggested that the first-time reader skip this section until he or she has become quite familiar with applying the interpretations to actual horoscopes. These keywords are given in preference to those in *A Vision*, since the latter are not (in this author's purview) particularly apt or evocative (except now and then). The reader who wishes to experiment with W.B.Y.'s original keywords will find them in Appendix I.

During the recapitulation (*Return* or *Dreaming Back*) at the moment of death, all the events in the life pass before a person's window in no time at all. Previously it was pointed out that it is the shift in attention from one level of memory (or *Faculty*) to another which creates the illusion of the passage of time. Just as Tarzan swings through the jungle by grabbing onto one vine after another, sentient beings swing through life by shooting out light fibers of desire from moment-to-moment in order to grasp (better said: create) the memories which lend a sense of continuity and familiarity to their existence. Thus the cessation of desire (which W.B.Y. characterizes as "Deception") would lead to the cessation of linear time and the entrance into a state of timelessness (at the expense of all sense of familiarity and importance). This occurs in the average life at certain *Critical Moments* – altered states of consciousness which, like bolts of lightning, disrupt all the routines of *Will*, from minor *Initiatory Moments* such as orgasm, to the final dissolution of the separated self into the *Beatific Vision* (Stopping the World).

This is a common experience resulting from the ingestion of psychedelics, as well as spiritual epiphanies and religious ecstasy. Timelessness is the hallmark of dreamless sleep: dream consciousness – which is the realm of the *Four Principles* – introduces the chronology of time (one thing happening after another in linear sequence instead of everything at once); and waking consciousness –

the realm of the *Four Faculties* – introduces the inexorability of time (the separation of past from future). Dreamless sleep – like psychedelics, religious ecstasy, and orgasm – is just pure NOW. It's the *Daimon*'s base of operations.

As Carlos Castaneda said (in *Tales of Power*) – and as anyone who has done some recapitulation soon realizes – "Something in the warrior is always aware of every change. It is precisely the aim of the warrior's way to foster and maintain that awareness. The warrior cleans it, shines it, and keeps it running. ... I knew that there was something in me that registered and was aware of everything I did. And yet it had nothing to do with the ordinary awareness of myself. It was something else which I could not pin down. ... It's an inner voice that tells you what's what." That something is the *Daimon* – pure awareness. It is filtered through the *Four Faculties*, which tend to obscure it or overlay it with contradictory programs. We suppress the voice of our *Daimon* because that information contradicts the agendas of our *Four Faculties*: whatever routines we are clinging to in order to feel secure (*Will*); our expectations of other people (*Body of Fate*); our karmic agendas (*Mask*); or our obedience to societal fiat (*Creative Mind*).

These *Faculties* represent one form or another of conditioning – by the *Zeitgeist* (cultural and epochal orientation = *C.M.*); personal karmic obligations and debts (*Mask*); or expectations by / of the quotidian social milieu (*B.F.*). The higher *Faculties* imbue *Will* with desire: *Will* by itself has no particular direction except "seeking its own continuance". *Will* only acquires purpose as it is animated by a need for higher meaning beyond mindless routine– i.e. one of the other *Faculties*.

The being becomes conscious of itself as a separate being, because of certain facts of Opposition and Discord, the emotional Opposition of Will *and* Mask [demands of one's everyday life vs. one's ideal self], *the intellectual Opposition of* Creative Mind *and* Body of Fate [one's cultural programming vs. the expectations of one's personal relationships], *Discords between* Will *and* Creative Mind [one's own convenience and comfort vs. one's higher duty to society], Creative Mind *and* Mask [the directives of one's society vs. the promptings of one's heart], Mask *and* Body of Fate [one's conscience vs. one's everyday desires], Body of Fate *and* Will [the needs of others vs. one's own needs; also one's wistful imaginings vs. playing it safe]. *A Discord is always the enforced understanding of the unlikeness of* Will *and* Mask [routine proclivities vs. underlying feelings] *or of* Creative Mind *and* Body of Fate [societal imperatives and values vs. exigencies of everyday relationships and one's investments in same. The *Discords* between *C.M.* and *B.F.* normally involve sex – what you're "supposed" to do vs. what you want to do]. *There is an enforced attraction between Opposites, for the* Will *has a natural desire for the* Mask [desire for some deeper meaning beyond mindless, everyday routine] *and the* Creative Mind *a natural perception of the* Body of Fate [appreciation of the possibility of relating to others spontaneously on a level beyond socially correct comportment]; *in one the dog bays the Moon, in the other the eagle stares on the Sun by natural right. When, however, the* Creative Mind *deceives the* Will *in an* antithetical *phase, by offering it some* primary *image of the* Mask [e.g. religious beliefs instead of true spirituality, or patriotism in lieu of heeding the Voices of the Ancestors], *or when the* Will *offers to the* Creative Mind *an emotion that should be turned towards the* Mask *alone* ["But for the present age, which prefers the sign to the thing signified, the copy to the original, representation to reality, appearance to essence … truth is considered profane, and only illusion is sacred. Sacredness is in fact held to be enhanced in proportion as truth decreases and illusion increases, so that the highest degree of illusion comes to be the highest degree of sacredness." – Ludwig Feuerbach, *The Essence of Christianity*], *the Discord emerges again in its simplicity because of the jarring of the emotion, the grinding out* [phoniness] *of the Image. On the other hand, it may be the* Mask *that slips on to the* Body of Fate *till we confuse what we would be* [B.F.] *with what we must be* [Mask]. *As the Discords through the circling* [filter] *of the* Four Faculties *become Oppositions, when as at Phase 15 (say) the* Creative Mind *comes to be opposite the* Mask [because at Phase 15 comes the realization that obedience to society's injunctions will *not* fulfill one's true purpose in incarnating], *they share the qualities of Opposition* [the carrot-and-stick of societal programming directly contradicts what hyper-aware Phase 15 natives know in their hearts they must do]. *As the* Faculties *approach to one another, on the other hand, Discord gradually becomes identity, and one or other, according to whether it takes place at Phase 1 or Phase 15, is weakened and finally absorbed,* Creative Mind *in* Will *at Phase 15* [the extreme *antithetical* expression of obedience to societal sanction is wholly mindless: Phase 15's comply with what society expects of them, but as one might slap a bothersome mosquito], Will *in* Creative Mind *at Phase 1* [the extreme *primary* expression of societal programming is high (albeit unconscious) sensitivity and adaptation to what is required at all times – usually monitored / enforced by a fear governor on the free expression of emotion], *and so on; while if it be at Phase 8 or Phase 22, first one predominates and then the other and there is instability* [these two phases waffle – they're never quite sure what's expected of them or how to fulfill it – so they go back and forth doing a soft-shoe shuffle in the effort to please].

Without this continual Discord through Deception there would be no conscience, no activity; Deception is a technical term of my teachers and may be substituted for "desire" [i.e., by Deception is meant "striving". Striving is not striving *after* something; desire is not desire *for* something – this is the Deception. Striving / desire are movements for their own sake – the object sought or desired is a conceptual thought form tacked on "after the fact", as a way of "remembering" or making a notation of the movement or light fiber. It isn't really the objects of desire which are sought but rather the hunger, the state of desire itself. The *primary* yearns for the *antithetical*, and the *antithetical* for the *primary*: we all crave that which we do not / cannot have – the grass is always greener on the other side of the fence. The objects of desire – thought forms, the stuff of waking consciousness – don't have any objective existence. This is what is meant by "reality is but a symbol" or "waking consciousness is but a more highly evolved form of dreaming"; and this is the Deception]. *Life is an endeavor, made vain by the four sails of its mill* [i.e. *Will, B.F., Mask,* and *C.M.* – symbolized by the four phases in each rectangle], *to come to a double contemplation, that of the chosen Image* [thought forms – the events of everyday life], *that of the fated Image* [light fibers – the direct experience / expression of the *Daimon* – what we have termed "true purpose", of which the events of everyday life are merely a symbolic reflection].

In other words, *Will* acquires its sense of continuity (experience of continuous self-existence) by turning to the higher *Faculties* which embed *Will* in a meaningful sequence – first this happens, then that happens, then the other thing happens; but there is a pot of gold at the end of the rainbow (a meaningfulness supplied by the higher *Faculties* – hope in the case of *B.F.*, social approval in the case of *C.M.*, destiny in the case of *Mask*) – a reason to keep on keeping on, no matter how boring the everyday routines of *Will* may be. The higher *Faculties* enable *Will* to take a break, to take a rest from itself (as will be explained below). Moreover, the entire exercise makes some kind of sense (at least when it is happening) – it's not all just helter-skelter ineffableness (except for some schizophrenics). However, running past life regressions and recapitulations often reveals that the thing doesn't necessarily make as much sense as it did when one was living it and making those decisions the first time around.

Unlike "normal" folks, crazy people don't have the luxury of being able to insulate themselves from what is going on around them with the mindlessness and insensitivity of taken-for-granted routines (pure *Will*) or taken-for-granted societal assumptions (*Creative Mind*). They aren't centered in a familiar "reality" in which their attention is focused on important this and important that and important the other thing every minute ("ME!" "ME!" "ME!"). Crazy people find so-called "reality" disorienting since they aren't armored in a phony "ME!" as a defense against the onslaughts of demons (unlike "normal" people, who are so lost in their "ME!" "ME!" "ME!" that they fail to see that they are basically soulless puppets whose every decision is being manipulated from outside themselves). Why do you suppose that it is the people who are mentally ill – Sir Isaac Newton, Wolfgang Mozart, Friedrich Nietzsche, Vincent van Gogh, Vaslav Nijinsky, Kurt Gödel come to mind – who most advance our civilization? Think on it.

The moment-to-moment attention is like a kaleidoscope or psychedelic light show of thoughts-sensations-feelings (sensory and conceptual thought forms) which saccade from object to object from instant to instant, blown hither and thither by the astrological winds of the time (this point is easiest to appreciate when you begin trying to control your moment-to-moment attention intentionally through some sort of mind-training technique such as *Vipassana*, which reveals the Herculean effort necessary to turn back that tide of incessant babble). It is the interplay of all these staccato impressions which produces the subjective sense of the continuous passage of time. As the attention flickers from thing to thing to thing, it creates a sense of a non-flickering, separated "ME" there which is paying attention. In fact, that sense of a separated, self-existent "ME" which is watching what's happening, is death. When the stroboscopic flickering slows down (due to shock, or mind training, or psychedelic drugs) death moves to the forefront; and when the flickering stops, that's all she wrote (the wheel stops turning).

In other words, "you" have no more substance than a motion picture – a series of still images which give the impression of motion and life – except where a motion picture is pre-scripted and filmed, "you" are an ongoing piece of work, with the next scene more or less randomly subject to the exigencies of your *Faculties* (dictated by whatever you consider to be familiar at that moment), unless death suddenly pops up in the midst of the show and says "Surprise!"

Death is just that – a joining of random flickers into cohesive wholes. A person doesn't have just one death (so to speak), but rather infinite deaths which are different ways of combining random thought forms (flickers) into chains of linear temporality. These are the probable realities for that person's life – the person's *Body of Fate*. At any given moment, the next flicker could be just about anything (and master magicians have this option – of choosing what to pay attention to next); but for the average person, the choice of the next flicker is constrained by the familiarity parameters of the person's habitual (routine) proclivities and predilections (*Will*), wistful fancies (*B.F.*), personal karma (*Mask*), and cultural expectations (*C.M.*).

WILL = HABIT (ROUTINE)
MASK = ACCEPTANCE when True and DENIAL when False
CREATIVE MIND = DUTY when True and STATUS when False
BODY OF FATE = SPONTANEITY

Body of Fate is what people see when they are primping themselves before the mirror; but *Mask* is what they see when they gaze intently into the mirror. *Body of Fate* is what people think about when they're whistling a happy tune; but *Mask* is what's on their minds when they lie awake late at night. Therefore,

In an antithetical *phase the being seeks by the help of the* Creative Mind [sense of DUTY] *to deliver the* Mask [ACCEPTANCE of karma] *from* Body of Fate [SPONTANEOUS impulses] – that is to say, *antithetical* phase natives (who rely on reflection to make decisions) rely on their intellectualized sense of responsibility to their group to raise their higher self above the lure of expectations of other people; they use their group identity and allegiance to still the clamor of their desire for approval / approbation / success in the eyes of others.

In a primary *phase the being seeks by the help of the* Body of Fate [SPONTANEOUS impulses] *to deliver the* Creative Mind [sense of DUTY] *from the* Mask [ACCEPTANCE of karma] – that is, *primary* phase natives use their gift for spur-of-the moment improvisation to rise above (cut across the quagmire of) their karmic "issues" to make their unique contribution to the group weal. In other words, where *antithetical* phase natives think things through to control their unruly impulses to serve their group and thus fulfill their true purpose, *primary* phase natives go with the flow of their impulses to get past their psychological hang-ups and fulfill their group responsibilities.

The term *"Automatonism"* is used to refer to people's "automatic pilot" – the compulsive, incessant inner dialogue or rumination which occupies their attention most of the time they are awake (and is almost entirely absent from dreaming). *Automatonism* (mindlessness) requires less energy of the organism than does constant alertness (mindfulness), and thus can be considered a form of rest. In *antithetical* phases, with their high degree of self-awareness and self-attunement, *Automatonism* takes the form of thinking on (absorption in) abstracts and arises from the higher *Faculties Mask* and *Creative Mind* as a respite from constant vigilance and attentiveness to the conflicts and petty demands of everyday life (represented by the *Body of Fate* and *Will*). In *primary* phases *Automatonism* takes the form of absent-minded woolgathering or perfunctory attentiveness to everyday routines (emphasizing *Body of Fate* and *Will*) when wearying of the struggle of having to think for oneself and take responsibility for one's decisions. Engaging in this internal dialogue does not make people untrue to themselves (*out of phase*); the most powerful natures are precisely those who most often need *Automatonism* as a rest; moreover, this focus on one's own mentation (as opposed to paying attention to the here and now) is an element in our enjoyment of art and literature, aesthetic pleasure being awakened in our minds by the rhythm and pattern available to the exercise of imagination, which transports us to a more perfect world than the here and now. People are, however, *out of phase* if – when in *antithetical* phases – they unduly indulge in this compulsive internal rumination as an escape from spontaneous participation in their everyday experience (*Body of Fate*); or – when in *primary* phases – they use *Automatonism* to focus upon trivialities and distractions in order to deny acknowledgment of and taking responsibility for their true karmic destiny (*Mask*).

By Will *is understood feeling that has not become desire because there is no object of desire; a bias by which the soul is classified and its phase fixed but which as yet is without result in action; an energy as yet uninfluenced by thought, action, or emotion; the first matter of a certain personality — choice.* That is to say, *Will* is the decision-making portion of the *Daimon* in its mechanical aspect – that which channels intent. *Will* is not intent per se, any more than a phonograph needle is sound; *Will* merely enables intent in the same fashion that a phonograph stylus instruments sound. The objects of desire upon which *Will* fixates (*thoughts, actions,* and *emotions*) are created by the three higher *Faculties*.

> As the Kinks described *Will*:
> 'Cause he gets up in the morning,
> And he goes to work at nine,
> And he comes back home at five-thirty,
> Gets the same train every time.
> 'Cause his world is built 'round punctuality,
> It never fails.
> And he's oh, so good,
> And he's oh, so fine,
> And he's oh, so healthy,
> In his body and his mind.
> He's a well respected man about town,
> Doing the best things so conservatively.

Will, or everyday conscious mind, is like a traffic cop at a busy intersection directing the flow of cars (impulses coming from other lives and probable realities as well as societal imperatives from this one) by deciding which car can go now (which impulse will be paid attention to in this now moment). When *Will* is not impinged upon by the higher *Faculties*, it becomes a soulless automaton – a zombie slave to mindless routines (Stasis) and automatic responses to everyday stimuli. It is the influence of the higher *Faculties* which imbue *Will* with the spark of life (Change), which is the basis of the illusion of linear time. Linear time is like a color-blindness test in that up close (caught up in the midst of it), it makes no sense; but when you step back (separate yourself more) you can see a recognizable (familiar) order and pattern to it. So too with linear time: the way an infant apprehends it is completely random and ineffable; but with some distance (separatedness) it gives the appearance of making sense: being sequential – one thing happening after another in a regular, logical order. It is the conditioning which infants receive at the hands of the adults around them which enables them to stabilize and operate in the midst of complete chaos by making that chaos appear sensible (and defensible).

In terms of *Automatonism*, *Will* is the cavalcade of thought forms – the automatic thoughts and knee-jerk responses – which in adults is focused on the mindless routines of everyday life – hence the keyword that describes *Will* is HABIT. *Will* has no "will" of its own, but is directed in its conceptualizing by the three higher *Faculties*, principally by *Creative Mind*, which first and foremost divides the thinkable from the unthinkable – what Freud would term the conscious from the unconscious. This is wholly a matter of cultural conditioning, and hence varies from society to society.

The basic assumption or building block underlying *Creative Mind* is the supposition that we are "awake"; and that there is an external "reality" out there which we all share. It is *Creative Mind* which defines common sense – what is popularly considered "real" vs. "unreal", "subjective" vs. "objective", "normalcy" vs. "insanity" – as this varies substantially from culture to culture and even from family to family.

Creative Mind is a matter of solidarity with the overarching cultural mores. True *Creative Mind* (whose keyword is DUTY) shows people's adaptation to those cultural traits which unite them with others (in a *primary* phase) or distinguish them from others (in an *antithetical* phase). True *Creative Mind* entails such things as sense of responsibility, honor, self-limitation and self-sacrifice willingly offered – i.e. using group identification to erase self-importance.

False or enforced *Creative Mind* (whose keyword is STATUS) describes people's adaptation to the traits which divide people from one another in a *primary* society or lump them together in an *antithetical* society – i.e. which increase self-importance. False *Creative Mind* is what in *Thought Forms* was described as hiding shame from other people and seeking glory from them. This constant concern with one's STATUS – saving "face" – in other people's eyes is the very basis of waking consciousness: the moment-to-moment "How'm I doing? Ain't I cool? How'm I doing? Ain't I cool?" inner dialogue serves to undergird and stabilize waking experience, without which it would dissolve into pure dreaming (of course there are other ways of keeping the two states separated without continual reference to "ME!" "ME!" "ME!" every second one is awake; awareness of the presence of one's death is actually a more effective way of doing it).

False *Creative Mind* subsumes SUPERIORITY (which was the keyword used for it in previous editions of this book), since one's sense of STATUS in society entails such things as xenophobia, racism, snobbery – i.e. using group identification to bolster self-importance. All judging other people, feeling oneself to be superior to other people, is False *C.M.* at work. False *C.M.* is based on fearfulness, whereas True *C.M.* is based on fearlessness (the same as for True and False *Mask*). Where True *Creative Mind* is animated by joy – a true sense of connectedness – False (or enforced) *Creative Mind* is animated by cowardice. Where True *Creative Mind* is based upon awe, False *C.M.* is based upon emotional repression (hence "enforced").

By "awe" we are not talking about anything mystical. We're talking about respect. Earlier human societies – *primary* societies – lived a circumscribed existence in which there was very little free choice (unlike today). But they had that magical quality of *respect* – for the gods, the earth, nature, themselves, and other people – which modern *antithetical* societies in their hubris and contempt for nature completely lack. Individuals then had a seriousness of purpose wholly missing from the frivolous, escapist lifestyle of today.

The main feature which distinguishes a truly *primary* from an *antithetical* society is that in the former the marriage partner is provided; whereas in the latter each individual must scout around for him or herself. In *primary* societies licit sex is only available within the context of marriage; hence marriage usually occurs at puberty. The institution of marriage doesn't fare so well in highly *antithetical* societies such as our own; it is a hangover from earlier times in which people never asked the question of whether they are happy with their lot or fulfilling their potential, but were concerned primarily with "belonging". One finds that individuals in *primary* societies are less individualized than in *antithetical* societies – they keep their heads down and mouths shut and try to fit in; whereas individuals in *antithetical* societies are encouraged to develop their individual abilities and seek their personal destinies. In *primary* societies (and phases) *Creative Mind* (traditional canons of suitable thought and behavior) and *Body of Fate* (expectations of others) bear more heavily upon *Will* than they do in *antithetical* societies (and phases); and in *antithetical* societies (and phases) *Mask* (sense of individual destiny – obsessive reflection on whether one is happy or not and why not) is the dominant influence upon *Will* (everyday mind).

Primary societies are usually more primitive and dreamier; a lot less thinking goes on in these societies than in *antithetical* ones. Individuals in *primary* societies define themselves by their family, religion, clan or social caste; and there is usually a greater awareness of and receptivity to messages from the spirit world and the Voices of the Ancestors than in *antithetical* societies. *Primary* societies have a great deal more sensory thought forms mixed in with their habitual moment-to-moment mentation than do *antithetical* societies (such as present-day America, whose *Creative Mind* consists principally of conceptual thought forms); or another way of saying this is, *Will* in *primary* societies is more dreamlike and ineffable than it is in wide-awake, hup-hup-hup *antithetical* societies. In *primary* societies (e.g. hunting-gathering, herding, subsistence agriculture) everyone does what everyone does, and that's why everyone does it. All the men do what all the men do and all the women do what all the women do (although there may be some specialization such as healers, priests / nobles, storytellers, etc.). No questions are asked, no thinking is required, and no disobedience is tolerated. Individuals in *primary* societies are not as "solid"; not as "there" as are people in *antithetical* societies. Individuals in such societies are encouraged from infancy to be passive and accepting, and not to rock the boat.

In *antithetical* societies, where people are confronted with a plethora of choices, the individual members are more awake, more aware, and more neurotic (asking too many questions that don't have answers). Individuals in *antithetical* societies spend a lot more of their everyday existence thinking (rather than spacing-out); and therefore, to paraphrase Descartes, they *are* (self-conscious, self-pitying, overburdened with *Angst*). The phases preceding Phase 15 are increasingly thoughtful and intellectual and filled with *Spiritual or supersensual Rage*; until at Phase 15 complete reliance is placed upon self-reflection, the native is little motivated by societal fiat and imperatives.

Creative Mind is not so much a matter of intellectualized beliefs as it is a sense of emotional allegiance and anchoring – the sum of people's loyalties, what they stand for. *Creative Mind* encompasses the ingroup / outgroup shibboleths of one's culture / clan / social class; and the particular professions, pastimes, proclivities, prejudices, proscriptions, psychoses, psychopathy, and patterns of marital dysfunction which "run in families" from generation to generation. For example, to understand the problems in a marriage it is necessary to examine not only how each person blames the other for their dashed expectations (*Body of Fate*); and the past lives that the two people have had with one another (*Mask*); but also the marital patterns which obtained between the respective partners' parents, their grandparents, and their great-grandparents (*Creative Mind*), since these are the mold in which present patterns of dysfunction have been cast.

In *primary* societies not only sexual expression, but also much "normal" (by *antithetical* standards) emotionality is staunchly repressed. Within certain parameters (which vary from society to society) the individual is taught from an early age (usually through corporal punishment) to keep his or her mouth shut, and only express emotions – particularly anger – in a group context (e.g. by persecuting minorities or – if the society is homogenous – women). For example, in traditional Mayan society babies are swaddled, held in darkness for the first forty days of life, and never held up vertically so that they can look around. In older children severe beatings are administered for even minor transgressions. As a result the Maya have a strong herd mentality (*Creative Mind*) which tends to discourage individual initiative.

True *Creative Mind* embraces the ideals and ideas which inspire and uplift people – the tales of heroes; whereas False *C.M.* is a matter of comparing oneself to other people – looking up to those whom we envy and down on those whose vulnerability we fear. It is people's (False) *Creative Mind* which is the basis of their attitudes of snobbishness and superiority to others – the petty backbiting and calumny (particularly noticeable in *primary* societies); the fear of what the neighbors might think or say; the threat of ostracism or violence for deviant thought or behavior – which holds society together.

According to don Juan, men of knowledge have no *Creative Mind*: "A man of knowledge has no honor, no dignity, no family, no name, no country, but only a life to be lived, and under these circumstances his only tie to his fellow men is his controlled folly. Thus a man of knowledge endeavors, and sweats, and puffs, and if one looks at him he is just like any ordinary man, except that the folly of has life is under control. Nothing being more important than anything else, a man of knowledge chooses any act, and acts it out as if it matters to him. His controlled folly makes him say that what he does matters and makes him act as if it did, and yet he knows that it doesn't; so when he fulfills his acts he retreats in peace, and whether his acts were good or bad, or worked or didn't, is in no way part of his concern." – Carlos Castaneda, *A Separate Reality*

The point is that whatever cultural traditions exist in a person's society – the *Creative Mind* of that society – circumscribe the range of choices available to *Will*, thus narrowing its focus. Thus the basic function of *Creative Mind* is to separate the thinkable from the unthinkable: this *Automatonism* enables *Will* to take a "rest from conflict" of having to pay conscious attention every moment because certain things can be safely assumed or taken completely for granted.

True and False *Creative Mind* for a given phase are found by the following rules (see the Table of Keywords for the Influence of the *Faculties* Upon the Phases):

When the Will *is in antithetical phases the True* Creative Mind *is derived from the* Creative Mind *phase* [the *antithetical* phase in the same rectangle with complementary planetary ruler], *modified by the* Creative Mind *of that phase* [i.e. the original *Will* phase]; *while the False* Creative Mind *is derived from the* Creative Mind *phase* [the *antithetical* phase in the same rectangle with complementary planetary ruler], *modified by the* Body of Fate *of that phase* [the phase opposite to the original *Will* phase].

When the Will *is in primary phases the True* Creative Mind *is derived from the* Creative Mind *phase* [*primary* phase in the same rectangle with complementary planetary ruler], *modified by the* Body of Fate *of that phase* [the phase opposite to the *Will* phase]; *while the* False Creative Mind *is derived from the* Creative Mind *phase* [*primary* phase in the same rectangle with complementary planetary ruler] *modified by the False* Creative Mind *of that phase* [the original *Will* phase].

In *primary* societies (and phases) True *Creative Mind* is modified by (learned from and enforced by) the *Body of Fate* (the expectations of one's family and social milieu); whereas in *antithetical* societies (and phases) True *Creative Mind* is beholden only unto itself. In other words, in *antithetical* phases False *Creative Mind*; and in *primary* phases True *Creative Mind*; are modified by a *Body of Fate* of the same planetary ruler but opposite dynamic (*primary* or *antithetical*) to reflect the effect of the formality and stiff dignity of everyday social interactions (on the positive side, a sense of community; on the negative side: pettiness, backbiting, judgmental gossip, and neighbor-spying-on-neighbor and putting their noses in each other's business) by which overarching societal norms (*C.M.*) are enforced by everyday social contacts (*B.F.*); which *antithetical* phases find odious – limiting to their self-expression; but *primary* phases find reassuring – a base of support / springboard to achievement.

Conversely, in *antithetical* phases True *Creative Mind*; and in *primary* phases False *Creative Mind*; are modified by a *Creative Mind* of the same phase as the *Will*, to reflect the fact that the individual's cultural adaptation is more thought-out and voluntarily assumed (or rejected, as the case may be) in *antithetical* phases; but is accepted willy-nilly, taken-for-granted with no questions asked, in *primary* phases. The everyday mentation of *primary* people (and societies) leans towards daydreams and fantasies – being "lost" in reverie – which comes under the rubric of *Body of Fate*; whereas the normal content of the everyday minds of *antithetical* people (and societies) leans towards thinking (words) – which is subsumed under *Creative Mind*. Thus it is said that when *Will* is in *primary* phases, the True *Creative Mind* is modified by the *Body of Fate* (of the opposite phase): because the everyday mind is dreamy and wistful – the "rules" it plays by are spontaneous expressions of the acceptable (or un-). *Primary* people are true to themselves as they rely on / go with their gut-level impressions and intuition.

When *Will* is in *antithetical* phases, the True *Creative Mind* is modified by the *Creative Mind* of the same phase, because the normal everyday mentation is reinforced and constrained by concepts inculcated by the ambient culture – the "rules" it obeys are abstract and self-measuring (as opposed to free-associating, as are the thought forms which occupy *primary* mind). *Antithetical* people are true to themselves as they uphold what they believe is morally right.

On the other hand, the spaced-out mindset of *primary* people implies that their False *Creative Mind* is modified by their own *Creative Mind* – in obeying what they take to be acceptable patterns of thought they run around in little circles, go through empty motions; whereas the rigid mindset of *antithetical* people implies that their False *Creative Mind* is modified by the *Body of Fate* (of the opposite phase) – they lose their center when they are flying with their fancies rather than ruminating and analyzing objectively.

Mask is the *Automatonism* that keeps *Will* on track, so that the whole enterprise doesn't degenerate into a chaotic game of bumper cars – a bunch of random collisions from moment to moment. Where *Creative Mind* provides a sense of belonging, *Mask* provides the native with a feeling of uniqueness – it provides the *Will* with a sense of selfhood from within (where *C.M.* delineates the bounds of the Other). Where *Creative Mind* draws the line between what is acceptable and unacceptable in social terms, *Mask* is conscience, inner voice, which tells the person right from wrong (regardless of what society says).

Mask is purposeful / purposiveness; determination; stick-to-it-iveness. Where *Will* is lower mind (random conceptual thought forms) *Mask* is higher mind (light fibers): a filter which orders the moment-to-moment saccade to keep it moving in a (more or less) constant direction. It is *Mask* which urges upon *Will* all the little decisions in life which make for enormous consequences – to turn left rather than right, to get on this plane or wait for a later one – which lead to the fulfillment of our destiny. As Carlos Castaneda put it (in *The Second Ring of Power*): "The force that rules our destinies is outside of ourselves and has nothing to do with our acts or volition. Sometimes that force would make us stop walking on our way and bend over to tie our shoelaces, as I had just done. And by making us stop, that force makes us gain a precious moment. If we had kept on walking, that enormous boulder would have most certainly crushed us to death. Some other day, however, in another ravine the same outside deciding force would make us stop again to bend over and tie our shoelaces while another boulder would get loose precisely above where we are standing. By making us stop, that force would have made us lose a precious moment. That time if we had kept on walking, we would have saved ourselves. Don Juan said that in view of my total lack of control over the forces which decide my destiny, my only possible freedom in that ravine consisted in my tying my shoelaces impeccably." So we can describe *Mask* as the *Automatonism* which urges us to tie our shoelaces impeccably.

Most people's representation of *Mask* is their ideals, morality, etc. inculcated through religious training (*C.M.*) but basically arising from / resonating with their own innate sense of justice and fair play. Even psychopaths have a *Mask* level, although it's pretty self-serving. But everyone fancies themselves to possess certain noble characteristics which they uphold – honor among thieves, or whatever; and this is their *Mask* level, which keeps people from making decisions which contradict their sense of what is right.

Mask describes what the person is passionate about (or deeply fears). It has reference to discipline (or lack of discipline); meaning, and sense of direction in life; long-range goals, willingness to sacrifice present comfort / convenience (*Will*) for higher (future) ends (as compared with *C.M.* which is willingness to sacrifice in the name of conformity to cultural / societal imperatives). When you feel as though you are caught in the clutches of some irresistible force which won't let you go but impels you forward (even in directions you fear to tread), that is your *Mask*. True Mask is ACCEPTANCE of your destiny – of playing the cards which life has dealt you; whereas False *Mask* is DENIAL, running away from your destiny (from yourself). While the *Mask* is always principally derived from the phase opposite *Will* (i.e., $\pm$ 14), the True and False *Mask*s for a given phase are found by the following rules (see the Table of Keywords for the Influence of the *Faculties* Upon the Phases):

When *Will* is in *antithetical* phases True *Mask*; and in *primary* phases False *Mask*; are modified by the *Creative Mind* of the phase in the same rectangle with complementary planetary ruler and opposite dynamic (*primary* or *antithetical*) to suggest that a person's obedience to his karmic destiny is fortified (in *antithetical* phases) or vitiated (in *primary* phases) by allegiance to the norms and taken-for-granted assumptions of the ambient culture and *Zeitgeist*: that is to say, *antithetical* phase natives ACCEPT their destinies by doing their DUTY to the common weal; whereas *primary* phase natives DENY their true purpose in life when they rely upon their STATUS in other people's eyes as a means of self-exculpation.

Conversely, when *Will* is in *antithetical* phases False *Mask*; and in *primary* phases True *Mask*; are modified by the *Body of Fate* of the phase in the same rectangle with complementary planetary ruler but same dynamic (*primary* or *antithetical*) to symbolize that a person's highest ideals are DENIED (*antithetical*) or ACCEPTED (*primary*) by SPONTANEOUS responses to his or her social milieu and personal relationships: that is to say, it's best for *antithetical* phase natives to ignore; and for *primary* phase natives to listen to and act on; the exigencies of everyday circumstances and relationships.

Since the *Mask* is always *antithetical* (a matter of the individual rather than related to other people) it is in sympathy with *antithetical* phases while it opposes *primary* phases – i.e., natives of *antithetical* phases – being reflective and self-aware – are in somewhat closer touch (for better if ACCEPTING or worse if in DENIAL) with their true purpose in life than are the outer-directed *primary* phase natives, who are more inclined to ACCEPT or DENY things at face value rather than puzzle them out.

Body of Fate consists of people's unconditioned impulses (where *Mask* and *Creative Mind* are conditioned and constrained by karmic or societal agendas) – whims, fancies, and flashes of unrestrained emotion (anger, joy, sexual turn-on). *Body of Fate* introduces an element of randomness into the whole enterprise – it's *Body of Fate* which leavens the ponderous inexorability of *Mask* and the onerous compulsion of *Creative Mind*. It is *Body of Fate* when two strangers look into each other's eyes and – in that *Critical Moment* – their *Masks* (instrumented by their *Bodies of Fate*) break through their *Creative Minds* and all the weight and intensity of their past and future lives together abrogates the prim propriety of social correctness. Sexual mores and the customs of and constraints on courtship are part of *C.M.*; whereas spontaneous sexual encounters (including one's fantasy life) are part of *B.F.* True *C.M.* entails conscientiousness (in contrast to the conscience of *Mask*); and False *C.M.* entails people going through empty motions of putative solidarity while actually devouring each other. But *Body of Fate* is too immediate, too here-and-now for such intellectualized constructs as "loyalty" and "solidarity" to have much meaning. *C.M.* includes roles such as mother-father-sister-brother-husband-wife-son-daughter-neighbor which people are forced to play out regardless of the actual karmic agendas of the persons involved; whereas *B.F.* includes roles such as baby – child – adolescent - young adult - middle-aged - old which are universal biological conditions; thus relationships with one's comrades (of the same age) are usually part of one's *Body of Fate*, and therefore relatively free and easy-going; whereas relationships with one's family are usually fraught with the social exigencies of *Creative Mind* and the karmic agendas of *Mask*.

The difference between *C.M.* and *B.F.* is one of immediacy; that is why there is no False *B.F.* – it's just too instinctive and unconditioned. As Roshi Philip Kapleau put it (in *Three Pillars of Zen*): "All thoughts, whether ennobling or debasing, are mutable and impermanent; they have a beginning and an end even as they are fleetingly with us, and this is as true of the thought of an era [*C.M.*] as of an individual [*B.F.*]. In Buddhism thought [what is here termed "*Automatonism*"] is referred to as 'the stream of life-and-death.' It is important in this connection to distinguish the role of transitory thoughts from that of fixed concepts. Random ideas [*Body of Fate*] are relatively innocuous [which is why there is no True or False *B.F.*], but ideologies, beliefs, opinions, and points of view [*Creative Mind*], not to mention the factual knowledge accumulated since birth (to which we attach ourselves) [*Will*] are the shadows which obscure the light of truth [the *Daimon*]."

The point is that all so-called "allegiances" and "proprieties" are part of *Creative Mind. Body of Fate* is too immediate and personal. When e.g. incest occurs, for example, it's a matter of *B.F.* trumping *C.M.* (and in our society it is usually demon-inspired – albeit in a society not as sexually repressed as ours it might be the normal way that adolescents are initiated into sex. If there were any truth to the Selfish Gene theory, one would expect incest to be the vogue throughout nature, not merely in human experience). The point is that it is *C.M.* which stamps "Unthinkable" upon incest. But kids playing "doctor" is a matter of *B.F.*, not *C.M. C.M.* is abstract whereas *B.F.* is personal, here-and-now (not a matter of loyalty or solidarity). In the same way *Mask* can be considered solidarity with one's destiny (as opposed to one's personal predilections, which are a matter of *Will*).

Body of Fate includes the expectations of other people in one's social circle. *C.M.* includes the taken-for-granted assumptions which shape one's thoughts – not so much the actual subject matter (*B.F.*) of the thoughts, but rather the constraints on them. E.g., it is assumed / expected that a mother will love her children. That is *C.M.* When a mother is rejecting, the child's reactions and thoughts on the subject are *B.F.* Similarly, it is assumed that children will obey (*C.M.*). When they rebel against their parents, that is *B.F.*

Expectations of other people include what one is disposed to offer as well as what is expected (or demanded) in return – fellowship, camaraderie, understanding, appreciation. *Body of Fate* starts with what infants desire from parents; at adolescence it takes a sexual turn; in marriage it can become utterly consuming. *Body of Fate* describes interpersonal relationships, since most of a person's expectations / hopes / fears are pinned to these: family, friends, lovers, enemies, neighbors, coworkers. *Body of Fate* includes the biological adaptation (as opposed to the abstract constraints of *C.M.*) to which people are subject by virtue of their sex (male or female) and age: young children have different concerns than do adolescents; or young adults; or the middle-aged; or the old. In terms of mental life *B.F.* is the person's fantasies, daydreams, and wistful imaginings (or fears of rejection); and in everyday life behaviors which are SPONTANEOUS expressions of desire. The *Body of Fate* of any particular phase is the effect of the phase in the same rectangle with complementary planetary ruler and opposite dynamic (*primary* or *antithetical*) – see the Table of Keywords for the Influence of the *Faculties* Upon the Phases. This means that a person's SPONTANEOUS responses to the people and happenings in his or her everyday environment are of exactly opposite character in every way from his or her customary HABIT of thinking and acting. Since the *Body of Fate* is always *primary* (having to do with others) it is in sympathy with *primary* phases while it opposes *antithetical* phases – i.e., natives of *antithetical* phases are somewhat more uptight stick-in-the-muds than are the lighter and looser *primary* phase natives, who are more inclined to seize opportunities as they arise or just go with the flow.

Will	Mask	Creative Mind	Body of Fate
HABIT, ROUTINE	T: ACCEPTANCE F: DENIAL	T: DUTY F: STATUS	SPONTAN-EITY
19 ♄♄ IP: UTILITARIAN OOP: EXIGENT	T: 5<CM 25 DECISIVE F: 5<BF 11 TYRANNICAL	T: 11<CM 19 TENDER F: 11<BF 5 SULLEN	25 SENSITIVE

< indicates "modified by"

As a practical example of how to use the keywords for the influence of the *Faculties* upon the phases, consider how the *Faculties* impacted W.B.Y.'s lunar phase. Phase 19 is a Saturn phase in a Saturn rectangle (phases 5, 11, 19, and 25), so he had a HABIT of no-nonsense, roll-up-your-sleeves-and-get-down-to-it practicality, with a gift for the political art of the possible (UTILITARIAN when *in phase* and EXIGENT when *out of phase*). His dominating (out-of-phase domineering) pragmatism made him a natural-born leader, and also the solid, stabilizing influence in all the groups to which he belonged (his family, occult and theatrical groups, the Irish Senate).

W.B.Y.'s *Mask* is derived from the opposite phase (5); when True (indicating ACCEPTANCE of his destiny) he was DECISIVE like Phase 5 yet SENSITIVE to his role in his group (modified by the *Creative Mind* of Phase 25). For example, W.B.Y.'s search for spiritual truth led him into conflicts with e.g. the Theosophical Society (in which he had become a leader) because he felt it was too dogmatic rather than practical and realistic. He ACCEPTED his destiny when he DECISIVELY followed his heart, even at the risk of censure (rather than bowing to political expedience and seeking approbation rather than truth).

W.B.Y.'s *Mask* was False when he DENIED his true purpose in life, lost his patience with others, and was TYRANNICAL in trying to impose his will upon people (with a SULLENLY overbearing *Body of Fate* of Phase 11); as for example when he attempted to shame and force his rejecting true love's daughter into marrying him (as a vicar for her mother) when the principal object of his sexual fantasies clearly wouldn't do so. It wasn't W.B.Y.'s destiny to marry either of these women (the object of his obsessive, life-long fantasies or her daughter), but rather the woman who channeled *A Vision* for him and thereby helped him realize his true destiny.

W.B.Y.'s True *Creative Mind* (sense of DUTY) derived from Phase 11 (TENDER) as modified by its own (Phase 19) UTILITARIANISM: in group situations his no-nonsense pragmatism was both kind and realistic in taking other people's feelings into account (supporting his dysfunctional family; and being the neutral, moderating voice in the midst of his political extremist friends, in the Irish theatre company he co-founded, and as senator in the new Irish government – always seeking good-faith, compromise solutions beneficial to all).

W.B.Y.'s False *Creative Mind* (STATUS) reflected the SULLENNESS of Phase 11 as modified by the TYRANNY of Phase 5's *Body of Fate*, so in group situations he tried to fit in as best he could under trying circumstances but was a self-righteous rebel and acerbic critic when disrespected; e.g., as an Irish Protestant writer he was frequently forced to bend himself to the will of the Catholic Church in order to get his plays performed; and he was on the defensive against – or else publicly attacking (and being attacked by) the Church – much of the time for most of his life.

W.B.Y.'s *Body of Fate* derived from Phase 25, so his SPONTANEOUS impulses were SENSITIVE – attuned to the nuances of the moment and taking everything that happened very much to heart. He was a basically a gentle, peace-loving person caught up in conflictive / oppressing everyday relationships (a mentally-ill mother and poverty-stricken family he had to support his entire life; a hopeless, life-long, non-love affair with a selfish, treacherous woman; a solitary voice of reason in the midst of revolutions and revolutionaries on all sides).

Keywords for the Influence of the *Faculties* Upon the Phases

< indicates "modified by"

Will	Mask	Creative Mind	Body of Fate
HABIT, ROUTINE	T: ACCEPTANCE F: DENIAL	T: DUTY F: STATUS	SPONTANEITY
1 ☉ IP: IRREPRESSIBLE OOP: PIGHEADED	15 T: ANGUISHED F: FRACTIOUS	1 T: IRREPRESSIBLE F: PIGHEADED	15 ANGUISHED
2 ♀♂ IP: COMPANIONABLE OOP: CURT	T: 16<BF 28 SELF-POSSESSED F: 16<CM 14 IMPASSIVE	T: 28<BF 16 CONSCIENTIOUS F: 28<CM 2 CHIMERICAL	14 DOUGHTY
3 ☿♃ IP: PERCEPTIVE OOP: TRIFLING	T: 17<BF 27 STAUNCH F: 17<CM 13 UNYIELDING	T: 27<BF 17 HUMANE F: 27<CM 3 SANCTIMONIOUS	13 FACILITATING
4 ☽ IP: GENTLE OOP: ABSTRACTED	T: 18<BF 26 INGENUOUS F: 18<CM 12 PERFUNCTORY	T: 26<BF 18 QUIRKY F: 26<CM 4 BULLHEADED	12 UPSTANDING
5 ♄ IP: DECISIVE OOP: TYRANNICAL	T: 19<BF 25 UTILITARIAN F: 19<CM 11 EXIGENT	T: 25<BF 19 SENSITIVE F: 25<CM 5 TOUCHY	11 TENDER
6 ♃☿ IP: BROADMINDED OOP: FINICKY	T: 20<BF 24 AUDACIOUS F: 20<CM 10 COCKY	T: 24<BF 20 IDEALISTIC F: 24<CM 6 CREDULOUS	10 DISCERNING
7 ♂♀ IP: INCISIVE OOP: CUTTING	T: 21<BF 23 RESOLUTE F: 21<CM 9 OBSTINATE	T: 23<BF 21 EMPATHIC F: 23<CM 7 MOODY	9 INGRATIATING

< indicates "modified by"

Will	Mask	Creative Mind	Body of Fate
HABIT, ROUTINE	T: ACCEPTANCE F: DENIAL	T: DUTY F: STATUS	SPONTAN-EITY
8 ☉ IP: SELF-SATISFIED OOP: SMUG	22 T: OBLIGING F: SUBMISSIVE	22 T: OBLIGING F: SUBMISSIVE	8 SELF-SATISFIED
9 ♀♀ IP: INGRATIATING OOP: MANIPULATIVE	T: 23<CM 7 EMPATHIC F: 23<BF 21 MOODY	T: 21<CM 9 RESOLUTE F: 21<BF 23 OBSTINATE	7 INCISIVE
10 ☿☿ IP: DISCERNING OOP: CAPRICIOUS	T: 24<CM 6 IDEALISTIC F: 24<BF 20 CREDULOUS	T: 20<CM 10 AUDACIOUS F: 20<BF 24 COCKY	6 BROAD-MINDED
11 ☽♄ IP: TENDER OOP: SULLEN	T: 25<CM 5 SENSITIVE F: 25<BF 19 TOUCHY	T: 19<CM 11 UTILITARIAN F: 19<BF 25 EXIGENT	5 DECISIVE
12 ♄☽ IP: UPSTANDING OOP: LOFTY	T: 26<CM 4 QUIRKY F: 26<BF 18 BULLHEADED	T: 18<CM 12 INGENUOUS F: 18<BF 26 PERFUNCTORY	4 GENTLE
13 ♃♃ IP: FACILITATING OOP: ABOVE-IT-ALL	T: 27<CM 3 HUMANE F: 27<BF 17 SANCTI-MONIOUS	T: 17<CM 13 STAUNCH F: 17<BF 27 UNYIELDING	3 PERCEPTIVE
14 ♂♂ IP: DOUGHTY OOP: HEADSTRONG	T: 28<CM 2 CONSCIEN-TIOUS F: 28<BF 16 CHIMERICAL	T: 16<CM 14 SELF-POSSESSED F: 16<BF 28 IMPASSIVE	2 COMPANION-ABLE

< indicates "modified by"

Will HABIT, ROUTINE	Mask T: ACCEPTANCE F: DENIAL	Creative Mind T: DUTY F: STATUS	Body of Fate SPONTANEITY
15 ☉ IP: ANGUISHED OOP: FRACTIOUS	1 T: IRREPRESSIBLE F: PIGHEADED	15 T: ANGUISHED F: FRACTIOUS	1 IRREPRESSIBLE
16 ♀♂ IP: SELF-POSSESSED OOP: IMPASSIVE	T: 2<CM 28 COMPANIONABLE F: 2< BF 14 CURT	T: 14<CM 16 DOUGHTY F: 14<BF 2 HEADSTRONG	28 CONSCIENTIOUS
17 ☿2 IP: STAUNCH OOP: UNYIELDING	T: 3<CM 27 PERCEPTIVE F: 3<BF13 TRIFLING	T: 13<CM 17 T: FACILITATING F: 13 <BF 3 ABOVE-IT-ALL	27 HUMANE
18 ☽ IP: INGENUOUS OOP: PERFUNCTORY	T: 4<CM 26 GENTLE F: 4<BF 12 ABSTRACTED	T: 12<CM 18 UPSTANDING F: 12<BF 4 LOFTY	26 QUIRKY
19 ♄♄ IP: UTILITARIAN OOP: EXIGENT	T: 5<CM 25 DECISIVE F: 5<BF 11 TYRANNICAL	T: 11<CM 19 TENDER F: 11<BF 5 SULLEN	25 SENSITIVE
20 ♃☿ IP: AUDACIOUS OOP: COCKY	T: 6<CM 24 BROADMINDED F: 6<BF 10 FINICKY	T: 10<CM 20 DISCERNING F: 10<BF 6 CAPRICIOUS	24 IDEALISTIC
21 ♂♀ IP: RESOLUTE OPP: OBSTINATE	T: 7<CM 23 INCISIVE F: 7<BF 9 CUTTING	T: 9<CM 21 INGRATIATING F: 9<BF 7 MANIPULATIVE	23 EMPATHIC

< indicates "modified by"

Will	Mask	Creative Mind	Body of Fate
HABIT, ROUTINE	T: ACCEPTANCE F: DENIAL	T: DUTY F: STATUS	SPONTAN-EITY
22 ☉ IP: OBLIGING OPP: SUBMISSIVE	8 T: SELF-SATISFIED F: SMUG	8 T: SELF-SATISFIED F: SMUG	22 OBLIGING
23 ♀♀ IP: EMPATHIC OOP: MOODY	T: 9<BF 7 INGRATIATING F: 9<CM 21 MANIPULATIVE	T: 7<BF 9 INCISIVE F: 7<CM 23 CUTTING	21 RESOLUTE
24 ☿☿ IP: IDEALISTIC OOP: CREDULOUS	T: 10<BF 6 DISCERNING F: 10<CM 20 CAPRICIOUS	T: 6<BF 10 BROAD-MINDED F: 6<CM 24 FINICKY	20 AUDA-CIOUS
25 ☽♄ IP: SENSITIVE OOP: TOUCHY	T: 11<BF 5 TENDER F: 11<CM 19 SULLEN	T: 5<BF 11 DECISIVE F: 5<CM 25 TYRANNICAL	19 UTILI-TARIAN
26 ♄☽ IP: QUIRKY OOP: BULLHEADED	T: 12<BF 4 UPSTANDING F: 12<CM 18 LOFTY	T: 4<BF 12 GENTLE F: 4<CM 26 ABSTRACTED	18 INGEN-UOUS
27 ♃♃ IP: HUMANE OOP: SANCTIMONIOUS	T: 13<BF 3 FACILITATING F: 13<CM 17 ABOVE-IT-ALL	T: 3<BF 13 PERCEPTIVE F: 3<CM 27 TRIFLING	17 STAUNCH
28 ♂♂ IP: CONSCIENTIOUS OOP: CHIMERICAL	T: 14<BF 2 DOUGHTY F: 14<CM 16 HEADSTRONG	T: 2<BF 14 COMPANION-ABLE F: 2<CM 28 CURT	16 SELF-POSSESSED

Interpretations for Individual Phases

Phase 1

INSTINCTIVE PURPOSE = IRREPRESSIBLE
Complete plasticity.

Phase 1 is a sun phase, so you have the HABIT of being IRREPRESSIBLY yourself at all times, with a great sense of fun and joie de vivre which lights up any group when you are acting *in phase*; but which can become an obstinate and capricious PIGHEADEDNESS – petty, self-centered, and demanding when you are *out of phase*: you just take your ball and go home. You are spunky, audacious and exuberant; with little need for explanations, apologies, or excuses (tactless). Where Phase 28 does nothing without first seriously deliberating all the possible consequences, Phase 1 leaps first and assumes there will be a pleasant place to land down there somewhere. You are unabashedly yourself at all times: *Thought and inclination, act and object of desire, are indistinguishable (Mask is submerged in Body of Fate, Will in Creative Mind)* [so you ACCEPT your destiny as you obey your SPONTANEOUS impulses; and you are perfectly content to adjust your everyday ROUTINES to whatever DUTY your society expects of / imposes on you] ... *that is to say, there is complete passivity, complete plasticity* [going with the flow of whatever presents itself, and quick to grasp opportunities as they arise ...]. *Mind has become indifferent to good and evil, to truth and falsehood* [... in a rather amoral – some might even say completely self-centered – fashion]. You are mischievous, light-hearted, intent on perfecting your particular skills and talents. You have a pioneering spirit and are always ready to fly with your hunches – everything is an adventure. You have a genius for riding the moment

– trusting in your own intuition and in the power of the universe to support you and to catch you when you jump: *Mind and body take whatever shape, accept whatever image is imprinted on them, transact whatever purpose is imposed upon them, are indeed the instruments of supernatural manifestation, the final link between the living and more powerful beings. There may be great joy; but it is the joy of a conscious plasticity.* You are cocky, jaunty and ready to tackle anything. Your naïve optimism is wholly centered in the moment, and lends you a zesty spontaneity. However you tend to eschew rebellion; but rather find all the freedom you need within a social context – the proverbial leader without followers – who quite consciously seeks admiration and applause for your derring-do – "Hey Ma – watch this!" You always play to the gallery; must always be the cynosure in any group. Your cute (or outrageous) antics are not so much ingenuous but rather designed to get attention (as a sun phase). You radiate a tremendous self-confidence and belief in yourself, and are mischievous, light-hearted, with a good sense of humor, dash, and panache.

Something of an interchange of the *tinctures* occurs at Phases 1 and 15: in true yin-yang fashion, at the heart of Phase 1's IRREPRESSIBILITY there lurks the dark ANGUISH of Phase 15 – and vice versa. On a True *Mask* (or ACCEPTANCE of karmic destiny) level; and also on a *Body of Fate* (SPONTANEOUS impulse) level; you sense a cosmic ANGUISH – emptiness – at the root of human belonging, which keeps you always glancing back furtively to see who or what is lurking there in the shadows; and which drives you forward and is the source of your devil-may-care courage and free-spirited leadership ability as a sun phase – an attempt to keep a step ahead of everyone else in order to maintain a sense of being in control. When in DENIAL of some deep-seated and unacknowledged ANGUISH from which you flinch or are running away –

when confronted with that terror of loss of self through *primary* engulfment which you so greatly fear – you withdraw into a FRACTIOUS rebelliousness with a damn-the-torpedoes heedlessness of consequences.

In a social setting your *Creative Mind* when True does its DUTY – serves as the example – with your IRREPRESSIBLE personal flair and élan which arouses admiration and acquiescence for your daring; but when False and you feel pierced to the core and naked before others you try to preserve your STATUS with an unshakeable self-certainty and insistence on doing things your own way, which can be extremely PIGHEADED, brazen, contrary, and recklessly obtuse – steamrolling over other people's sensibilities with utter indifference. Your staunch independence and willfulness then are eccentric, feisty, and overly pugnacious. *In phase* you possess a calm self-assurance, single-mindedness, and a genius for riding the moment which cannot be deflected or halted.

Phase 2

INSTINCTIVE ENJOYMENT = COMPANIONABLE
Beginning of energy.

Phase 2 is a Venus phase in a Mars rectangle, so your HABITUAL mindset is both pleasure-loving and cocksure, which makes you artless, out-front, and unabashedly real. *In phase* your bright-eyed, bushy-tailed perkiness and the mischievous glint in your eye give you a COMPANIONABLE alacrity; *out of phase* you can be dogmatic, outspoken, and CURT to the point of rudeness. Unlike the oblivious, self-centered Phase 1 types, however, Phase 2 natives are capable of taking other people's views and needs into account, if only to thereby facilitate the fulfillment of their own. Thus while you are as self-promoting as Phase 1, you are more objective about your own aims, so here collaboration and cooperation become possible. Phase 2 natives want to be perceived as nice people – accepted as harmless, amusing, witty, and non-threatening – and win acceptance (or at least acquiescence) thereby. You are pert, and unruffled, and – like Phase 1 – you possess an unabashed alacrity and gusto. Your *Mask* from Phase 16 lends you a CONSCIENTIOUS (from Phase 28) SELF-POSSESSION – a sincerity and earnestness which are a reliance for people when True and you ACCEPT your destiny by being accepting of others in turn: then your optimism and ironic good humor immediately put you on a friendly basis with everyone you meet, and you are able to make yourself quite at home in any company. Your cool efficiency and your unbothered, blithe insouciance keep the group setting light and on an even keel: *He would be remembered as a form of joy, for he would seem more entirely living than all other men, a personification or summing up of all natural life. He would decide on this or that by no balance of the reason but by an infallible joy.* Although you take a benevolent interest in other people, you nonetheless keep yourself rather loose and aloof, and don't permit anyone to bring you down. When living out your False *Mask* your DENIAL gives you a HEADSTRONG (from Phase 14) IMPASSIVITY and aloof indifference to everyone and everything except your own short-term plans and aims. *Out of phase*, you are inclined to play the prissy prima donna: you go your own way without a care and just can't be bothered about other people's issues (or their sensibilities), and thereby *he copies the emotional explosion of Phase 16* with its coldly detached unconcern. When your *Creative Mind* is False you uphold your STATUS by CURTLY pushing other people's feelings aside to indulge your own CHIMERICAL (from Phase 28) fancies and whims. ... *But if he live according to phase, ... He gives himself up to Nature as the Fool (Phase 28) gave himself to God*: then your *True Creative Mind* is CONSCIENTIOUS (with something of Phase 16's SELF-POSSESSION), so in group situations your DUTY is to act the role of the disinterested and aboveboard arbitrator – the straight-shooter who plays fair, by the rules (whatever you conceive the rules to be). You have a simple faith in the power of reasonableness to convince others: *He is neither immoral nor violent but innocent; is as it were the breath stirring on the face of the deep; the smile on the face of a but half-awakened child.* Your *Body of Fate* (from Phase 14) gives you a DOUGHTY SPONTANEITY which is refreshing and disarming in its naïve, can-do spiritedness. You win people over with your enthusiasm and good cheer: *He would decide on this or that by no balance of the reason but by an infallible joy, and if born amid a rigid mechanical order, he would make for himself a place, as a dog will scratch a hole for itself in loose earth.*

Phase 3

INSTINCTIVE MENTALITY = PERCEPTIVE
Beginning of ambition.

Like Phase 2 natives, Phase 3's have a broad spread of acquaintances and a strong desire to be liked and accepted. However Phase 3 types make a real effort to understand other people – not in the calculating mode of Phase 2, but rather as a sincere expression of interest and intellectual curiosity. In Phase 3 *simplicity and intensity are united* (unlike the rather cool and matter-of-fact Phase 2's). Phase 3 is a Mercury phase in a Jupiter rectangle, which endows you with a HABITUALLY nervous, high-wire energy together with a broad grasp which is PERCEPTIVE when *in phase* and you can dominate the moment with your inquisitiveness, droll point of view, and pointed insights on the passing scene; but when *out of phase* becomes a TRIFLING refusal to get serious and a tendency to strew your attention ineffectually hither and thither like a hummingbird. You are brisk, breezy, and saucy, with a sardonic sense of humor and the ability to see the irony in any situation. You are unbothered and carefree, refusing to take things too seriously or to bog yourself down in sticky involvements (flighty). You are very clear mentally, possessing a shrewd understanding of human frailty and the Machiavellian convolutions of everyday society. Your *Mask* derives from Phase 17 and when True, and you ACCEPT your destiny, lends you a STAUNCH, stick-to-your guns certainty which is HUMANE (from Phase 27), grounded, and concerned with the well-being of all. You are then quick on your feet and ever ready with a pithy response or remark which reveals a sympathetic concern for other people and the realities of the situation. Your *Creative Mind* (from Phase 27) endows your sense of DUTY when True with a HUMANE view of other people from their own side: a charitable, benefit-of-the-doubt impulse and a STAUNCH (from Phase 17) willingness to reach out to, protect, and defend the helpless: *He takes delight in all that passes; but because he claims nothing of his own, chooses nothing, thinks that no one thing is better than another, he will not endure a pang because all passes.* When your *Mask* is False and you are in DENIAL you exhibit an UNYIELDING, ABOVE-IT-ALL (from Phase 13) orneriness which is huffy and overly zealous in guarding your petty prerogatives; and which believes your paltry insights make you such hot stuff. When your *Creative Mind* (from Phase 27) is False your sense of STATUS becomes a SANCTIMONIOUS self-justification: TRIFLING and brusquely dismissive of any views which do not conform to your rather simplistic and categorical thinking: *a kind of clodhopper folly, that keeps his intellect moving among conventional ideas with a sort of make-believe* which in turn can make you impossible to talk to. Your blasé and chintzy flippancy can be extremely annoying to others: *Incapable of consecutive thought and of moral purpose, miserably seeking to hold together some consistent plan of life, patching rags upon rags because that is expected of him* you are scattered and marooned in your own threadbare rationalizations. *In phase*, your blithe cheerfulness and your clever and PERCEPTIVE patter provide a leavening of lively confabulation to your social milieu. Your *Body of Fate* (from Phase 13) makes your SPONTANEOUS impulse that of the detached FACILITATOR whose mental clarity, eagerness to please, and communicative skill enlivens any group of which you are a part: *Eyes and ears are open; one instinct balances another; every season brings its delight.*

Phase 4

☽

INSTINCTIVE ASSURANCE = GENTLE
Desire for primary objects (Exterior World).

Although friendly and outgoing, Phase 4 lacks the driving need to connect with others which characterizes Phases 2 and 3, hence you relate to people in a more relaxed and natural fashion than these earlier phases do. You don't have the crucial dependence of Phases 2 and 3 upon validation from others, but instead have found a way of validating yourself. Thus while you are as light and sociable as the previous phases, you have no need to be constantly performing or proving something to yourself and to other people as in the preceding phases (greater ASSURANCE). Phase 4 is a lunar phase in a lunar rectangle, so your HABITUAL approach to people and situations is soft-spoken, straightforward, kindly, and

GENTLE when *in phase*; and annoyingly ABSTRACTED – dreamy, oblivious, head-in-the-clouds, and out-of-reach and hearing when *out of phase*: *he separates himself from instinct and tries to enforce upon himself all kinds of abstract or conventional ideas which are for him, being outside his experience, mere make-believe.* You are enthusiastic, easy-going, good-natured and hopeful – always looking for the best in people and situations. You have a matter-of-fact nonchalance which disarms people and puts them at their ease. They can see right through you because you have nothing in particular to hide – what they see is what they get. Your *Mask* is a mixture of Phase 18's INGENUOUSNESS with a touch of the SPONTANEOUS QUIRKINESS of Phase 26, so when True you ACCEPT your destiny by being completely open to other people and to whatever comes your way, following your star wherever it leads with no particular plan or ulterior motive in mind: *It is as though he woke suddenly out of sleep and thereupon saw more and remembered more than others.* When your *Mask* is False you are in DENIAL as you adopt the PERFUNCTORINESS of Phase 18 (touched with the LOFTINESS of Phase 12) and withdraw into a fog of daydreams and misplaced idealism – a crybaby self-coddling or a shoulder-shrugging helplessness. Your usual self is full of good cheer and fellowship. You have no particular axes to grind; and your unaffected, aboveboard reasonableness is convincing and reassuring: people find your thoughts and ideas sensible and realistic; and they appreciate your good common sense and integrity: *He is full of a practical wisdom, a wisdom of saws and proverbs, or founded upon concrete examples.* Your *Creative Mind* derives from Phase 26, so when True you do your DUTY as you leaven the group proceedings with your own good-natured, optimistic, humorous, QUIRKY, and INGENUOUS (from Phase 18) contribution: *He has 'the wisdom of instinct', a wisdom perpetually excited by all those hopes and needs which concern his well-being or that of the race.* Unconventional and obeying your own heart rather than canons of social approval, you stand out from your family, schoolmates, coworkers, as not quite fitting the mold. When False you assert your STATUS with the BULLHEADED stubbornness of Phase 26, off on your own woolly-minded schemes, bolstered by your own ABSTRACTED deafness to reason and blindness to what you don't want to see. You try to keep things on a positive, upbeat note – to dodge contention if it cannot be ameliorated amicably (close your eyes to unpleasantness, or shirk irksome responsibilities). *Out of phase*, affecting the tactful sagacity and intellection of Phase 18 in the attempt to maintain stability and control, you can be blissfully ABSTRACTED – indifferent and off on your own tangent when difficult decisions or obligations are called for: *Lacking* antithetical *capacity, and* primary *observation* [for here the *tinctures* close and the preexistent *primary* will give way in the next phase to a nascent *antithetical* – which, however, is beyond your present compass] *he is aimless and blundering, possesses nothing except the knowledge that there is something known to others that is not mere instinct. True to phase, his interest in everything that happens, in all that excites his instinct ("search"), is so keen that he has no desire to claim anything for his own will.* Your *Body of Fate* derives from Phase 12, so your SPONTANEOUS, knee-jerk response is always informed by the UPSTANDING morality of that phase – you are mild-mannered and unruffled no matter what the provocation and always do the fair and honorable thing even if it redounds to your disadvantage. There's no way anyone can get angry at a Phase 4, at least not for long (whereas Phase 5's, by contrast, specialize in pissing people off). *In phase*, your GENTILITY and good will win the affection of everyone who knows you: *He can see nothing beyond sense, but sense expands and contracts to meet his needs, and the needs of those who trust him.*

At Phase 4 the *primary tincture* closes and in the next phase the *antithetical tincture* opens [N.b.: this usage of the terms "opening" and "closing" of the *tinctures* differs from the one given in *A Vision*, wherein it is said that at Phase 4 the *primary tincture* – open since Phase 26 – closes; and at Phase 5 the *antithetical tincture* – open since Phase 25 – closes. In the present book the meaning of the terms "opening" and "closing" of the *tinctures* refers to the inchoate appearance of the opposite *tincture* in the middle of each quarter where the break in the Chaldean cycle occurs – i.e. between the moon and Saturn phases]. *Since Phase 26 the* primary tincture *has so predominated, man is so sunk in Fate, in life, that there is no reflection, no experience, because that which reflects, that which acquires experience, has been drowned* [before Phase 5 the natives are "lost in the funhouse" – exhibiting little objectivity or direction. At Phase 5 there emerges ego, a sense of captaincy, a drive for control, an *antithetical* separation of the self from experience]. *Between Phase 4 and Phase 5 the tinctures ceased to be drowned in the One, and reflection begins. ... When Man identifies himself with his Fate, when he is able to say 'Thy Will is our freedom' or when he is perfectly natural, that is to say, perfectly a portion of his surroundings* [utterly *primary*], *he is free even though all his actions can be foreseen, even though every action is a logical deduction from all that went before it. He is all Fate* [B.F.] *but has no Destiny* [Mask].

Phase 5

INSTINCTIVE RESPONSIBILITY = DECISIVE
Separation from innocence.

Like the preceding phases, *he lives in the moment but with an intensity Phases 2, 3 and 4 have never known, the* Will *approaches its climax* [i.e. the *primary tincture* has just closed and the *antithetical* now opens with a bang]. Phase 5 is a double Saturn phase so your HABITUAL take on everyday affairs is a hard-nosed, no-nonsense pragmatism which *in phase* makes you DECISIVE – quick to spot potential opportunities and threats, and quick to act and react, taking other people by a storm. When *out of phase* your TYRANNICAL streak – utter lack of diplomacy or even common courtesy – is not only gratuitously bruising but engenders friction and opposition where none would otherwise be met. You are concentrated, focused, assiduous, and hard-charging. You take pride in your competence and you punctiliously discharge your responsibilities. Your *Creative Mind*, from Phase 25, is SENSITIVE to nuances, so when True you are able to pick up on and exploit (with something of Phase 19's UTILITARIANISM) whatever unspoken feelings and vibrations are in the air in order to carry out what you feel is your DUTY to your group. When False you assert your STATUS with a TOUCHY, prickly, TYRANNICAL streak that strikes fear in the hearts of everyone around you. You visualize a goal and drive straight for it, glancing neither to the right nor left, and smash through any obstacles (or people) in your path: *at conflict with a world which offers him nothing but temptation and affront.* You demand complete freedom of action (and damn the torpedoes). You are not so much a loner as isolated within yourself; not so much born to lead as imperious and congenitally incapable of adapting yourself to anyone else. This is what is meant by the *antithetical tincture* opening here – *antithetical* individualism makes its appearance in the middle of a *primary* phase (comparing oneself to others for self-definition): *He no longer touches, eats, drinks, thinks and feels Nature, but sees her as something from which he is separating himself, something he may dominate, though only for a moment and by some fragmentary violence of sensation or of thought.* Your *Mask* derives from Phase 19; when True and ACCEPTING your destiny your down-to-earth UTILITARIANISM (tinged with shrewdness from the SENSITIVITY of Phase 25) is adept at the art of the possible, making the best use of whatever is at hand and capable of bringing off miracles. When False and in DENIAL your EXIGENT impatience and SULLEN (from Phase 11) intransigence stonewalls all communications and good faith. You follow your own star come hell or high water, and your single-mindedness and utter confidence in yourself bowl people right over, or at least incline them to yield rather than try to obstruct you. You have a serious demeanor and (unless e.g. Venus or Jupiter rise) little in the way of social grace, tact, or patience. Indeed, you are not much of a social animal, but keep your own counsel and – because you are quite conscious of your own motives and tendencies – you are wary and suspicious of others. You are vigilant, quick to spot opportunities, and quick to act without hesitation or fear (or forethought). *Out of phase*, attempting the rationalization and justification of Phase 19 for what is basically just grabbing what you want, you are hard-headed and hard-hearted – autocratic and coldly dismissive of anyone in your circle who does not offer total loyalty or subservience: *he is sterile, passing from one insincere attitude to another, moving through a round of moral images torn from their context and so without meaning ... he becomes a sort of angry or smiling Punch with a lath between his wooden arms striking here and there.* You then become a hammerer who bludgeons other people into submission. However your *Body of Fate*, from Phase 11, does endow you with a SPONTANEOUS ameliorating impulse of TENDERNESS which at your best gives you a saving mercy and willingness to use your personal power to help and protect the weak and defenseless. *In phase*, your staunch single-mindedness and willingness to risk all make you an ideal trail-blazer and champion: *he is a corrupter, disturber, wanderer, a founder of sects and peoples, and works with extravagant energy, and his reward is but to live in its glare.*

Phase 6
♃

INSTINCTIVE UNDERSTANDING = BROADMINDED
Artificial individuality.

In contrast to the brash heavy-handedness of Phase 5, these natives are genial, poised, and self-controlled. Phase 6 natives are acute observers of life who reach for understanding rather than dominance. Phase 6 is a Jupiter phase in a Mercury rectangle, so your jovial expansiveness is direct and plainspoken – you say exactly what's on your mind with no hesitation (or tact or diplomacy). You are HABITUALLY BROADMINDED, discriminating, and democratic in your impulses when acting *in phase*, with a Virgo-ish punctiliousness and attention to details; but you can be rather FINICKY – antsy, impatient, and brusque with people when *out of phase*. You place great reliance on your reasoning powers – not (as in phase 5) to outsmart other people or be one up on them, but rather to encompass as much as possible of human experience within your own world-view: *interest in crowds, in casual loves and affections, in all summary human experience.* There is an unceasing intellection (on the negative side, self-justification) going on here. You are prim, sedate, conventional, and socially correct (touchy and testy): *Abstraction had been born, but it remained the abstraction of a community, of a tradition.* Your *Mask* derives from Phase 20, so when True and you are ACCEPTING your destiny you are AUDACIOUS – fearlessly brash and outspoken with an IDEALISTIC (from Phase 24) ability to see the good in people and hope in any circumstances, which gives you a composed demeanor and an unerring sense of being at the helm in the face of confusion and turmoil. When False your DENIAL manifests as a CAPRICIOUS (from Phase 10) COCKINESS which struts and blusters and always knows better than anyone else. You engage in an unending rumination and self-examination, as if to ask yourself: *"I have such and such a feeling. I have such and such a belief. What follows from feeling, what from belief?"* Your calm and businesslike manner takes situations and people in your stride – you may not always know where you are going, but you do give that impression. You are unhurried, unbothered, unruffled, and uninvolved (remote, unresponsive). You are a good listener, and readily go out of your way to give other people a lift. You seek accord and consensus, and you always remain true to your principles. You "take charge" and are quick to defend the helpless and downtrodden: *All his thought and impulse a product of democratic bonhomie, of schools, of colleges, of public discussion.* You are punctilious in discharging your own responsibilities: your *Creative Mind* derives from Phase 24, which when True gives you an IDEALISTIC sense of DUTY so you willingly put yourself at the service of others with the AUDACITY (from Phase 20) of your expertise and love of teaching and holding forth in any group. When False, your need for STATUS becomes a prissy, FINICKY tendency with a CREDULITY which is snidely critical of anyone and anything that doesn't meet your exalted standards of perfection. You certainly don't shrink from conflict, but neither do you provoke it yourself when it can possibly be avoided. Insofar as it is in your power, you always hasten to spread oil on troubled waters and to keep things on an even keel. Your *Body of Fate*, from Phase 10, makes your SPONTANEOUS approach to people highly aware and

DISCERNING: you are quick to pick up on subtleties and the petty politicking of everyday relationships, and not much escapes your scrutiny. *Out of phase* and feigning the brass and sauciness of Phase 20, you can be the busybody know-it-all with a head-in-the-clouds optimism spouting empty platitudes, who takes situations (and other people) for granted: *some kind of jibing demagogue; ... that he might believe in himself, have compelled others to believe. In phase* your steady deliberateness is a rock-solid reliance in the face of any confusion: *Experience is all-absorbing, subordinating observed fact, drowning even truth itself.*

Phase 7

INSTINCTIVE ACCOMPLISHMENT = INCISIVE
Assertion of individuality.

At Phases 2, 3 and 4 the man moved within traditional or seasonable limits, but since [the *antithetical tincture* opened at] *Phase 5 limits have grown indefinite; public codes, all that depend upon habit, are all but dissolved, even the catalogues and categories of Phase 6 are no longer sufficient.* Since the closing of the *primary tincture* and opening of the *antithetical* the last phases of the first quarter have become more and more self-aware; and at Phase 7 the *primary* succumbs to a new spirit of individualistic self-expression. The last three phases of the first quarter are all rather cool and impersonal in their handling of people and situations; but in contrast with the restrained, demure Phase 6 types, you Phase 7 natives are bold and brash. Phase 7 is a Mars phase in a Venus rectangle, so your HABITUAL frame of mind combines the dynamism of the former with the social awareness of the latter: when *in phase* you are INCISIVE in your acute grasp of and (droll take on) the passing scene, possess a pioneering spirit, and unhesitatingly reach out to take whatever you desire with an unapologetic sense of fitness of place and just deserts. When *out of phase* you can be CUTTING and peevish, with a prissy, prima donna streak and a mannered self-righteousness. You are fresh (in all senses of that word): sharp, forthright, and direct – a good talker who doesn't mince words and is always quick with a ready retort. You are clear-minded and insightful, with a highly original point of view and a wry sense of humor. You have little gift for guile, and – unlike Phase 6 natives – completely lack diplomacy (or tact). You are outspoken, sassy, and impudent (swaggering), with a saucy mischievousness (wiseacre). Your *Creative Mind* from Phase 23 reflects (from Phase 21) a RESOLUTE EMPATHY and sense of justice and fair play when True and you are being DUTIFUL and responsible within your group; and when False and you are vaunting your own STATUS it becomes a theatrical MOODINESS with which you assuage yourself and hold yourself above others. You get your way with people by charm and cleverness when possible; but you are also capable of digging in your heels and stonewalling – wearing down any opponent with adamant obduracy – when your shrewdness and wiles fail you. You are gutsy and daring; fearlessly willing to risk all in pursuing your own designs with little regard for the consequences (blunt and bruising). You don't shy from contention but usually avoid it by just charging right ahead and relying on the fait accompli to convince others, rather than waste your breath with explanation or expostulation. *Out of phase* and attempting the deliberate, Machiavellian empire-building and calculation of Phase 21 rather than going with your *primary*, seat-of-the-pants instincts, you tend to trip yourself up, make needless enemies, and bog yourself down: *If out of phase the man desires to be the man of Phase 21; an impossible desire, for that man is all but the climax of intellectual complexity, and all men, from Phase*

2 to Phase 7 inclusive, are intellectually simple. His instincts are all but at their apex of complexity, and he is bewildered and soon must be helpless. Your *Mask* derives from Phase 21: when True you ACCEPT your destiny with a RESOLUTE nobility of purpose and (from Phase 23) EMPATHIC concern for the well-being of all, which inspires respect and compels admiration; but when False and you are in DENIAL your OBSTINATE stonewalling makes you (from Phase 9) petty, narcissistic, and MANIPULATIVE in getting your own way. You exhibit a thorny, sharp-tongued impatience which brushes other people aside; an overweening, know-it-all haughtiness: *seeing that its thoughts and emotions are common to all, it can create a grandiloquent phantom and by deceiving others deceive itself. In phase* your youthful vigor, dash, and unabashed showmanship spice up any group of which you are a part: *a last act of courage, a defiance of the dogs that must soon tear the man into pieces* [at Phase 8]. *Such men have a passion for history, for the scene, for the adventure.* Your *Body of Fate* from Phase 9 gives you an INGRATIATING SPONTANEITY which delights everyone with your glib and witty commentary which is both apropos and illuminating: *They delight in actions, which they cannot consider apart from the setting sun or a storm at sea or some great battle, and that are inspired by emotions that move all hearers because such that all understand.*

From Phase 1 to Phase 7 there has been a gradual weakening of all that is primary. *Character ... has become individuality. ... but now, though individuality persists through another phase, personality ... must predominate. So long as the* primary tincture *predominated, the* antithetical tincture *accepted its manner of perception. ... But now the bottle must be burst. The struggle of idealised or habitual theologised thought with instinct, mind with body, of the waning* primary *with the growing* antithetical, *must be decided, and the vegetative and sensitive faculties must for a while take the sway. ... It must now feel that it can create order no longer.*

Through the first quarter the concern has been with "making it" in the world. The focus has been on oneself: one's own goals, dreams, ambitions. *At Phase 7, he had tried out of ambition to change his nature, as though a man should make love who had no heart, but now shock can give him back his heart. Only a shock resulting from the greatest possible conflict can make the greatest possible change.*

Phase 8

EMOTIONAL PURPOSE = SELF-SATISFIED
War between individuality and race. A struggle, where the soul must lose all form received from the objectively accepted conscience of the world

At Phase 8 is the 'Discovery of Strength', its embodiment in sensuality. The imitation that held it to the enforced Mask, *the norm of the race now a hated convention, has ceased and its own norm has not begun.* Primary *and* antithetical *are equal and fight for mastery; and when this fight is ended through the conviction of weakness and the preparation for rage, the* Mask *becomes once more voluntary.* Like all sun phases, Phases 8 and 22 are disconnected from their social milieu; but they feel it more acutely than do the oblivious Phase 1's (who don't worry about it) or Phase 15's (who don't care). Where Phase 15 natives proudly wear their sojourner badge, Phase 8 and 22 natives desperately try to hide their maladjusted state from everyone around them (and from themselves). It's not that phases 8 and 22 have any more emotional and spiritual problems than anyone else; it's just that in these two phases these issues result in acute contradictions which cannot be evaded or run from, but must be faced directly in one fashion or another; hence their lives tend to be continual exercises in crisis management. They sense something amiss, something out-of-kilter somewhere; and the world agrees. The basic problem the natives of Phases 8 and 22 face lies in knowing where to put their boundaries – to cease looking to others to define who they are. At the inversion of the *tinctures* from *primary* to *antithetical* (or the reverse in Phase 22), Phase 8 is struggling to break free of the herd, where Phase 22 is struggling to fit in somehow. The challenge of these phases is to free themselves from thralldom to their social milieu. Phase 8 is a sun phase, so you HABITUALLY possess a proud and masterful bearing which is rightly SELF-SATISFIED when *in phase* and exalting in your competence, craftsmanship, or in a job well done; but can become a SMUG self-stroking, preening and imperiousness when *out of phase* and insisting on special privileges and dispensation. Phase 8, like the other sun phases, is unconcerned and nonchalant, and finds emotional entanglements bothersome. You are dignified, self-possessed, and self-contained. You have a highly original point of view, and you are also very creative. You may possess considerable artistic ability, or some other talent or skill which other people admire; but in any case you have a unique vision and novel ideas – cleverness, originality, and joy in accomplishment (and in strutting your stuff). You have something of a blasé insouciance – you don't permit anyone to enter your space or to get to you. Your *Mask* and *Creative Mind*, from Phase 22, give you an OBLIGING noblesse which takes others under your wing when you ACCEPT your destined role in life and DUTY to your social group, making you the perfect mentor or shining exemplar – the one whom others naturally look up to; but when False and in DENIAL you maintain your STATUS with an obsequiously SUBMISSIVE wheedling or intriguing to get your own way. You maintain your unruffled façade of equanimity by living in your own idealized fantasy world – your own secret corner of the universe – from which everyone else is excluded – and you believe that it all revolves around you: *The man is inseparable from his fate, he cannot see himself apart, nor can he distinguish between emotion and intellect.* Although you are outgoing and sociable – even chatty – you nonetheless hold yourself above the common throng and can be vague or perfunctory in relationships – it's all such a nuisance, beneath you. You bid to be the cynosure, the center of attention, the one everybody applauds. Phase 8 natives possess a gift for self-promotion and have a strong need to feel one-up, on top of things (on top of other people); and you are not above coldly exploiting them for your own benefit and then discarding them without a second thought. You have a commanding presence – a control born of the intense feelings you hold back inside yourself – which in turn exerts a controlling influence upon the world around you. Like all sun phase types, you rather expect to be served or deferred to (autocratic). You resist commitment and compromise, but expect this of others to accommodate you (exploitative). Intimates may find you indifferent and insensitive; or complain that you withdraw completely into yourself leaving a smug Cheshire Cat smile behind. The crises in your life, of course, arise due to the not-infrequent intrusion of disruptive reality into your careful arrangements. You don't want to be bogged down in "issues" and complexities – you want to see everything in black-and-white, good-vs.-evil, me-vs.-them terms. The crises of Phase 8 arise when you try to deal instinctively with matters which require greater sensitivity and delicacy: your struggle is to open yourself to feelings – your own and other people's – rather than operate thoughtlessly on automatic pilot. The crises are due to your own indifference to what other people – and your own conscience –

are trying to tell you. You want them to bow down to you; to lionize you; to become your faithful chelas (or servants). You don't address them as people, who are as confused, lost, and desperately trying to understand who they are, as yourself. You need to develop a bit more compassion for other people instead of just using them to glorify yourself. *Out of phase* you cling to a dying *primary* by shamelessly projecting your inner turmoil on other people. Unlike Phase 22 which struggles to adapt itself to social norms as best it can (and thereby loses its sense of center), you bend the rules of the game your way to justify the most overweening and callous narcissism. You are a survivor: by hook or by crook, you usually manage to come out on top smelling like a rose. You trifle with issues of the greatest gravity, concocting patches-on-patches expedients and making threadbare excuses for yourself: *Here for the most part are those obscure wastrels who seem powerless to free themselves from some sensual temptation – drink, women, drugs – and who cannot in a life of continual crisis create any lasting thing. In phase* you permit the *antithetical* to take the baton from the *primary*: you shine when you expect much of yourself and little of others; *when He chooses himself and not his Fate.* Your *Body of Fate* from your own Phase 8 makes your SPONTANEOUS persona that of the SELF-SATISFIED hail-fellow-well-met, with an upbeat, can-do spirit and a saucy, cheeky, "How'm I doing?" alacrity. At your best your positive self-assurance and unlimited faith in yourself give you the ability to stay loose and open, and to improvise or capitalize upon whatever opportunities present themselves: *When his fingers close upon a straw, that is courage, and his versatility is that any wave may float a straw.* The self-doubts and fears which haunt *out of phase* 8 natives become a spur to action: *He must be aware of nothing but the conflict, his despair is necessary, he is of all men the most tempted – 'Eloi, Eloi, why hast thou forsaken me?'*

Phases 8 through 12 are characterized by *Rage* (the need to prove one's worth in other people's eyes); and Phases 12 through 15 by *Spiritual or supersensual Rage* (the need to separate from other people's approval / disapproval and measure oneself against an ideal or abstract). This is because in these phases the being struggles to be free of all restraint and encumbrance; and this struggle becomes more desperate until the final release, which is achieved effortlessly in phase 15.

In phase 8 *The being clings like a drowning man to every straw, and it is precisely this clinging, this seemingly vain reaching forth for strength, amidst the collapse of all those public thoughts and habits that are the support of primary man, that enables it to enter at last upon Phase 9.*

Phase 9

EMOTIONAL ENJOYMENT = INGRATIATING
Belief takes place of individuality.

Phase 9 is a Venus phase in a Venus rectangle, which is the mark of great poise and ease of manner – you are relaxed, open, and unabashedly yourself under all circumstances. Your HABITUAL demeanor when *in phase* is INGRATIATING: you have a winning style – a jaunty, self-assured, and rakish panache; a humorous and ironic view of life and your fellow bipeds; and the ability to take things evenly as they come. You have a frank, candid manner, a knowing twinkle in your eye, and a keen sense of fun. Your childlike mischievousness and joie de vivre are quite infectious, and give you excellent people skills. You are a keen observer of the passing scene and are quite clear mentally: you possess a good sense of humor and are not afraid to say out loud that which everyone else is thinking secretly: *Phase 9 (is) without restraint ... the greatest possible "belief in its own desire"*. Because you are reflective and care about people, you are attuned to subtleties and nuances; hence are quick to pick up and address underlying feelings and the mood of the moment. *Out of phase* you use your considerable charm and bonhomie to shamelessly MANIPULATE people to your will to get whatever you want from them. Your *Creative Mind* derives from Phase 21 so when True you do your DUTY to your group with a RESOLUTE iron fist beneath your own INGRATIATING, soft-spoken manner – although reserved and undemonstrative, your masterful influence is strongly felt and obeyed. But when False and you are merely affirming your STATUS, your OBSTINATE MOODINESS (from Phase 23) and recalcitrance herds people around and bends situations your way: *behind all that muddy, flooded, brutal [outspoken] self, there is perhaps a vague timid soul knowing itself caught in an antithesis, an alternation it cannot control. It is said of it, 'The soul having found its weakness at Phase 8 begins the inward discipline of the soul in the fury of Phase 9.'* You are resourceful and clever; a supreme realist who is not fooled by appearances; and you possess a can-do ebullience; so (like Phase 8 *in phase*) you are always able to make the best of things and to take advantage of whatever opportunities are at hand: *immense confidence in self-expression, a vehement self, working through mathematical calculation, a delight in straight line and right angle.* Your facility for shrugging off disappointment and not taking setbacks to heart – distancing yourself from unpleasantness with a lofty reserve – shows itself as a daintiness or pedantry: *the man instead of mastering this sensuality, through his dramatisation of himself as a form of passionate self-mastery ... becomes stupid and blundering. ... Phase 9 has no interest in others except in relation to itself.* In phase you are self-assured and confident, positive and idealistic, *powerful and accomplished*. Your *Mask* from Phase 23, when True and

ACCEPTING of your destiny, is both EMPATHIC and (from Phase 7) INCISIVE: your immediate impulse is protective and nurturing, endeavoring to spread oil on troubled waters and make peace wherever you can. When False and you are in DENIAL and on the warpath your dour MOODINESS and forbidding (from Phase 21) OBSTINACY warn people to just keep the hell out of your way. Although you play fair and take other people's feelings into account, you are nonetheless always sure of what you want and are unhesitating in reaching out and taking it with no shame or need for excuses. Your *Body of Fate*, from Phase 7, gives you an INCISIVE SPONTANEITY: you don't mince words but let it all hang out; and when you speak it's directly to the point. This is why it is said that *Phase 9 has the most sincere belief any man has ever had in his own desire.*

Phase 10

EMOTIONAL MENTALITY = DISCERNING
The image-breaker

Here is rage, desire to escape, but not now by mere destruction of the opposing fate; for a vague abstract sense of some world, some image, some circumstance, harmonious to emotion, has begun.

Like the preceding phase, Phase 10 natives are friendly and welcoming: *sees all his life as a stage play where there is only one good acting part; yet* [unlike Phase 9] *no one will accuse him of being a stage player. Where Phase 9 was without restraint ... now restraint has come and with it pride ... a kind of burning restraint, a something that suggests a savage statue to which one offers sacrifice. This sacrifice is code, personality no longer perceived as power only.* Phase 10 is a Mercury phase in a Mercury rectangle, so your HABITUAL mindset is naturally rather mercurial: DISCERNING and efficient, with little pother or wasted motion when *in phase* and you know just what you're about and how to accomplish your goals; but CAPRICIOUS when *out of phase* and you are merely buzzing about aimlessly and insisting just to insist. I.e., Phase 10 is like Phase 3 but without all the cocksure clatter and demonstrativeness; it's more judicious, controlled, and shrewd. You are scrupulous, perspicacious, and sincere, with a strong-willed self-control and endurance. Your considerable personal power is held in tight check and reserve *like that god of Norse mythology who hung from the cliff's side for three days, a sacrifice to himself.* You do not act on impulse, but are careful, diligent, and painstaking. Although you are emotionally guarded and play your cards close to your chest, you are a good listener and quick learner. You are a good problem-solver since your penetrating intellect is observant and thorough; good at picking up and addressing subtleties; and attentive to the feelings of other people (like Phase 9, but more vis à vis taking them into account rather than using them or playing to them as an audience). You possess a clear intuition into human motivation and a sympathetic appreciation of human limitation. Like Phase 9 you are able to pick up the undercurrents of the situation at hand, and can see clearly through hypocrisy and pretense. You seek harmony and accord, and make a good ombudsman or mediator. You possess a humane, concerned affability; are level-headed, fair-minded, and dependable; and you put everything on a basis of good faith and common sense. Phase 10 is the most realistic of the Mercury phases: *all practical curiosity has been lost wherever some personal aim is not involved* [in contrast to the simplicity of Phase 3], *while philosophical and artistic curiosity are still undiscovered* [in contrast to the idealism of Phase 24]. And, in contrast to the shrewd jockeying for advantage that characterizes

Phase 17, Phase 10 natives have a severe inner discipline which is based upon nobility of character and a strong sense of principled acquittal. Your True *Mask* evinces the IDEALISM of Phase 24 informed by the BROAD-MINDEDNESS of Phase 6 – when you ACCEPT your destiny you seek to model in your own life the highest standards of reasonableness and decency, and you are always open to new ideas and the points of view of other people so as to deepen your own understanding, scope, and competence. Your False *Mask* from Phase 24 tends to CREDULITY combined with the COCKINESS of Phase 20, so when you are in DENIAL there are times when you delude yourself with pipe dream fantasies of how you, embattled, all alone, stand for the right; and how marvelous and clever and noble you are. Then you lose your seriousness of purpose and instead indulge in wishful thinking, going through empty motions of serving a higher aim; *If he live like the opposite phase ... he lacks all emotional power ... and gives himself up to rudderless change, reform without a vision of form. He accepts what form ... those about him admire and, on discovering that it is alien, casts it away with brutal violence, to choose some other form as alien.* Your *Creative Mind* comes from Phase 20, so when True you fulfill your sense of DUTY to your social group with an AUDACITY fortified by your own razor-sharp DISCERNMENT, which endows you with a rock-solid authoritativeness which is both commanding and discriminating, so other people instinctively trust and rely upon your judgment and honorableness in times of doubt. When your *Creative Mind* is False you maintain your STATUS with the COCKINESS of Phase 20 influenced by the CREDULITY of Phase 24, producing a wrong-headed bravado and hubris which is the more adamant the more erroneous is your thinking. If you merely try to make your point or defend abstract principle (rather than confront realities) *the life remains troubled, a conflict between pride and race, and passes from crisis to crisis.* But if you remain careful, attentive, and punctilious, your *Body of Fate* from Phase 6 makes your SPONTANEOUS reaction to people and new situations one of BROADMINDED openness, fair play, and willingness to suspend judgment and listen to others with detached good will: *If ... he be true to phase ... and so create some code of personal conduct which implies always "divine right", he becomes proud, masterful and practical.*

Phase 11

☾

EMOTIONAL ASSURANCE = TENDER
The consumer – The pyre-builder

All phases before Phase 15 are in nature, as distinguished from God, and at Phase 11 that nature becomes intellectually conscious of its relations to all created things.

Like the preceding phases, Phase 11 natives are alert and judicious, but are more low-key, humble, and unprepossessing – without the cheeky alacrity and confident self-certainty of Phase 10: *While Phase 9 was kept from its subjectivity by personal relations, by sensuality, by various kinds of grossness; and Phase 10 by associations of men for practical purposes and by the emotions that arise out of such associations ... Phase 11 is impeded by the excitement of conviction ... The man of the phase is a half-solitary, one who defends a solitude he cannot or will not inhabit.* You are basically a private person, a loner at heart, with a distracted wistfulness and harmlessness which other people find appealing (mousey). Phase 11 is moon phase in a Saturn rectangle, which makes for a wariness and also endurance – the ability to bear up under burdens and uncomplainingly go the distance. Your

HABITUAL approach to people and situations when *in phase* is mild and TENDER, in the hope that life will be similarly soft with you; but *out of phase* and feeling unfairly put upon you retreat to a SULLEN silence, maintaining a stiff upper lip with an air of disgruntlement. You are called the "pyre builder" because you consume yourself in flames (sacrifice for others). You are soul-searching and self-effacing, and don't push yourself forward. You are soft-spoken, with nothing to hide or be ashamed of, so you are inimitably yourself at all times. Your *Mask* (from Phase 25) is SENSITIVE to other people's feelings and needs when True: you ACCEPT your destiny with (from Phase 5) a DECISIVENESS in standing up for others which you rarely employ in defending yourself. But in DENIAL you can be TOUCHY and EXIGENT (from Phase 19) with people in salving your hurt feelings and hiding yourself away. You possess an ease and naturalness of manner which makes itself at home in any surroundings. You are pensive, reflective, and conscientious in thinking things through before acting: *the man of Phase 11 systematises, runs to some frenzy of conviction, to make intellect, intellect for its own sake, possible, and perhaps, in his rage against rough-and-ready customary thought* [of the previous phases], *to make all but intellect impossible.* Because you shy from disharmony and don't like being pinned down, you may keep yourself loose by being evasive (wishy-washy) in contrast to the definite (and definitive) Phase 25 natives. Your *Creative Mind* (from Phase 19) is UTILITARIAN with a touch of your own TENDERNESS, so when True your DUTY to your group is to be the practical, down-to-earth worker with no axes to grind or petty agendas of your own; but when False and proclaiming your STATUS over others your TOUCHY (from Phase 25) EXIGENCE makes you huffy, thorny, and impossible to please. *Out of phase* you can be morbid and indwelling; and at the same time mulishly stubborn and nitpicking, a stickler for playing by your own personal rules: *compelled to substitute for intellectual rage some form of personal pride and so to become the proud prelate of tradition.* Your *Body of Fate* (from Phase 5) surprises people who are accustomed to your wonted plaintiveness and passive acquiescence, when your SPONTANEOUS DECISIVENESS breaks through in times of uncertainty and you take command with a no-nonsense confidence in your own abilities and the power of the universe to sustain you. *In phase*, your calm presence and unimpeachable integrity make you a model of forbearance for other people: *He [sees] the divine energy in whatever is the most individual expression of the soul.*

At Phases 11 and 12 occurs what is called the opening of the tinctures, *at Phase 11 the* antithetical *opens, at Phase 12 the* primary [in this book we say that the *antithetical tincture* closes at the end of Phase 11 and the *primary* opens with Phase 12]. ... *The opening means the reflection inward of the* Four Faculties: *all are as it were mirrored in personality, Unity of Being becomes possible. Hitherto we have been part of something else, but now discover everything within our own nature.*

Phases 12 – 14 are phases of supersensual Rage because they are struggling to be what Phase 15 manifests naturally – effortless self-adequacy, with no need to prove anything to anybody. Phases 12 -14 are still trying to prove something to themselves; hence they are driven (not at peace): *The phases of action where the man mainly defines himself by his practical relations are finished, or finishing, and the phases where he defines himself mainly through an image of the mind begun or beginning; phases of hatred for some external fate are giving way to phases of self-hatred.*

Phase 12

EMOTIONAL RESPONSIBILITY = UPSTANDING
The Forerunner

The Phase 12 native *no longer needs, like Phase 10, the submission of others, or, like Phase 11, conviction of others to prove his victory* because his sense of self-worth arises from within. Phase 12 is a Saturn phase softened by being in a moon rectangle, so your HABITUAL mode of action when *in phase* is UPSTANDING – you're a stand up person who always knows where you stand and what you stand for. You will not sully yourself with questionable or insincere behavior; which – when *out of phase* – can make you a bit of a crusty fuddy-duddy, with a LOFTY pride and a condescending, holier-than-thou attitude. You are scrupulous, honorable, diligent, respectful of others and demanding of respect in return. You have little capacity for duplicity or guile, so people know you to be true to your word and unshakeable in your convictions. Nonplussed by subtleties, you prefer "open covenants openly arrived at" – laying all your cards on the table and expecting others to do the same: *we shall meet with men and women to whom facts are a dangerous narcotic or intoxicant.* Your *Mask* derives from Phase 26, so when True and ACCEPTING of your destiny you exhibit a wry, QUIRKY humor which is GENTLE (from Phase 4), philosophical, indulgent, and able to take other people and the things that happen in stride; but when False and you are in DENIAL becomes a PERFUNCTORY (from Phase 18) BULLHEADEDNESS which is overweening, patronizing, and snooty. You are proud, serious-minded, and have firm lines which are not to be crossed. You jealously guard your private space; and you take pains to keep out of other people's space as well: *Solitude has been born at last, though solitude invaded, and hard to defend.* You stick to your principles through thick and thin, even when (sometimes – when playing the martyr – especially when) doing so redounds to your own disadvantage: *Intellectual abstraction ceased at Phase 11.* You are pensive and introspective, and you have a unique and well thought-out philosophy of life: *Having by philosophic intellect ... delivered it from all that is topical and temporary, announces a philosophy which is the logical expression of a mind alone with the object of its desire.* You are unshakeable in your convictions and you possess a frank, forward, and bluff social manner: *The nature is conscious of the most extreme degree of deception, and is wrought to a frenzy of desire for truth of self.* The *primary tincture* opening at Phase 12 means that the awareness of a higher imperative than the self's desires begins to inject itself into what is basically an *antithetical* (self-interested) quarter: *The man is pursued by a series of accidents* [outside reality forcibly intruding upon your version of it], *which, unless he meet them* antithetically [with some degree of detachment], *drive him into all sorts of temporary ambitions, opposed to his nature, unite him perhaps to some small protesting sect (the family or neighbourhood of Phase 4 intellectualised); and these ambitions he defends by some kind of superficial intellectual action, the pamphlet, the violent speech, the sword of the swashbuckler. He spends his life in oscillation between the violent assertion of some commonplace pose, and a dogmatism which means nothing apart from the circumstances that created it. If, however, he meets these accidents by the awakening of his* antithetical *being, there is a noble extravagance, an overflowing fountain of personal life.* The opening of the *primary tincture* at this point in the cycle (as mentioned previously) symbolizes sexual awakening: *It has become personal; there is now, though not so decisively as later, but one form of chosen beauty, and the sexual Image is drawn as with a diamond, and tinted those pale colours sculptors sometimes put on a statue.* Your *Creative Mind* derives from Phase 18, so when True the role you play in your social group is INGENUOUS – caring nothing for yourself except to discharge your DUTY in your own UPSTANDING, punctilious, faithful fashion. When False your sense of STATUS manifests as a PERFUNCTORY passive-resistance-under-protest rather than a whole-hearted giving of yourself, with a BULLHEADED (from Phase 26) refusal to collaborate on any terms but your own. You are driven, always trying to do more than is absolutely required to obey your conscience. This is what is meant by the *primary tincture* opening at this point in the cycle (a tilt towards self-effacement in the middle of an *antithetical* quarter): *It is a phase of immense energy* [intensity] *because the* Four Faculties *are equidistant* [= W.B.Y.'s interpretation; in this book we would say it's because the Chaldean cycle breaks between moon and Saturn]. ... *The nature is conscious of the most extreme degree of deception, and is wrought to a frenzy of desire for truth of self.* This is why your grave and stern manner notwithstanding, you do possess a droll, ironic, or gallows sense of humor; and are able to take a detached and long-range view of things. You thoroughly weigh the consequences before acting in order to anticipate possible pitfalls, and you try to take everyone's viewpoint into your calculations: *the greatest subtlety of sensitiveness, and more and more conscious of its frailty. Out of phase*, emulating Phase 26, your unrealistic assessment of realities or what people will stand for; together with your grim, suspicious, fortress mentality; can lead to a self-righteous huffiness, and undue strictness with other people as well as yourself: *driven from one self-conscious pose to another ... He spends his life in oscillation between the violent assertion of some commonplace pose, and a dogmatism which means nothing apart from the circumstance that created it. In phase* you are scrupulous, punctilious, and always undertake more than your fair share of the load so as to be able to acquit yourself with dignity and honor: *a noble extravagance, an overflowing fountain of personal life.* Your *Body of Fate* comes from Phase 4's GENTLENESS – your SPONTANEOUS impulses are genteel and gentlemanly; polite, well-mannered, considerate of others. Your high principles and unswerving allegiance to what you believe is right – *the greatest possible belief in all values created by personality* – win the admiration and respect of everyone: *before all else the phase of the hero, of the man who overcomes himself.*

After Phase 12, when true personality begins, brutality gives place to an evasive, capricious coldness ... a lack of good faith in their primary relation, often accompanied in their antithetical relation by the most self-torturing scruples.

There are moments of triumph and moments of defeat, each in its extreme form, for the subjective intellect knows nothing of moderation.

Phase 13

2

EMOTIONAL UNDERSTANDING = FACILITATING
The sensuous man – Perfection of Self-knowledge

Phase 13 continues the trend which began in the previous phase away from dependence upon the feedback of others for self-definition and towards a deeper sense of inner conviction; but in contrast to the gravity and self-seriousness of Phase 12, Phase 13 natives are cheerful, gregarious and inviting: *This is said to be the only phase where entire sensuality is possible, that is to say, sensuality without the intermixture of any other element. There is now a possible complete intellectual unity.* Phase 13's are far more willing than the stodgy Phase 12's to trust their impulses and intuition. Phase 13 is the phase of the student, the scholar, the open-minded investigator. These natives need an idealized system of belief to which they can refer their actions (whereas Phase 12's refer their actions to a sense of morality / right conduct). Phase 13 is a double Jupiter phase which gives you your optimistic, upbeat jollity with the HABIT when *in phase* of playing the disinterested, FACILITATING doyen or master-of-ceremonies in any group of which you are a part; and when *out of phase* puts people on with an ABOVE-IT-ALL sniffiness and condescension. You are amiable and inviting; intellectually curious and idealistic. You hold to abstract standards of fairness and truth, and you project a charitable and benevolent civility which lends a touch of good manners and decorum to any group situation. You prefer to see things carried out in good order, with a minimum of fuss. Your genial bonhomie and benign interest in other people soothes them and puts them at their ease. You are not so much the hail-fellow-well-met as the avuncular well-wisher or sage: *At this phase the self discovers, within itself, while struggling with the* Body of Fate, *forms of emotional morbidity which others recognize as their own; as the Saint may take upon himself the physical diseases of others.* Your *Mask* from Phase 27 is HUMANE: PERCEPTIVE (from Phase 3), thoughtful, judicious, and sympathetic when True and you are ACCEPTING your destiny – seeking to ensure that everyone gets a sympathetic hearing and a fair shake; but SANCTIMONIOUS when in DENIAL, with an UNYIELDING (from Phase 17), holier-than-thou self-righteousness: playing the role of the impartial arbiter or ombudsman while always keeping the focus on yourself. Albeit chatty, you decline to reveal what you are truly thinking or feeling. In contrast to Phase 6 you are personal and considerate rather than brisk and matter-of-fact; and you rely upon collaboration (rather than adherence to social norms) to maintain peace and harmony: *Phase 13 is a phase of great importance, because the most intellectually subjective phase, and because only here can be achieved in perfection that in the* antithetical *life which corresponds to sanctity in the* primary: *not self-denial but expression for expression's sake.* Your *Creative Mind* derives from Phase 17, so when performing your DUTY you naturally gravitate towards leadership roles as the STAUNCH FACILITATOR or impartial referee who advocates pondering and thinking things through rather than acting on impulse; but when False and you are merely avowing your STATUS you resort to an UNYIELDING SANCTIMONY (from Phase 27) to enforce your will rather than reason or good faith. You keep your cool and try your best not to let things get to you (or at least you make a show of things not getting to you). *Out of phase* your studied neutrality, dislike of unpleasantness, and disinclination to get too involved can make you wishy-washy and vacillating when decisiveness is called for, and patronizing when what is needed is resolution – *If it live objectively, that is to say, surrender itself to sensation, it becomes morbid* – a helpless onlooker inclined to grump at your misfortune: *Self-hatred now reaches its height, and through this hatred comes the slow liberation of intellectual love* [the wholeheartedness characteristic of Phase 27]. Your *Body of Fate* from Phase 3 makes your SPONTANEOUS approach to people that of the PERCEPTIVE, objective observer whose pithy insights are both entertaining and illuminating. Your patient dispassion is calming, reassuring, and wins the trust of others. *In phase* you always try to smooth out any points of dispute; your unselfish concern for the well-being of others and your commitment to rapprochement ensure a mutual respect and accommodation: *Though wax* [responsive] *to every impression of emotion, or of sense, it would yet through its passion for truth (*Creative Mind*) become its* *opposite and receive from the* Mask *(Phase 27), which is at the phase of the Saint, a virginal purity of emotion.*

From now, if not from Phase 12, and until Phase 17 or Phase 18 has passed, happy love is rare, for ... the range of choice grows smaller, and all life grows more tragic. As the woman grows harder to find, so does every beloved object. Lacking suitable objects of desire, the relation between man and Daimon *becomes more clearly a struggle or even a relation of enmity.*

> *... Eleven pass, and then*
> *Athene takes Achilles by the hair,*
> *Hector is in the dust, Nietzsche is born,*
> *Because the hero's crescent is the twelfth.*
> *And yet, twice born, twice buried, grow he must,*
> *Before the full moon, helpless as a worm.*
> *The thirteenth moon but sets the soul at war*
> *In its own being, and when that war's begun*
> *There is no muscle in the arm; and after,*
> *Under the frenzy of the fourteenth moon,*
> *The soul begins to tremble into stillness,*
> *To die into the labyrinth of itself.*
>
> (W.B.Y., *The Phases of the Moon*)

Phase 14

EMOTIONAL ACCOMPLISHMENT = DOUGHTY
The obsessed man

Ever since the *primary tincture* opened the emphasis has been on finding (*antithetical*) personal fulfillment and realization in the midst of (*primary*) community pressure to conform. Phase 14 is as idealistic as Phase 13, but here the reach is for freedom from restriction rather than towards intellectual understanding.

In contrast to the genial and sociable Phase 13 types, Phase 14 natives are self-willed and combative – they bristle at any sort of constraint or direction, and they go their own way and do their own thing without a fare-thee-well. Phase 14 is a double Mars phase, so your HABITUAL mindset *in phase* is a DOUGHTY spiritedness which leads you to fearlessly strike out on your own path in life; but when *out of phase* becomes a HEADSTRONG defiance of convention, restraint, or even ordinary social niceties. Your dislike of depending on other people makes you extremely hard-working and highly responsible, but you must decide for yourself where your responsibilities lie: *At Phase 16 will be discovered a desire to accept every possible responsibility; but now responsibility is renounced and this renunciation becomes an instrument of power, dropped burdens being taken upon by others.* You don't play the game by anyone's rules but your own: you are perfectly willing – and indeed prefer – to go it alone. You stoutly reject any attempt at coercion or being dictated to, nor do you give a damn about what other people say or think about you. You are a lone wolf, and the only thing that matters to you is preserving your honor, integrity, and independence. You are self-assured, audacious, and uncompromising – an unbridled maverick – and you are not afraid to call a spade a spade: *Fate thrusts an aimless excitement upon Phase 14:* a taste for adventure; for pushing the envelope; for being on the cutting edge. You are bold and defiant, with a heroic willingness to go to any extreme and endure any hardship in order to realize your goals. Your *Mask* from Phase 28 when True and ACCEPTING your karma exhibits CONSCIENTIOUS diligence, thoroughness, and meticulousness, with a COMPANIONABLE (from Phase 2) roll-up-your-sleeves-and-get-down-to-it cheerfulness; but when False and in DENIAL becomes a cold, unreachable, and CHIMERICAL IMPASSIVITY (from Phase 16) which digs in your heels and refuses to play by any rules but your own. You are feisty, rebellious, and outspoken, (a smug know-it-all); and on the negative side your indignant, sharp-tongued, and insubordinate contempt for any authority you disrespect is an extreme caricature of *antithetical* individualism, here as the quarter is about to end: *Her early life has perhaps been perilous because of that nobility, that excess of* antithetical *energies. The greater the peril the nearer has she approached to the final union of* primary *and* antithetical [at Phase 15], *where she will desire nothing.* Your staunch insistence on maintaining your freedom of action will not be circumscribed; and your contumacy can come to regard even the necessity of adhering to everyday social conventions as an insult to you personally. Your *Body of Fate*, from Phase 2, gives you a SPONTANEOUS insouciance, straightforwardness, and inability to dissemble which is COMPANIONABLE and relates to people with no need for guardedness or pretense; but which also ill-equips you for the rough-and-tumble of everyday society (whose rewards therefore tend to elude you). Since you don't have very good defenses, you are puzzled and very hurt by rebuff, and your naïve trust in other people's motives can make you a mark for the unscrupulous: *All born at the* antithetical *phases before Phase 15 are subject to violence ... this violence seems accidental, unforeseen and cruel.* Because you refuse to rely upon anyone else, you are dedicated and assiduous, and make a fetish of self-sufficiency; and *in phase* you tend to choose a simple, frugal, uncomplicated lifestyle. Your *Creative Mind* derives from Phase 16, so when True your own DOUGHTY SELF-POSSESSION lets you relax, be yourself, and fit right in to any group situation, particularly since you take pride in discharging your DUTY, have no objection to grunt work, and regard mean tasks as a challenge. You learn early on that you will receive no help or support on your journey, and as a result you are dogged, exacting, and capable of tremendous stick-to-itiveness.

You would rather live and work unaided than compromise your autonomy one iota: *Phase 14 finds within itself an antithetical self-absorbing dream.* When False your *Creative Mind* descends to seeking STATUS in the eyes of others with a superficially IMPASSIVE (but seething underneath) vanity or CHIMERICAL (from Phase 28) self-exaltation, hubris, and demand for special privileges and indulgence. *Out of phase* and pretending to the super-innocence and purity of motive characteristic of Phase 28, you are self-righteous and self-justifying: seeking the validation and approval of others you become a pitiful, cringing beggar or performing buffoon who deserves and receives nothing but their contempt: *When the being is out of phase ... its intellect becomes but a passion of apprehension or a shrinking from solitude; it may even become mad; or it may use its conscious feebleness and its consequent terror as a magnet for the sympathy of others, as a means of domination,* as if to Trump people with your bravado, braggadocio, and vindictiveness. *In phase* your stouthearted indomitability of spirit, unwavering (if at times wrong-headed) nobility of purpose, and resolute courage of your convictions assure your ultimate success and vindication.

The struggle for *antithetical*, uninhibited self-expression climaxes at Phase 15. Phase 14 is the clinging – the rage and intensity – before the release. Phase 14 is super-driven; Phase 15 is utterly undriven. Where Phase 14's are constantly trying prove their worth to themselves, Phase 15's just *are* – they don't have to prove anything to anyone, least of all themselves. All of the Phases 8 – 14 are phases of rage because they try to throw off social conditioning, to free themselves to become what Phase 15's achieve effortlessly: extreme individuation and separatedness – "I am a rock, I am an island."

At Phase 15 and Phase 1 occurs what is called the interchange of the tinctures, *those thoughts, emotions, energies, which were* primary *before Phase 15 or Phase 1 are* antithetical *after, those that were* antithetical *are* primary. *I was told, for instance, that before the historical Phase 15 the* antithetical tincture *of the average European was dominated by reason and desire, the* primary *by race and emotion, and that after Phase 15 this was reversed, his subjective nature had been passionate and logical but was now enthusiastic and sentimental.*

Phase 15

INTELLECTUAL PURPOSE = ANGUISHED
Complete beauty

Where phase 14 natives are determined and drive themselves relentlessly, Phase 15 natives have "arrived" – they are not going anywhere in particular. You are dreamy, eccentric, and otherworldly: you are tuned in to your own wavelength and always follow your own star. You stand apart from your social milieu, not so much because you are a nonconformist as because you are very intuitive and live in your own private universe. You are calm, cool, remote, and dislike perturbation and effusiveness. You have no concern for what others think of you; thus you are free of the striving for acceptance and approval which motivates most people: *All that the being has experienced as thought is visible to its eyes as a whole, and in this way it perceives, not as they are to others, but according to its own perception, all orders of existence. Its own body possesses the greatest possible beauty* [not physical beauty in the common sense but an incorruptibility and transparency] *being indeed that body which the soul will permanently inhabit, when all its phases have been repeated according to the number allotted: that which we call the clarified or Celestial Body.* It's not so much that you desire nothing as that you care about nothing (which can be a vexation to your intimates). You are immune to second thoughts and the fears of failure or censure which inhibit most people; and you are willing to throw all caution to the winds in order to follow your own destiny. You often feel isolated and nonplussed by the demands of the "real" world, and possess a childlike perplexity at the artificiality and arbitrariness of everyday society, which you disdain. You tend to hold other people at arm's length and let no one in. You don't form close friendships or need the emotional support of a family. You may be a dutiful spouse and parent, but this is more in response to your own sense of obligation than it is a heartfelt warmth or sympathy. Phase 15 is marked by a HABITUAL mindset of ANGUISHED self-absorption (which is also your True *Creative Mind*'s sense of DUTY): acknowledging the emotional and spiritual barrenness of all human longing and belonging, and pointing to the goal of the second half of the lunation cycle which entails forsaking the world and uniting with the Godhead. You are always on the outside looking in, acutely aware of your essential aloneness – within your family, society, and the universe – which knowledge nonetheless provides you with a strength of character and firmness of will (being a sun phase) based upon self-reliance and utter indifference to what other people think of you. Phase 15 is said to represent complete beauty because the Antithetical *of this phase perceives the world with the greatest detachment and wonder* (or *out of phase*: trivial bemusement). Phase 15 intuits its own answers directly from the Spirit rather than relying upon socially sanctioned channels of communication – thus it has the least sense of connection or security of connectedness of any phase (or, *in phase*, the greatest). The original version of this book gave the keyword of VISIONARY for Phase 15, so as to sound upbeat; but truthfully – while you are indeed a visionary in the sense that you see and feel things which no one else sees or feels – it is when you are experiencing the greatest degree of separatedness (isolation) that you are the most *in phase*, the most alive; and any effort you make to deaden this feeling (such as imitating Phase 1's brash playing to the crowd) puts you *out of phase*. Phase 14 is as isolated within itself as is Phase 15; however these natives shield themselves from the feeling of *Angst* – of cosmic aloneness – by always having some obsessive aim or other in mind that they strenuously cling to in order to distract themselves (it is this feeling of being relentlessly driven which gives rise to their indomitability). By contrast, Phase 15 natives experience relative freedom from compulsion (and compunction) – you are not motivated by the carrot or the stick; and you have a concomitant *out of phase* potential for obsessions, addictions, and – reproducing the Phase 1 exuberance – unbridled extremism generally. *Out of phase* and asserting your STATUS over others with your False *Creative Mind*, you hide your vulnerability behind a FRACTIOUS, thorny, taciturnity; (and you are quite conscious of when you are doing this, inasmuch as Phase 15 is the most self-aware of all the phases). When your *Mask* is False your DENIAL takes the form of demanding special favor or consideration from others for your suffering, with a PIGHEADED contumely and contrariety: a hatchet-faced stoicism, a low growl, which keeps people in a continual tizzy, walking on eggs around you and never knowing what to expect next. Then Phase 15 lacks a firm sense of direction; gropes for guideposts in life; and grabs for dear life onto any flotsam at random (the applause of the crowd). The other phases – especially the *primary* phases – are more constrained by their social training (*Will* – particularly first quarter phases); or else are primarily responsive to ideals (*Mask*– particularly second quarter phases); or perhaps are motivated by a sense of intellectual right (*C.M.* – particularly third quarter phases); or else act out of a sense of solidarity and belonging (*B.F.* – particularly last quarter phases). But Phase 15 acts out of an inner knowing; or, *out of phase*, inner despair. *Out of phase, complete beauty can become complete self-indulgence and self-obsession: you retreat into yourself and become secretive, uncommunicative, impervious and imperious – like Phase 1, a demanding tyrant, preening and prancing, quite capable of turning stone cold and cutting other people off emotionally, with a concomitant terror of solitude, its forced, painful and slow acceptance, and a life haunted by terrible dreams.* The yin-yang interchange of *tinctures* at Phase 15 means that when your *Mask* is True and you ACCEPT your true life's purpose – when you are standing there completely naked, in all your wretchedness, hiding nothing (least of all from yourself) – the flip side of your solitariness is a delightfully IRREPRESSIBLE élan (similar to that of Phase 1) – a live-for-the-moment *Body of Fate* SPONTANEITY (since you know you have nothing to lose or defend); a faith in yourself and the power of the universe to sustain you; a craziness and willingness to fly with your impulses and not care where you land. *In phase* you possess an unshakeable faith in your own inner voice and are a model of originality and fearlessness.

> *Although I saw it all in the mind's eye*
> *There can be nothing solider till I die;*
> *I saw by the moon's light*
> *Now at its fifteenth night.*
>
> *One lashed her tail; her eyes lit by the moon*
> *Gazed upon all things known, all things unknown,*
> *In triumph of intellect*
> *With motionless head erect.*
>
> *The other's moonlit eyeballs never moved,*

*Being fixed on all things loved, all things
unloved,
Yet little peace he had,
For those that love are sad.*

After Phase 15, but before Phase 19, the being is full of phantasy, a continual escape from and yet acknowledgement of all that allures in the world, a continual playing with all that must engulf it. In other words, these are phases of pulling away from isolation from other people and joining together with them in voluntary association which eventually must lead to servitude – or at least loss of individual freedom. Where Phase 14 struggles against the bonds of socialization to attain at phase 15 an effortless freedom of self-expression, Phase 16 takes this new-found freedom of self-expression back to other people, to share with them (Phase 16 sees other people in terms of collaboration; where phase 14 sees them in terms of combat).

All Phases after Phase 15 and before Phase 22 unweave that which is woven by the equivalent phases before Phase 15 and after Phase 8.

Phase 16

INTELLECTUAL ENJOYMENT = SELF-POSSESSED
The positive man

Where the striving for or assumption of freedom from all social restraint which climaxes in phases 14 and 15 leads the natives of these phases to lightheartedly drop social burdens for others to pick up, by contrast *At Phase 16 will be discovered a desire to accept every possible responsibility.* There is a sense of social obligation and service to others – a desire to help, to be useful – present here which is absent in the preceding phases. Phase 16 is a

Venus phase in a Mars rectangle so your outgoing and gregarious disposition is based upon a strong will and unshakeable sense of self-at-center. Your HABITUAL manner is SELF-POSSESSED equipoise when *in phase* – tranquil, unhurried, unbothered – not allowing other people's turmoil to knock you off your pins. You have an agreeable, charming personality, a genteel manner, and a hopeful and optimistic take on life. You make good eye contact and immediately get on a cordial basis with everyone you meet. You have nothing to hide; are quite candid and outfront about what is on your mind; and you are nonjudgmental and accepting of the viewpoints and foibles of others. Since you are so unabashedly yourself at all times and under all circumstances, it's easy for other people to relax and be themselves around you too. You are very popular, with a wide circle of friends and acquaintances and an active round of social engagements. You are poised, easygoing, laid-back, and mannerly, with an unruffled gentility: no matter how badly things are going, you always look on the bright side and try to see the best in people and situations. Your *Creative Mind* from Phase 14 is a DOUGHTY SELF-POSSESSION which when True does its DUTY by being the voice of calm reason in any group and keeping things on a relaxed, placid, even-keel; but when False and concerned only with your STATUS you evince a HEADSTRONG CURTNESS (from Phase 2) – hard, cold, and ruthless in the face of conflict or obstruction – which doesn't much care what anyone thinks or feels. You take things in stride and avoid confrontation, needless unpleasantness, and distasteful uproars (fastidious). When *out of phase* you are given to an IMPASSIVE, noncommittal coolness – a blasé indifference to other people and their welfare. You have a strong sense of inner equilibrium and it takes deliberate malice to throw you off your stride or bend you out of shape. Like Phase 13 you have great intellectual curiosity and an adventurous, independent spirit. There's a love of travel and of meeting new people and confronting novel situations. You have artistic talent, or at least considerable originality and creativity; and you bring a disarming naturalness and a sense of style and flair – your special touch – to whatever you do. You are encouraging of other people and appreciative of their efforts; hence you make a patient teacher and enthusiastic helper – *boundless in generosity*. As an extreme antithetical phase, you may find the bonds of matrimony stifling, preferring to keep your relationships light and loose. You are impersonal and brisk and rather than warm or empathic; and you have a facility for shrugging things off rather than taking them to heart. Indeed, one of the fascinating conundrums of Phase 16 is how it is possible for a person to be so caught up in the social whirl without evincing much in the way of sympathy beyond well-meaning pleasantries; or forming any compromising alliances or intimate relationships (perhaps because you don't belong to anyone – you belong to the world). In spite of your outward conviviality, you are quite capable of dismissing or discarding other people coldly and without a second thought when they have outlived their usefulness. Your *Mask* derives from Phase 2's COMPANIONABILITY, making you friendly, inviting, and upbeat when True, with a CONSCIENTIOUS (from Phase 28) live-and-let-live, laissez faire ACCEPTANCE of yourself and other people; but when False and in DENIAL can become a CURT and brusque HEADSTRONG (from Phase 14) and headlong tendency to do your own thing come what may. *Out of phase*, the Phase 2 insistence on maintaining your cool and keeping the peace at all costs can make you overly compliant and put-upon. Then you become resentful and turn the cold shoulder, and you can be quite sharp-tongued and tactless in closing up and lashing out: *they turn termagant ... All the cruelty and narrowness of that intellect are displayed in service of preposterous purpose after purpose ...Capable of nothing but an incapable idealism ... it must, because it sees one side as all white, see the other side all black.* Your *Body of Fate* derives from Phase 28, so your SPONTANEOUS impulse towards others is a CONSCIENTIOUS and democratic sense of justice and fair play – a disinterested impartiality which wins people's trust. *In phase*, your cheerfulness, genuineness, and upbeat attitude bring harmony and conciliation to any group: *It finds the soul's most radiant expression and surrounds itself with some fairyland, some mythology of wisdom or laughter.*

Phase 17

INTELLECTUAL MENTALITY = STAUNCH
The Daimonic man

Phase 17 is a Mercury phase in a Jupiter rectangle so your astute mentality is broadened with a patient forbearance, which when *in phase* makes your HABITUAL mindset STAUNCH independence of thought and action – a capable person who must fearlessly follow your own will wherever it leads you; but when *out of phase* becomes an UNYIELDING eccentricity or hard-edged and sassy wrong-headedness which doesn't listen to anyone. You possess a penetrating, analytical mind, and are logical (as opposed to thoughtful, which is the province of Phase 24) and resourceful. You are agile and adaptable – able to make the best of any situation in which you happen to find yourself and quick to see and exploit opportunities as they arise. Crafty and calculating, you possess a fitful, nervous energy which is never at rest but is constantly scouting about: *As contrasted with Phase 13 and Phase 14, where mental images were separated from one another that they might be subject to knowledge, all now flow, change, flutter, cry out, or mix into something else.* Your *Mask* from Phase 3 is PERCEPTIVE and HUMANE (from Phase 27) when True and ACCEPTING: you must always find your own truths and illuminate your own path in life; and are solitary even in the midst of people, depending on no one for help or support. When False and in DENIAL your ABOVE-IT-ALL (from Phase 13) TRIFLING with people and refusal to get serious makes you callous and oblivious to consequences. You are prudent (suspicious) and constantly try to have all bases covered; to outfox and outmaneuver; to keep one step ahead of other people (and yourself): *... can never see anything that opposes him as it really is* but only in terms of whether it might serve or threaten you. You're tough, you're a survivor, you understand how to play (game) the system and come out on top. You are ever alert so as not be caught with your guard down, or unprepared: *The being has for its supreme aim, as it had in Phase 16 (and as all subsequent* antithetical *phases shall have), to hide from itself and others this separation and disorder, and it conceals them under the emotional Image of Phase 3* [assumed ease of manner]; which however is belied by your intense single-mindedness. It's important to you that others see you in the terms in which you see yourself; that they buy into your image of cleverness; and that you impress them with your acuity. You are rather taken with your own adroitness and have a tendency to be judgmental and opinionated, posturing and attitudinizing: *men of this phase are almost always partisans, propagandists and gregarious* [associate themselves with a cause or wrap their motives in the mantle of higher truth]; *yet ... they hate parties, crowds, propaganda* [will not be fooled; or trust too much; or permit themselves to be used]. Your *Creative Mind* derives from Phase 13, so when True you do your DUTY to your group by being the objective and FACILITATING mediator who is STAUNCH in fearlessly standing up for what you know is right and making sure that everyone plays by the rules; but when False you affirm your STATUS with an ABOVE-IT-ALL attitudinizing which is TRIFLING (from Phase 3) and insulting. *Out of phase* and attempting the flip impertinence and impersonal detachment of Phase 3 you tend to be petty, picky, and paranoiac: *it will avoid the subjective conflict, acquiesce ... feel itself betrayed, and persecuted till, entangled in* primary *conflict it rages ... It may even dream of escaping from ill-luck by possessing the impersonal* Body of Fate *of its opposite phase and of exchanging passion for desk and ledger. In phase* there is truthfulness in both your speech and comportment, so people take you at your word and appreciate your candor. Your *Body of Fate* comes from Phase 27 so your SPONTANEITY – when you get down to brass tacks and are being real – has a HUMANE sincerity and compassion – a plaintive honesty which brings out the best in people. Your unflagging faith in your ability to deal with whatever may come provides a reliance and reassurance for everyone: *When true to phase the intellect must turn all its synthetic power to (finding) ... simplicity that is also intensity ...The* Will, *when true to phase, assumes ... an intensity which is never dramatic but always lyrical and personal, and this intensity, though always a deliberate assumption, is to others but the charm of the being.*

Phase 18

INTELLECTUAL ASSURANCE = INGENUOUS
The emotional man

Like Phase 17, Phase 18 is lively, sassy, in-the-know; but these natives are softer, less prickly and prissy; and their aims are more collaborative than competitive: *Now for the first time since Phase 12, Goethe's saying is almost true: "Man knows himself by action only, by thought never."* Phase 18 is a lunar phase in a lunar rectangle, so your HABITUAL approach to people and situations is INGENUOUS – aboveboard, plain-dealing, and incapable of guile when *in phase*; and PERFUNCTORY or not altogether present – not exactly spaced-out, but distracted and on your own wavelength, looking past people rather than engaging them directly – when *out of phase*. You have a friendly, intimate manner and a pixie-like good humor; and your earthy naturalness and unvarnished frankness incline people to take you at your word: *The* Will, *with its closing antithetical, is turning away from the life of images to that of ideas, it is vacillating and curious, and it seeks ...a wisdom of the emotions.* You are conciliatory, tolerant, and decent; with high standards of comportment and a keen sense of justice: *The antithetical tincture begins to attain, without previous struggle or self-analysis, its active form which is love – love being the union of emotion and instinct – or when out of phase, sentimentality.* You brim with enthusiastic geniality: you are gregarious and chatty, and are a simple person who is quite open and forthcoming about what is on your mind. You dislike complexities and nuances; and are determined to cut across and get down to the truth. Although you try to avoid disharmony and conflict, you are by no means feeble or lax. Normally, you strive to strike a balance and find some common ground; yet you are more than willing to hold fast to what you know is right and to stand up for yourself (and others) than are the laid-back Phase 4 natives (who tend to walk away from unpleasantness and turn their attention elsewhere). Your *Mask* is derived from Phase 4, so when True you ACCEPT people as they are by being GENTLE and open to their feelings, withholding judgment and criticism, and seeking the best in them (with something of the mischievous and conspiratorial QUIRKINESS of Phase 26 mixed in). When False (in DENIAL) you are ABSTRACTED and feign a can't-be-bothered reverie – up on your own cloud that no one can pull you down from – TOPLOFTY like Phase 12 at its worst. You can't be forced or bullied – you stick to your guns and stand your ground whenever you are pushed beyond your limits. As Chögyam Trungpa put it: "The ideal of warriorship is that the warrior should be sad and tender, and because of that, the warrior can be very brave as well. Without that heartfelt sadness, bravery is brittle, like a china cup. If you drop it, it will break or chip. But the bravery of the warrior is like a lacquer cup, which has a wooden base covered with layers of lacquer. If the cup drops, it will bounce rather than break. It is soft and hard at the same time." Your *Creative Mind* is derived from Phase 12; when True your sense of DUTY, modified by your own INGENUOUSNESS, gives you an UPSTANDING moral imperative which dominates any group with a low-key presence (moon); you prefer to keep in the background, but you always stand up for what you know is right and willingly make great sacrifices with no thought of personal gain. When False you indulge a LOFTY sense of STATUS tinged with a Phase 4 ABSTRACTEDNESS – a disinclination to dirty your hands or soil yourself with other people's issues when things get down to the nitty-gritty. Since (like all moon phase natives) you are on your own wavelength much of the time, when *out of phase* you can be overly sensitive, easily wounded (thin-skinned, huffy), or excessively blunt and brusque: *When he seeks to live objectively, he will substitute curiosity for emotional wisdom* [i.e. try to remain aloof, like Phase 4], *he will invent objects of desire artificially ... The nightingale will refuse the thorn and so remain among images instead of passing to ideas. In phase*, your lack of pretense and guile, unadorned simplicity, and aboveboard right-mindedness inspire confidence and trust. Your Body of Fate is derived from the phase of the Hunchback, so your SPONTAN-

EOUS impulses are QUIRKY, surprising, and delightful – you shoot from the hip, say exactly what's on your mind, and no one can predict what you will do next (or in response to any situation). Your friendly interest in people – in sharing experience and learning what you can from your fellows rather than in impressing or controlling them (as does Phase 17) – means that you are always ready to defend others who are incapable of defending themselves: *the man seeks to become not a sage, not Ahasuerus, but a wise king.*

The antithetical tincture *closes during this phase* [18], *the being is losing direct knowledge of its old antithetical life. The conflict between that portion of the life of feeling which appertains to his unity, and that portion he has in common with others, coming to an end, has begun to destroy that knowledge.*

At Phase 18 the primary tincture *closes once more, and at Phase 19 the* antithetical [in this book we say the *antithetical tincture* closes now and the *primary* opens at Phase 19] ... *The* primary tincture *is closing, direct knowledge of self in relation to action is ceasing to be possible. The being only completely knows that portion of itself which judges fact for the sake of action.... it is well to find before (the nineteenth night counting from the start) – a sudden change, as when a cloud becomes rain, or water freezes, for the great transitions are sudden; popular, typical men have grown more ugly and more argument-tative. ... In phases 19, 20 and 21 genius grows professional, something taken up when work is taken up, it begins to be possible to record the stupidities of men of genius in a scrapbook.*

Phase 19

INTELLECTUAL RESPONSIBILITY = UTILITARIAN
The assertive man

Phase 19 is a double Saturn phase: hardy, hard-headed, hard-edged, hard-driving, hardworking. Your HABITUAL *in phase* mindset of UTILITARIAN practicality – getting the job at hand done as smoothly and with as little pother as possible – willingly undertakes whatever burdens or sacrifices are necessary, no matter how mean or thankless, in order to uphold your ideals. *Out of phase* and in DENIAL your assertive, forbidding EXIGENCE and call for special privileges more closely resembles the self-aggrandizing dictatorial streak of Phase 5. You demonstrate much of the incisive and no-nonsense practicality of Phase 17, but you dedicate it to abstract principle rather than self-service: *This phase is the beginning of the artificial, the abstract, the fragmentary, and the dramatic.* You follow the road less taken: you know what you want and how to get it. You are a crusader, possessing the hearty ebullience of Phase 18, but without the ameliorating humility; on the contrary, you are stubborn, outspoken, and emphatic (pushy). Your *Mask* from Phase 5 is DECISIVE: positive and self-assured, with an admirable nobility of spirit when True and you are able to ACCEPT other people (and yourself) with a SENSITIVE (from Phase 25) appreciation of their (and your) limitations; but when False and you are in DENIAL, your TYRANNICAL absolutism runs roughshod over the people around you, who scurry to avoid your SULLEN (from Phase 11) disapproval: *When lived out-of-phase there is a hatred or contempt of others, and instead of seeking conviction for its own sake, the man takes up opinions that he may impose himself on others. He is tyrannical and capricious.* At this point in the cycle *the* primary tincture *is closing, direct knowledge of self in relation to action is ceasing to be possible* [in this book we say that the *primary tincture* opens here – there is a single-minded dedication to higher principle at work in Phase 19 than has been evident previously in the Third Quarter]. You have high ideals and possess a genius for translating thought into action: *The being only completely knows that portion of itself which judges fact for the sake of action.* Your *Creative Mind* comes from Phase 11, so when True you fulfill your DUTY to your group with a TENDER protectiveness (with your own UTILITARIAN slant on what is practicable and possible) towards the helpless and those who depend on you; but when False and you are merely certifying your own STATUS, your outta-my-way-buddy intransigence becomes a SULLEN TYRANNY (from Phase 5) which refuses to participate on any terms but your own: *His aim is to use an intellect which turns easily to declamation, emotional emphasis, that it serves conviction in a life where effort, just in so far as its object is passionately desired, comes to nothing.* The opening of the *primary tincture* at this point in the cycle symbolizes the appearance of a *primary* impulse in what is basically an *antithetical* quarter: *he is doomed to attempt the destruction of all that breaks or encumbers personality, but this personality is conceived of as a fragmentary, momentary intensity. ... now the weakness of the* antithetical *has begun, for though still the stronger it cannot ignore the growing* primary. *... there is the desire to escape from Unity of Being or any approximation towards it, for Unity can be but a simulacrum now. And in so far as the soul keeps its memory of that potential Unity there is conscious* antithetical *weakness.* You are vocal and adamant (sharp-tongued), and always insist upon making your point (getting in the last word): *His thought is immensely effective and dramatic, arising always from some immediate situation, a situation found or created by* *himself, and may have great permanent value as the expression of an exciting personality.* Your opportunism is utterly realistic – you are a skillful practitioner of the art of the possible; with a flair for the histrionic: *when they are tempted to dramatise it, the dramatisation is fitful, and brings no conviction of strength, for they dislike emphasis.* You rush to defend the weak and helpless – not so much out of compassion, perhaps, as for the opportunity to get up on your soap box and take a heroic stand: *He desires to be strong and stable, but as Unity of Being and self-knowledge are both gone, and it is too soon to grasp at another unity through* primary *mind, he passes from emphasis to emphasis. ... The strength from conviction, derived from a* Mask *of the first quarter* antithetically *transformed, is not founded upon social duty, though that may seem so to others, but is temperamentally formed to fit some crisis of personal life.* While you ultimately depend upon no one but yourself, you are nonetheless quite sociable and outgoing (as long as no one crosses you). Your seriousness of purpose convinces people: you have a passion for life, and your self-discipline, high-minded idealism, and thorough dedication to everything you do gives you a knack for enlisting the enthusiastic support of others in implementing your own goals and dreams: *There is no "disillusionment", for they have found that which they have sought, but that which they have sought and found is a fragment. ... Here one finds men and women who love those who rob them or beat them, as though the soul were intoxicated by its discovery of human nature, or found even a secret delight in the shattering of the image of its desire.* Your *Body of Fate* derives from Phase 25, and makes your SPONTANEOUS outpourings unexpectedly (considering your wonted short and brusque manner) SENSITIVE, willing to listen, and attuned to where other people are coming from and what they really need. *In phase* your high-minded integrity is a shining example for everyone:

When the man lives according to phase, he is now governed by conviction, instead of by a ruling mood, and is effective only in so far as he can find this conviction. ... Vitality from dreams has died out [with the closing of the *antithetical* tincture in Phase 18], *and a vitality from fact has begun which has for its ultimate aim the mastery of the real world.*

At Phase 19 we create through the externalised Mask *an imaginary world, in whose real existence we believe, while remaining separate from it; at Phase 20 we enter that world and become a portion of it; we study it, we amass historical evidence, and, that we may dominate it the more, drive out myth and symbol, and compel it to seem the real world where our lives are lived.*

Phase 20

2

INTELLECTUAL UNDERSTANDING = AUDACIOUS
The concrete man – A Phase of ambition ...a creative energy

Phase 20 is a Jupiter phase in a Mercury rectangle, which gives you a quick mental acuity based upon originality of vision and uninhibited self-expression. Your HABITUAL stock-in-trade when *in phase* is the pithy observation, knowing witticism, or ready retort which startles everyone with its AUDACITY and apropos coherence; but when *out of phase* and you are merely strutting your stuff and showing off can become a shamelessly COCKY grab for attention. Like Phase 19 you make your own rules and define your own path (vocation and relationships) in life; but *Unlike Phase 19 he fails in situations wholly created by himself.* Phase 20 is as perceptive as Phase 19, and has much of the same cheek and panache, but you are rather more judicious and politic, and more adaptable and attuned to subtleties: *There is a delight in concrete images that, unlike the impassioned images of Phase 17 and Phase 18, or the declamatory images of Phase 19, reveal through complex suffering the general destiny of man.* You possess a smooth, suave, ease of manner; maintain a humorous running commentary on the passing scene; and you handily accomplish your goals because your sassy, sprightly alacrity and insouciance sway people to see things your way and to go along with your ideas and plans: *His phase is called "The Concrete Man", because the isolation of parts that began at Phase 19 is overcome at the second phase of the triad; subordination of parts is achieved by the discovery of concrete relations* [instead of dogmatism]. Your *Mask*, from Phase 6, is BROADMINDED (with something of Phase 24's IDEALISM) when True and you are ACCEPTING of people and their thinking: you are then impelled by a great intellectual curiosity to reach for a conceptual grasp of life and an understanding of other people's behavior; but when False (and being something of a smart-ass) you can exhibit a CAPRICIOUS (from Phase 10) FINICKINESS or temperamental hairsplitting which is obstinate rather than thoughtful. *Out of phase* and appealing to the social norms and political correctness of Phase 6 for justification instead of relying on your own insight and the message of your own heart, you can be overly smug and self-exculpating. You are shrewd and clever, and think that you have figured out all the angles and anticipated all the pitfalls (at least until life pulls the rug out from under you), which can make you seem immune to the caution and second thoughts which inhibit most people: *The energy is always seeking those facts which being separable can be seen more clearly, or expressed more clearly.* In contrast to the earlier Jupiter phases you maintain an inner equilibrium instead of tying your current mood and sense of worth to the attention of the people around you: *He no longer seeks to unify what is broken through conviction, by imposing those very convictions upon himself and others, but by projecting a dramatisation or many dramatisations.* Your ironic wit and deft and easy handling of other people make you the cynosure of any group. Your *Creative Mind* comes from Phase 10, so when True your DUTY is to be the DISCERNING analyst whose own AUDACIOUS force of personality dominates your milieu with its penetrating discrimination and refusal to be anybody's fool: you are truly an original; you invent yourself as you go along; and there's no one else in your circle even remotely like you. When False you are given to a CAPRICIOUS and (from Phase 6) FINICKY posturing which demands special STATUS due to your superior perspicacity. Your *Body of Fate* derives from Phase 24, so your SPONTANEOUS cleverness is – at its best – employed in the service of a selfless IDEALISM which always has your eyes gazing beyond the horizon to a hopeful outcome and a better tomorrow. *In phase* you have a conspiratorial twinkle in your eye and a tongue-in-cheek manner that wins people over: *In a man of action this multiplicity gives the greatest possible richness of resource where he is not thwarted by his horoscope, great ductability, a gift for adopting any rôle that stirs imagination, a philosophy of impulse and audacity.*

Phase 21

INTELLECTUAL ACCOMPLISHMENT = RESOLUTE
The acquisitive man

Like the preceding phase, Phase 21 is astute, mentally clear, attuned to subtleties, and possesses a broad understanding of human motivation and frailty. But in contrast to the humorous detachment of the Phase 20 types, you are ambitious and enterprising, and are quick to turn your insights to personal account. Phase 21 is a Mars phase in a Venus rectangle, so your dynamism and mettle have a certain delicacy, restraint, and sense of the politic. You look people directly in the eye and have an unvarnished directness of manner – a detached noblesse oblige. When *in phase* your HABITUAL mindset is an unshakeable and RESOLUTE focus on your own ends, yet with a disinclination to make waves or incite open conflict: you are shrewd, circumspect, and inclined to keep your own counsel. When *out of phase* you can be OBSTINATE in guarding your secrets and charging on ahead – grimly uncommunicative and indifferent to anyone else's opinion or needs. *The antithetical tincture is noble, and, judged by the standards of the primary, evil, whereas the primary is good and banal* [of course this is the opinion of one born in an *antithetical* phase]; *and this phase, the last before the antithetical surrenders its control, would be almost wholly good did it not hate its own banality* [a sense of being special, on the inside track]. You are high-minded, with a well-developed sense of honor and punctiliousness and a can-do spirit. You are bold and original, with a droll point of view: *A man of Phase 21 has a personality that seems a creation of his circumstance and his faults, a manner peculiar to himself and impossible to others. We say at once, "How individual he is"*. Your *Mask*, from Phase 7, is clear-sighted and INCISIVE when True – ACCEPTING of people with an EMPATHIC (from Phase 23) and philosophical understanding of human motivation; but when False and in DENIAL exhibits an impatient and CUTTING dismissal of others which you use to bend and MANIPULATE (from Phase 9) them to your will (or brusquely toss them aside). You are cool, businesslike, and efficient, doing what is required in the moment with a minimum of pother or taking things personally. You are cagey, secretive, and play your cards very close to your chest. You revel in the chess game aspects of human relations – you are reserved and calculating, and need to feel yourself to be one-up on everyone, a step ahead in the game of life: *we find in practice that nobody of this phase has personal imitators, or has given his name to a form of manners.* Since you are quite consciously aware of your own designs, you tend to be suspicious and distrustful of the motives of others as well: *Precisely because his adaptability can be turned in any direction, when lived according to the* primary, *he is driven into all that is freakish or grotesque, mind-created passions, simulated emotions; he adopts all that can suggest the burning heart he longs for in vain; he turns braggart or buffoon.* Your *Creative Mind* derives from Phase 9 and when True and you DUTIFULLY put yourself at the service of others, you can be most INGRATIATING in your own RESOLUTE insistence on equality, justice, and a fair shake for everyone; but when False your need for STATUS manifests as a MANIPULATIVE, shamelessly CUTTING (from Phase 7) adamancy which simply grabs whatever it is you want, regardless of the consequences. You hold people at arm's length and tend to be equivocal and evasive, disinclined to be pinned down: *In phase he strengthens conflict to the utmost by refusing all activity that is not* antithetical: *he becomes intellectually dominating, intellectually unique ... for he is a tyrant and must kill his adversary.* Out of phase, forfeiting the advantage of careful deliberation and attempting the headstrong dynamism and bold strokes characteristic of Phase 7, you tend to be vociferous but ineffectual; going through empty, meaningless motions: *In so far as he lives out of phase he weakens conflict, refuses to resist, floats upon the stream*; and you are left high and dry in your own rationalizations, which so often miss the actual point: *Phase 7 shuddered at its intellectual simplicity, whereas he must shudder at his complexity.* Out of phase, *instead of seeking this simplicity through his own dominating constructive will, he will parade an imaginary naïveté, even blunder in his work, encourage in himself stupidities of spite or sentiment, or commit calculated indiscretions simulating impulse.* Your Body of Fate derives from Phase 23, so when you are acting SPONTANEOUSLY you can be very EMPATHIC – willing to overlook frailty and give other people the benefit of the doubt. *In phase your caution, reserve, and level-headed judgment are rewarded with allegiance and trust: the aim of the individual, when true to phase, is to realise, by his own complete domination over all circumstance, a self-analysing, self-conscious simplicity.*

The quarter of Intellect was a quarter of dispersal and generalization, a play of shuttlecock with the first quarter of animal burgeoning, but the fourth quarter is a quarter of withdrawal and concentration, in which active moral man should receive into himself, and transform into primary *sympathy the emotional self-realisation of the second quarter.*

That which at Phase 21 was a longing for self-conscious simplicity, as an escape from logical complication and subdivision, is now ... a desire for the death of the intellect. At Phase 21 it still sought to change the world ... but now it will seek to change nothing, it needs nothing but what it may call 'reality', 'truth', 'God's Will': confused and weary, through trying to grasp too much, the hand must loosen.

At Phase 22 is the "Breaking of Strength', for here the being makes its last attempt to impose its personality upon the world before the Mask *becomes enforced once more, character substituted for personality.*

Phase 22

MORAL PURPOSE = OBLIGING
Balance between ambition and contemplation

Phase 22 is ruled by the sun, so you possess a sunny optimism, innocence, and hopefulness which *in phase* gives you the HABIT of being OBLIGING and ready to put yourself at the service of other people to keep things on a light, positive track. *Out of phase* and feeling powerless or despairing (since you are incapable of dealing with the phoniness and game-playing inherent in everyday society) you take on a SUBMISSIVE role, drifting helplessly or going along with what other people seem to want of you, in order not to rock the boat. Phases 8 and 22, like all solar phases, are relatively detached and self-contained. But these are phases of turmoil: Phase 8 and 22 natives feel themselves to be misfits, out of step somehow, inextricably entangled in an incomprehensible world. In their desperate efforts to avoid involvement they become embroiled in the very conflicts they seek to avoid. Where Phase 8 tends to shameless self-promotion, Phase 22 tends to neurosis (overburdened with shame). Where Phase 8 natives tend to feel superior to other people and ignore their opinions, Phase 22 natives tend to submerge themselves in others, craving an approval and recognition which – even when forthcoming – leaves them with a feeling of emptiness and nonfulfillment: rudderless at sea. Where Phase 8 erects stout boundaries to protect the self, Phase 22 relinquishes boundaries in an attempt to erase the self: *Phase 8 and Phase 22 are phases of struggle and tragedy, the first a struggle to find personality, the second to lose it.* Both your *Mask* and *Creative Mind* derive from Phase 8, so when True and ACCEPTING your destiny and obeying your sense of DUTY to your group you take SELF-

SATISFACTION in being a model citizen and team player – one who takes others into account and puts the well-being of all ahead of your own personal needs and desires. But when False and in DENIAL, you defend your STATUS with a SMUG pettiness which is quick to perceive slights (where perhaps none are intended), to take ready offense, salve your wounds, and close up into yourself. You are natural, unpretentious, and unobtrusive (a sad sack); and you have a gentle and approachable personal manner. In conversation you are straightforward and unassuming – glib without being pushy or presumptuous – with a dignity born of calm and patient resignation. You are nonplussed by disharmony and therefore are at pains not to make waves, but to keep everything on an even keel. You feel yourself to be blown hither and thither, trying to find where you belong: ... *confused and weary, through trying to grasp too much, the hand must loosen. .... the mind exhausts all knowledge within its reach and sinks exhausted to a conscious futility.* You always try to put on a happy face, to maintain that things are just fine and dandy. Although you are gregarious and gracious with people, nonetheless you are basically a private person. Your sun-phase detachment makes it easy for you to play by the rules and to live up to the expectations of others (even at your own expense). And, if your horoscope is not otherwise terribly afflicted, you readily receive acknowledgement, pre-ferment, and advancement in return – a pat on the back for a job well done. But somehow this is not you. There is something plaintive about you: good-natured, but overshadowed by an ineffable sadness or preoccupation – perhaps a tragedy in early life – which lends you an air of straining to keep up your spirits in the face of enforced renunciation: *It is a phase as tragic as its opposite, and more terrible, for* [where Phase 8 destroys and persecutes] *... his system will become an instrument of destruction and of persecution in the hands of others.* The crises of Phase

22 result when – with the dying of the *antithetical* and onset of the *primary* – you refuse command of your own destiny and instead bend yourself out of whack to please other people until something snaps; then you suddenly become, like Phase 8, *strangely hard, cold and invulnerable, that this mirror is not brittle but of unbreakable steel*, going off half-cocked and making a mess of things. Phase 22 spends too much time thinking (in terms of what is acceptable) – seeking an intellectual grasp on matters which are not intellectually graspable but must be intuited instead – *a desire for the death of the intellect*. *Out of phase* and defensively projecting the blasé indifference of Phase 8, you are in thrall to everyone around you, passively looking to others for some sort of clue as to who you are and what you should be doing. You keep a stiff upper lip and endure, and permit others to project their turmoil onto you. Where Phase 8 victimizes, Phase 22 plays victim: *The mind that has shown a predominantly emotional character, called that of the* Victim, *through the* antithetical *phases, now shows a predominantly intellectual character, called that of the* Sage; ... *whereas the mind that has been predominantly that of the* Sage *puts on* Victimage. When *in phase* you find true self-respect in your self-effacement and willingness to sacrifice. Your spirit of service to others lends you a nobility of character which shines through and illuminates all your actions: *Intellect knows itself as its own object of desire; and the* Will *knows itself to be the world; there is neither change nor desire of change. For the moment the desire for a form has ceased and an absolute realism becomes possible. ... A man of Phase 22 will commonly not only systematise, to the exhaustion of his will, but discover this exhaustion of will in all that he studies. ...* [*In phase*] *The man himself is never weak, never vague or fluctuating in his thought, for if he brings all to silence, it is a silence that results from tension, and till the*

moment of balance, nothing interests him that is not wrought up to the greatest effort of which it is capable. Your *Body of Fate* is OBLIGING like your *Will*, so your SPONTANEOUS response to people is the same friendly outreach and helpful solicitousness for their well-being that is your usual wont: you are a straightforward, unsophisticated, uncompli-cated person – what people see is what they get, and what they get is a nice, kindly person who is rather baffled by it all and is trying to fit in as best you can.

Before the self passes from Phase 22 it is said to attain what is called the 'Emotion of Sanctity', and this emotion is described as a contact with life beyond death. It comes at the instant when synthesis is abandoned, when fate is accepted.

After Phase 22 the man becomes aware of something which the intellect cannot grasp, and this something is a supersensual environment of the soul ... Every achievement of a being, after Phase 22, is an elimination of the individual intellect and a discovery of the moral life. ... After Phase 22, desire creates no longer, will has taken its place; but that which they reveal is joyous.

Phase 23

MORAL ENJOYMENT = EMPATHIC
The receptive man

The primary tincture *is now greater than the* antithetical, *and the man must free the intellect from all motives founded upon personal desire, by the help of the external world, now for the first time studied and mastered for its own sake.* Where Phase 22 natives defer to others as a defensive strategy (arising from a sense of insecurity about where they belong), in Phase 23 there is a true moral sensibility: *At Phase 23 events seem startling because they elude intellect.* Phase 23 is a Venus phase in a Venus rectangle – sociable, well-mannered, and pleasant. It is your HABIT to be EMPATHIC when *in phase*: soft-spoken, modest, inviting, so other people seek you out to share their confidences. But when *out of phase* your MOODY heaviness of spirit engulfs and oppresses the people around you. You possess a disinterested good will and a readiness to serve and uplift others: you are natural, earthy, and real. Always polite, gentle, and soft-spoken, you have genuinely benevolent impulses: *The man wipes his breath from the window-pane, and laughs in his delight at all the varied scene.* You are candid and sincere, subdued and self-effacing; with high and honorable intentions. You possess a strong sense of personal accountability and rectitude, and your fundamental decency and fairness lead other people to instinctively trust and rely upon you: *In reality he cares only for what is human, individual and moral.* You are meticulous in playing by the rules, but they are rules of your own heart rather than (as in Phase 22) what you believe other people expect: *His energy escapes in a condition of explosive joy from systematisation and abstraction. ... He sees all things from the point of view of his own technique, touches and tastes and investigates technically. He is, however, because of the nature of his energy, violent, anarchic* [fierce in your convictions and in standing your ground], *like all who are of the first phase of a quarter.* Your *Mask* (from Phase 9) is INGRATIATING and agreeable when True and ACCEPTING of yourself and others, with an INCISIVE (Phase 7) and humorous twinkle in your eye which wins people over. When False and in DENIAL, you can be heavy-handed and OBSTINATE (like Phase 21), using your forbidding intractability to MANIPULATE people by making them fearful of crossing you. When *out of phase* and seeking the perfunctory unconcern of Phase 9, your depth and delicacy of feeling can make you overly touchy, self-serious, and morose; liable to feeling ill-used and inclined to withdraw and brood; to be *tyrannical, gloomy and self-absorbed ... gloomy with the gloom of others, and tyrannical with the tyranny of others, because he cannot create.* Your *Creative Mind* derives from Phase 7: when doing your DUTY to your group you are INCISIVE, practical, no-nonsense; you roll up your sleeves and get right to work at whatever task is at hand with the INGRATIATING good cheer and camaraderie of Phase 9. When False you uphold your STATUS over others with a harsh, CUTTING dismissal of people and their feelings, and a withdrawal into your own dark dejection. Your somber moods can weigh heavily upon the people around you, and call for a need to lighten up and just let go: *At Phase 23, because there must be delight in the unforeseen, he may be brutal and outrageous ... ignorant of or indifferent to the feelings of others.* Your *Body of Fate* comes from the RESOLUTENESS of Phase 21, so when you break out of your shell your SPONTANEOUS self is courageous, assured, and always ready to strike out on your own or stand up for what you know is right. When *in phase* your constancy and faithfulness inspire optimism and hopefulness in everyone you meet: *Only by his technical mastery* [scrupulousness] *can he escape from the sense of being thwarted and opposed by other men; and his technical mastery must exist, not for its own sake, though for its own sake it has been done, but for that which it reveals, for its laying bare – to hand and eye, as distinguished from thought and emotion – general humanity ... free the intellect and rid pity of desire and turn belief into wisdom.*

Phase 24

MORAL MENTALITY = IDEALISTIC
The end of ambition

Phase 24 is a double Mercury phase, which makes you lively, voluble, and self-assured; and you possess a strong sense of intellectual competence and a philosophical bent: *Men and women of the phase create an art where individuals only exist to express some historical code, or some historical tradition of action and of feeling.* Like Phase 23, the natives of Phase 24 are rather fixated on themselves; but here the fixation is rationalized, missionary, and optimistic rather than personal, subdued and concerned: *At Phase 23, when in what seemed the natural self, the man was full of gloomy self-absorption and its appropriate abstractions, but now the abstractions are those that feed self-righteousness and scorn of others* [reliance on pat solutions and uncritical thinking], *the nearest the natural self can come to the self-expressing mastery of Phase 10.* You are a dreamer: intuitive and other-worldly, not altogether of this planet (flakey). You go off on your own tangent with a cocksure bravado that is not without its charm, and which others find endearing: *It is always seemingly fated, for its subconscious purpose is to compel surrender of every personal ambition; and though it is obeyed in pain ... the man is flooded with the joy of self-surrender* [trusting in the basic goodness of your own impulses and willing to fly with them]. *... Unmerciful to those who serve and to himself, merciful in contemplating those who are served, he never wearies of forgiveness.* Your *Mask* derives from Phase 10, so when True and ACCEPTING your karma in life, your DISCERNING and purposive insight goes right to the heart of matters, with a BROADMINDED (from Phase 6) and daring willingness to defy convention and speak the truth; but when False and in DENIAL your CAPRICIOUS and judgmental absolutism alienates people with its COCKY (from Phase 20) self-certainty (which you, yourself, ascribe to purity of motive). You are imperturbable and possess an unshakeable rectitude: *Instead of burning, as did Phase 23, intellectual abstraction in a technical fire, it grinds moral abstraction in a mill. This mill, created by the freed intellect, is a code of personal conduct, which, being formed from social and historical tradition* [in contrast to the code of Phase 10, which is felt rather than intellectualized] *remains always concrete in the mind. All is sacrificed to this code; moral strength reaches its climax.* Your one-track tenacity and overbearing self-certainty can make you gratuitously brusque and heedless: *There may be great intolerance for all who break or resist the code* [in contrast to the humanistic impartiality of Phase 10]. Your *Creative Mind*, from Phase 6, gives you a BROADMINDED and DISCERNING (from Phase 10) objectivity when True and you are DUTIFULLY contributing your sober judgment and sui generis insights to your group; but when False can become a rigid and FINICKY adherence to whatever canons of social STATUS – such as race, creed, religion, caste – your own CREDULITY deems superior; and an endless repetition of the same trite cant. You are definite, even blunt, and in conversation you cut directly to the chase with a minimum of double-talk or pother, so people tend to believe in you (or think that you're crazy – you're just not there: you're always somewhere else, above this world). You always try to figure things out for yourself: not in the one-upsmanship fashion of phase 17, but with a fidelity to principle and with your sight on ultimate ends: a staunch idealism in contrast to the staunch realism of Phase 10: *They submit all their actions to the most unflinching examination, and yet are without psychology, or self-knowledge, or self-created standard of any kind, for they but ask without ceasing, "Have I done my duty as well as So-and-So?" "Am I as unflinching as my fathers before me?" and though they can stand utterly alone, indifferent though all the world condemn, it is not that they have found themselves, but that they have been found faithful.* Out of phase your woolly-minded indefiniteness can render your words empty homilies and your actions self-exculpating gestures: *Morality, grown passive and pompous, dwindles to unmeaning forms and formulae.* Your ivory tower absolutism (trying to uphold – like Phase 10 – some abstract code of conduct, but one in which making your point becomes the most important consideration), *seeking emotion instead of impersonal action, there is – desire being impossible – self-pity, and therefore discontent with people and circumstance, and an overwhelming sense of loneliness, of being abandoned. All criticism is resented ... there is great indifference to others' rights and predilections; ... a tyrant who is incapable of insight or of hesitation. ... When* out of phase *they take from Phase 10 isolation, which is good for that phase but destructive to a phase that should live for others and from others; and they take from Phase 6 a bundle of race instincts, and turn them to abstract moral or social convention. ... when* in phase *they turn these instincts to a concrete code, founded upon dead or living example* and reassure others with your calm certainty and faith in yourself. Your *Body of Fate* derives from Phase 20, so your SPONTANEOUS, off-the-cuff remarks are outspoken and AUDACIOUS, calling a spade a spade with no concern for tact or what anyone thinks or says about you. Your positive and winning enthusiasm convinces people and makes you an inspiring teacher and mentor.

That which characterises all phases of the last quarter, with an increasing intensity, begins now to be plain: persecution of instinct – race is transformed into a moral conception – whereas the intellectual phases, with an increasing intensity as they approached Phase 22, persecuted emotion. Morality and intellect persecute instinct and emotion respectively, which seek their protection.

Before the self passes from Phase 22 it is said to attain what is called the 'Emotion of Sanctity', and this emotion is described as a contact with life beyond death. It comes at the instant when synthesis is abandoned, when fate is accepted. At Phases 23, 24, and 25 we are said to use this emotion, but not to pass from Phase 25 till we have intellectually realised the nature of sanctity itself, and sanctity is described as the renunciation of personal salvation.

Phase 25

☽

MORAL ASSURANCE = SENSITIVE
The conditional man

Like Phase 24, these natives have their eyes lifted to the horizon; but they look inward rather than outward – they are more watchers and waiters rather than go-getters: *unlike Phase 24, he has no pride to nourish upon the past.* Phase 25 is a moon phase in a Saturn rectangle, which entails keeping a gleam of hope alive in the midst of disappointment and disillusionment. Your HABIT when *in phase* is to be the SENSITIVE one in your environment – the one picks up the unspoken vibrations and who feels what's going on beneath the surface; but when *out of phase* you retreat into a TOUCHY, irascible defensiveness which withdraws into yourself or strikes out like a snake at the slightest sign of disrespect. Your childhood may have been emotionally barren, your parents dysfunctional or rejecting, which forced you early on to attune yourself to higher imperatives: *Born as it seems to the arrogance of belief, as Phase 24 was born to moral arrogance, the man of the phase must reverse himself, must change from Phase 11 to Phase 25... till this intellect accepts some social order, some condition of life, some organised belief: the convictions of Christendom perhaps. He must eliminate all that is personal from belief; eliminate the necessity for intellect by the contagion of some common agreement* [i.e. forgo the pat on the back] *as did Phase 23 by its technique, Phase 24 by its code.* Your *Mask* derives from Phase 11, so when True and ACCEPTING your destiny you are the TENDER yet (from Phase 5) DECISIVE defender of those who are more vulnerable and helpless than yourself; but when False and in DENIAL you keep a stiff upper lip and bear in SULLEN silence; put on your resentful scowl and EXIGENT (from Phase 19) manners; and either shut down completely or else bark at people: *if it pursue the* False Mask, *to the persecution of others, if found by the* True Mask, *to suffer persecution.* You have a rough, headstrong simplicity; and you are plainspoken and overt in manner: *There may be great eloquence, a mastery of all concrete imagery that is not personal expression, because though as yet there is no sinking into the world but much distinctiveness, clear identity, there is an overflowing social conscience. No man of any phase can produce the same instant effect upon great crowds; for codes have passed, the universal conscience takes their place.* You are more intense and solitary than the other lunar phases, and possess a greater inner assurance and rootedness: *the last phase where the artificial is possible.* You have firm walls that are not to be breached (as compared to the hail-fellow-well-met Phase 4 natives, the endless rumination of the Phase 11's, or the peace-making Phase 18 types): *At Phase 25 men seek to master the multitude, not through expressing it, nor through surprising it, but by imposing upon it a spiritual norm.* Where Phase 25 resembles the other lunar phases is in its vulnerability and otherworldliness. You are utopian; synchronized to a higher vibration, but more thin-skinned and out-of-kilter with your environment – you are not so much the loner as the outsider, the one who just doesn't fit in, the round peg in a square hole: *when the* Will *is at Phase 25* [there is a] *breaking by belief or condition. In this it finds impulse and joy.* You have an endless capacity for selfless devotion. Your *Creative Mind*, from Phase 5, is DECISIVE when True and you are extremely scrupulous, punctilious, and disciplined in discharging your DUTY and responsibilities, yet TENDER (from Phase 11) and forgiving to others who are not as capable as you are. You may take on the role of mother hen, protective and willing to pick up burdens for others: *He is strong, full of initiative, full of social intellect; absorption has scarcely begun; but his object is to limit and bind, to make men better, by making it impossible that they should be otherwise, to so arrange prohibitions and habits that men may be naturally good, as they are naturally black, white, or yellow.* You wear your heart on your sleeve; can be overly naïve and trusting; and have little ability to dissemble or finesse to parry attacks; so when your *Creative Mind* is False and you are defending your STATUS, your TYRANNICAL streak (from Phase 5, aggravated by your own TOUCHY sense of propriety) can be harsh, hatchet-faced, and hurtful. Phase 25 is often very conflicted, having been born into harsh or unresponsive karmic circumstances and forced to bear thralldom as best you could – perhaps by withdrawal or denial. You are misunderstood – especially by yourself – and when *out of phase* you can be extremely imperious, self-righteous and quick to take offense; bristling with frustrated rage; or simply shut yourself down and turn yourself off: *he may, because Phase 11 is a phase of diffused personality and pantheistic dreaming, grow sentimental and vague, drift into some emotional abstract, his head full of images long separated from life, and ideas long separated from experience, turn tactless and tasteless, affirm his position with the greatest arrogance possible to man*: strutting, overweening, and full of yourself. Your *Body Fate* comes from Phase 19, so your SPONTANEOUS response to any situation is a no-frills, no-nonsense UTILITARIAN pragmatism which gets the job done with the least pother, posturing, or politicking. When *in phase*, your unwavering faith and your assurance that everything will work out for the best bolster the confidence and security of the people around you: *He has but one overwhelming passion, to make all men good, and this good is something at once concrete and impersonal.*

At Phase 25 the *primary tincture* closes and at Phase 26 the *antithetical tincture* opens. The *tinctures* closing / opening here seems to invert the usual planetary meanings: i.e., Phase 25 (a moon phase) is burdened, seething, barely under control (perhaps by being in severe denial); whereas Phase 26 (a Saturn phase) is spritely, eccentric, and free-spirited.

> *Hunchback and Saint and Fool are the last crescents.*
> *The burning bow that once could shoot an arrow*
> *Out of the up and down, the wagon-wheel*
> *Of beauty's cruelty and wisdom's chatter –*
> *Out of that raving tide – is drawn betwixt*
> *Deformity of body and of mind*
>
> (W. B. Y., *The Phases of the Moon*)

In the last phases, Phases 26, 27, and 28, the Faculties *wear away, grow transparent, and man may see himself as it were arrayed against the supersensual. ... From Phase 26 to Phase 28 there is, when the phase is truly lived, contact with supersensual life, or a sinking-in of the body upon its supersensual source, or desire for that contact and sinking. ... At Phases 26, 27, and 28 he permits those* [bodily] *senses and those faculties to sink in upon their environment. He will, if it be possible, not even touch or taste or see.*

Phase 26
♄

MORAL RESPONSIBILITY = QUIRKY
The hunchback – the most difficult of the phases

The terrible Phase 26, called the phase of the Hunchback, is the reverse of all that is emotional, being emotionally cold. Phase 26 natives are called hunchbacks because they're freaks. Phase 26 is a Saturn phase in a moon rectangle, which lightens the Saturnine tendency towards moroseness and makes your HABITUAL mindset when *in phase* QUIRKY and quixotic, with considerable daring and panache, a quick wit and irreverent sense of humor, and a sprightly spirit of adventure. *Out of phase* and feeling your oats you put on a BULLHEADED contrariety that delights in being outrageous and rebellious for its own sake. Like the preceding phases, Phase 26 natives are dreamers; but these natives are doers rather than talkers (unlike those of Phase 24); and compared to the wait-and-see Phase 25 natives, they are more willing to strike out in new directions and actually act out their dreams. Where Phase 25 natives come into this life weighted down with very heavy karmic burdens, you Phase 26 types are relatively light-hearted, experimentative, and fancy-free. This is why the *antithetical tincture* opens at this point in the cycle: more than any other phase, you insist on living out your fantasies and fancies willy-nilly. This *antithetical*ity in the midst of a *primary* quarter is a contradiction – which is why Phase 26 is said to be so difficult (in the sense of ornery) – and why the *tincture* is said to open (reverse polarity) here: *but at this time the tinctures open not into personality, but into its negation. The whole objectively perceived* ... Hitherto he could say to primary *man, "Am I as good as So-and-so?"* and when still antithetical *he could say, "After all I have not failed in my good intentions taken as a whole"*. Like all the Saturn phases you possess great determination and focus, but Phase 26 is the least Saturnine of the four: you live in a world of your own in the midst of this one, with little comprehension of the difference between the two. You are self-assured and know that you are any person's equal; thus you are able to relate to people from all walks of life without shame or shyness: *There may be hatred of solitude, perpetual forced bonhomie; yet that which it seeks is without social morality, something radical and incredible.* You are strong-willed and possess a gritty, eccentric, even rebellious spirit of independence*: If he live amid a theologically minded people, his greatest temptation may be to defy God, to become a Judas, who betrays, not for thirty pieces of silver, but that he may call himself creator.* You have a shrewd, analytical mind; are perspicacious and insightful; and you possess a strong sense of irony: *He will, because he can see lives and actions in relation to their source and not in their relations to one another, see their deformities and incapacities with extraordinary acuteness.* Like Phase 12 you possess a noble bearing and carriage; and you hold your head up high. Your *Mask* from Phase 12 when True and you are ACCEPTING your destiny lends you an UPSTANDING nobility – similar to that of the Don – which is GENTLE (from Phase 4), chivalrous, well-mannered and well-bred; you take pride in your fitness and have a strong sense of stateliness and dignity. But when your *Mask* is False and you are in DENIAL, it becomes a LOFTY, can't-be-bothered indifference to other people's feelings and a PERFUNCTORY (from Phase 18) and contemptuous discharge of your minimal responsibilities to them. You fly with your impulses and enjoy being something of the bad boy or girl – breaking the rules and counting on your considerable charm and winning appeal to smooth over any negative consequences of your rapscallion capers. You possess an unswerving allegiance to higher ends – or at least, non-material ends – not the ends which the people around you are pursuing: *All the old abstraction, whether of morality or of belief, has now been exhausted; but in the seemingly natural man.* More than any other phase you delight in "creating your own reality." You are not so much whimsical as off on your own tangent (out of it), so people tend to treat you with benign indulgence. From the outside your behavior may appear as nonconformist for the sake of nonconformity; but in truth you are not striving for any particular effect – you are a law unto yourself: *At Phase 26 has come a subconscious exhaustion of the moral life, whether in belief or in conduct, and of the life of imitation, the life of judgment and approval* [which is why the hunchback is said to be his own *Body of Fate*, since your spontaneity has no reference to or interest in the judgment or approval of others]. *Out of phase* your insistence on doing your own thing come what may can become (as in Phase 12) an obstinate wrong-headedness masquerading as a sense of honor: *in Phase 26 out of phase, there is an attempt to substitute a new abstraction, a simulacrum of self-expression. Desiring emotion the man becomes the most completely solitary of all possible men, for all normal communication with his kind, that of a condition of life, a code, a belief shared, has passed; and without personality he is forced to create its artificial semblance.* Your *Creative Mind* derives from Phase 4 so when True your DUTY to your group is to be a GENTLE guide whose UPSTANDING (from Phase 12) decorum is a model of impeccable comportment; but when False and asserting your STATUS becomes a negligent ABSTRACTEDNESS which refuses to listen or to deal with anything which contradicts your own QUIRKY eccentricities. Your antipathy for any sort of restriction can be quite intimidating, and your cool indifference can lead you to shirk obligations: *He is full of malice because, finding no impulse but in his own ambition, he is made jealous by the impulse of others. He is all emphasis, and the greater that emphasis the more does he show himself incapable of emotion, the more does he display his sterility.* People may find your swaggering overdone even though they respect your well-meaning and honorable intentions. Your *Body of Fate*, from Phase 18, gives your SPONTANEITY an INGENUOUS impulsiveness and an undaunted readiness to undertake any enterprise as long as it looks like fun. Phase 26 (and Phase 28) are said to be their own *Bodies of Fate* because spontaneity is their habitual equilibrium state – free-wheeling and unpredictable, imperturbably themselves (in contrast to the irrepressibility of Phase 1 which is mannered and designed for popular consumption). *In phase* your jaunty, devil-may-care self-certainty; your refusal to be daunted by the social conventions and expectations that inhibit most people; and your outspoken candor and willingness to give things a shot just for the hell of it; buoy the spirits of all who know you: *He stands in the presence of a terrible blinding light, and would, were that possible, be born as worm or mole.*

Phase 27

2

MORAL UNDERSTANDING = HUMANE
The Saint - Perfection of Sanctity

At Phase 3 ... there should be perfect physical well-being or balance, though not beauty or emotional intensity, but at Phase 27 are those who turn away from all that Phase 3 represents and seek all those things it is blind to.

Like Phase 26 these natives live in a self-created isolation from the exactions of the world around them; but they are rather less flamboyant and individualistic, more self-effacing and refined: *He does not, like Phase 26, perceive separated lives and actions more clearly than the total life, for the total life has suddenly displayed its source.* Phase 27 is a double Jupiter phase, which makes you soft-spoken and unassuming yet possessing a moral authoritativeness which, when *in phase*, has a HABITUAL mindset of HUMANE benevolence born of an ineffable sadness or resignation; but when *out of phase* can turn into a SANCTIMONIOUS self-salving which leads you to wring your hands ineffectually rather than take sides or make a stand. You are gentle, restrained, and amiable, with a disinterested beneficence and an avuncular spirit of good will. You are considerate and appreciative of other people, and deal with them honorably and civilly. Your *Mask*, from Phase 13, is FACILITATING when True and you ACCEPT your karmic role of being the disinterested voice of reason whose PERCEPTIVE (from Phase 3) discrimination and unimpeachable decency influence other people to do the right thing; but when False and in DENIAL produces an ABOVE-IT-ALL complacency with an UNYIELDING (from Phase 17) aversion to soiling yourself with unpleasant involvements. You are tactful and diplomatic and are a good mediator or negotiator: clear-thinking, astute, and disinterested. Your down-to-earth realism observes things with great clarity, sensitivity and compassion; and your soft, inviting manner and impartiality make you the sort of person others instinctively turn to for advice and guidance. You are motivated by a deep sense of moral responsibility and stand for equability and moderation in any group. Your calm and resolute conduct is a steadying influence upon other people: *In his seemingly natural man ... there is an extreme desire for spiritual authority; and thought and action have for their object display of zeal of some claim of authority.* Your dedication and conscientiousness, as well as your charitable impulses, are a model of right-mindedness: *He must renounce even his desire for his own salvation, and that this total life is in love with his nothingness.* Your *Creative Mind* derives from Phase 3, which when True makes you a natural-born leader with a highly PERCEPTIVE and objective view of the people in your social group – their skills, needs, and limitations – when you are FACILITATING (from Phase 13) the orderly carrying out of everyone's several DUTIES; but when False you uphold your STATUS by TRIFLING with people and withdrawing into your own SANCTIMONIOUS self-righteousness. *Out of phase*, emulating the cool nonchalance of Phase 13, you can seem insular and indifferent: *the man asserts when out of phase his claim to faculty or to supersensitive privilege beyond that of other men; he has a secret that makes him better than other men.* In phase your tenderness and harmlessness provide a cushion of repose for everyone who knows you: *True to phase, he substitutes for emulation an emotion of renunciation, and for the old toil of judgment and discovery of sin, a beating upon his breast and an ecstatical crying out that he must do penance, that he is even the worst of men.* Your *Body of Fate* from Phase 17 gives you a SPONTANEOUS STAUNCHNESS of character – always solitary even in the midst of people – but with an unshakeable conviction and belief in the good which sustains you and keeps you looking on the bright side when the going gets tough: *Man does not perceive the truth; God perceives the truth in man.* Your high idealism and unruffled sang-froid cope with all problems with a dignified composure and detachment, and you are a model of unselfish forbearance: *His joy is to be nothing, to do nothing, to think nothing; but to permit the total life, expressed in its humanity, to flow in upon him and to express itself through his acts and thoughts.*

Phase 28

MORAL ACCOMPLISHMENT = CONSCIENTIOUS
The Fool

Where Phase 27 is high-minded and is selflessly dedicated to the general weal, Phase 28 natives – like those of all Mars phases – are basically out for themselves (but in this most *primary* of phases are the least successful at it). Phase 28 is a Mars phase in a Mars rectangle, which indicates a strong-willed self-certainty and intrepidity which when *in phase* has the HABIT of being dedicated, CONSCIENTIOUS, and modest: more concerned with acquitting yourself honorably than with receiving any special praise or credit. When *out of phase* you can exhibit a CHIMERICAL orneriness which is unwilling to contribute or go along but must always be off on your own tangent or living in your own fantasy world. Phase 27 is the Saint; and while Phase 28 is by no means the Sinner, nonetheless this is a phase of expiation: *One finds his many shapes on passing from the village fool to the Fool of Shakespeare.* Here "Fool" doesn't mean simpleton, but rather unselfconscious naïf: Phase 28 is the Fool because – in contrast with the other Mars phases, who know what they want and how to get it (or think they do) – Phase 28 natives are animated by a wistful yearning, and follow their fancy wherever it leads them. In contrast to Phase 1 natives who are canny in their impulsiveness, Phase 28 natives are ingenuous – as fresh and innocent as puppies, striking out with a bold (foolhardy) assurance that all's for the best in this best of all possible worlds, and that the good guys will triumph in the end. Also unlike Phase 1, while you are friendly and outgoing on the surface, you are far more self-contained and circumspect – basically a watcher who keeps your own counsel. You maintain your distance with a wary vigilance over the proceedings, and zealously guard your personal space – very guarded, cagey, and furtive beneath your bland, smiling veneer (in contrast to the blatant, confrontational Phase 14's). Your *Mask* derives from Phase 14, so when True and you are ACCEPTING your destiny your DOUGHTY, sanguine alacrity and upbeat COMPANIONABILITY (from Phase 2) keep things on an even keel (especially in difficult times); but when False and you are in DENIAL your HEADSTRONG perversity and cool, IMPASSIVE (from Phase 16) demeanor leave the people who depend upon you in the lurch. Fate seems to deal rather more harshly with you than with most people; you are held on a tighter leash or are more circumscribed in your available options; and your true purpose is to find your joy in the midst of it: *for having no active intelligence he owns nothing of the exterior world but his mind and body. He is but a straw blown by the wind, with no mind but the wind and no act but a nameless drifting and turning, and is sometimes called "The Child of God".* This is the quietest and least pushy of the Mars phases: you tend to hold yourself in the background and not make waves or draw undue attention to yourself. You are reflective and cautious; subdued and concentrated; and (unlike the other Mars phases) you rely more upon cunning and manipulation rather than bravado to enforce your will and get your way. You are thorough and meticulous, with considerable staying power, and it is quite difficult to disconcert you or to knock you off your pins. You are mindful and painstaking, with a remarkable capacity for taking things as they come – evenly, with a profound acceptance – and for trying to deal with situations and relationships to the best of your ability, without pother or complaint. Your *Creative Mind* from Phase 2 when True and you fulfill your DUTY gives you your COMPANION-ABLE spirit of collaboration and joy in serving others, with a DOUGHTY (from Phase 14) unwillingness to surrender to doubt or to admit defeat (even when others have given up hope); but when False and you are emphasizing your own STATUS becomes a CURT, dig-in-your-heels refusal to play unless your own CHIMERICAL ideas (such as receiving special treatment or consideration because you feel you are carrying more than your fair share of the load) are accepted by all. You are an intensely private person, and you feel like a misfit much of the time – ignored or futile – and you carry that cross for everyone: *The physical world suggests to his mind pictures and events that have no relation to his needs or even to his desires; his thoughts are an aimless reverie; his acts are aimless like his thoughts; and it is in this aimlessness that he finds his joy.* You may be called upon to make enormous sacrifices for the sake of other people; or perhaps illness, poverty, or lack of opportunity forces you to release and deny your own predilections. This enforced surrender and resignation leads, as the phase progresses, to an increased lightening up and letting go of all that impedes your feeling content with yourself and your life no matter what:

> *Out of the pool,*
> *Where love the slain with love the slayer lies,*
> *Bubbles the wan mirth of the mirthless fool.*

Out of phase, when you try to imitate Phase 14's blithe unconcern and readiness to strike out on its own come what may, you soon find yourself facing insuperable limitations or responsibilities which cannot and will not be budged or ducked, but must be faced squarely and accepted willy-nilly. Your *Body of Fate* comes from Phase 16 so your SPONTANEOUS role amongst your fellows is the SELF-POSSESSED savant who knows what you are doing and are in control of things (even when you don't and aren't); but who thereby has a calming effect upon the people around you. *In phase* your simplicity, honorableness, and ability to deal with reality is a rock of stability in your social circle: *At his worst his hands and feet and eyes, his will and his feelings, obey obscure subconscious fantasies, while at his best he would know all wisdom if he could know anything.*

IV. The Nature of the *Daimon*

Daimon is timeless, it has present before it <a man's> past and future, or it has no present and is that past and future, and as the dramatisations recede from his waking mind and from the dreams that reproduce his waking desires they begin to express that knowledge.

(W.B.Y., commentary to *Words upon the Window-pane*)

Mind and Memory

Mind can be easily dispensed with. Most animals, for example, have very little of it and they do quite nicely. The universe runs along quite well with very little conscious mind at all. But feeling cannot be dispensed with, because that is fundamentally what you, and everything else in the universe, are made of. Molecules and atoms and subatomic particles are but a crude conceptual approximation of but one aspect of what the universe is in fact made of. It's made of feelings (light fibers), and what you are, is a knot or node or nexus or agglomeration of light fibers. That's *all* you are. All the yada-yada nonsense about a "real world" out there is just a gloss, a distraction. The "real world" has actually nothing to do with what's really going on. It's a bunch of baloney, really, and doesn't rate much more than a belly laugh. What's actually going on out there is your feelings. Your feelings are your true contact with the truth, with life, with the Spirit.

So it's not true that you first have a conscious experience and then have a memory of it, but rather the other way around. The memory, which is a feeling, exists "first"; and the conscious experience, which is a thought form, comes to symbolize that memory. If you allow your life, your consciousness, to be dominated by your mind, then what you get is conscious memory on the one hand

and forgetfulness on the other. Conscious memory and forgetfulness arise at the same time, and this is where death enters into it.

The chief function of waking mind is forgetting – it has to forget 99.99% of what is happening (being felt) in order to conceptualize. The purpose of magical training is to reach to recapture that 99.99% as need be. You don't have to remember every breath you've ever taken because there's no need for doing so; but if there were such a need, it would be nice to have that information available. And that's what magical training is – it's memory training: training your mind to access whatever memories are needed at a given moment. This training has nothing to do with survival value, but is dictated by the Spirit. You don't train your mind to access memories *in order to* ... (do this, that, or the other); but rather you train your mind to access memories so as to be responsive to the Spirit's commands.

Each of your conceptual memories – memories that give you a twinge; that you try not to think about; that you purposely try to forget – is a sticking point, a position being defended, a place where you are constricting energy into yourself (where you are clenching up against death). Memories didn't happen long ago; they're happening *right now*, including all the future ones that haven't happened yet (in your time frame). All of your memories are happening this very second, under your nose, but you're too busy conceptualizing (clenching up your feelings) to see them. All that ever was and ever will be is right here, right now, and this is no metaphor. This statement is literally true. What we call "time" and "space" are the metaphor – a complete distortion of reality.

As in Bergman's *Seventh Seal*, conscious mind plays a chess game with death, and this is the cutting edge between conscious mind and forgetfulness. When you've forgotten everything, death takes all. In the beginning you start life with a finite number of light fibers (this isn't true, but it makes a simpler analogy). As life goes on you throw light fiber after light fiber to memory after memory, until you eventually lose control. You can only balance a finite number of memories at a time; death claims more and more of them. At the moment of death you lose your conceptual memory altogether (though you soon recover your actual memory, the *real* feelings that were going down at the time rather than your conceptual, whitewashed version of it).

Forgetfulness is but a game played with death. Death is not part of your *Daimon*, the totality of who you are; it only exists in this or that incarnation (set of memories from a single probable reality chain of a single lifetime). Any memory can be the death of you. Any memory at all opens you up to your death, just as your desires do. That's why death always seems so familiar when you experience it – it comes to you on one of your memories. Ideally you should not have light fibers in *any* memory at all, since death can get at you through any one of your memories. This is the purpose of recapitulation – to pull back all your light fibers out of your memories of this life, to remove death's handle over you.

There is no "self" in the way you are accustomed to thinking. All "you" are is a collection of thought forms at a given moment. The closest thing to a continuous, abiding "you" that exists is your instincts, or memories. But these are feelings, not thoughts. Memories are in fact attached to thought forms, and it is this attachment which binds beings, ties them down, makes them heavy. Master magicians aren't caught up in this flow since they don't act on memory / instinct but rather intent (the now moment).

A memory is no different from a desire line (a feeling, or light fiber of desire): it's just a different way of looking at the same phenomenon. Every desire arises in / is created by / is associated with a memory. And these light fibers are not always associated with thought forms: there are desire lines / memories which have no thought forms attached. These are dream memories not usually available to conscious mind, but which can be accessed obliquely, in symbolic form, through dreaming techniques such as gazing, lucid dreaming, etc.

Observe that just as mind and desire are mutually dependent and couldn't exist without each other, neither can memory exist without them, nor they without memory. Mind is essentially a different activity than desire / memory, but just as mind commands desire, so too does memory command mind (this is what Carlos Castaneda meant by "our command becomes the Spirit's command"). Memory precedes mind; it's all just a feeling at first. Originally, all that's there, is feeling. Mind is what attaches feeling to a scene in the world "out there". But the memory (feeling) exists before (at least in an anterior or primal sense) to the concept of it, the actual experience of it in the so-called "real world".

* * * * *

Waking and Dreaming

Certain Upanishads describe three states of the soul, that of waking, that of dreaming, that of dreamless sleep, and say man passes from waking through dreaming to dreamless sleep every night and when he dies. Dreamless sleep is a state of pure light, or of utter darkness according to our liking, and in dreams 'the spirit serves as light for itself'. 'There are no carts, horses, roads [i.e., thought forms] *but he makes them for himself.'*

It's difficult to understand why the dreams which you can remember should consist of thought forms. To most people, that just "proves" that waking consciousness is primary and dream consciousness is secondary or derived from waking consciousness. But dreams which consist of thought forms (which can be remembered in waking consciousness) are a tiny part of what goes on while you are asleep. Most dreaming is pure feeling. Some feelings get passed up to thought form dreaming and there take on a dream shape; and some feelings get passed up to waking consciousness and there take on a physical shape. The same dream (feeling) is dreamt over and over again in different lifetimes.

Another way of saying this is that all of your incarnations as a human being are just subtle little variations on the same theme, the theme "you" are playing as an individual. The next guy over is playing some other theme. Actually, two different individuals are more different than they are alike: most people think that our individual perceptions of the world are more or less the same, that there is some outside reality there that we can agree on; but this is not true. In actual fact we are more unalike than alike. We are just pretending to be more or less alike, just as soldiers like to dress the same and march in step, so that by submerging their individual identities (differences) they can get a feeling of power or joint purpose going that would be more difficult to achieve if everyone was just dressed as he liked and wandering off in any old direction. In the same way, all human beings are submerging their individual identities in order to achieve a joint purpose; but the fact is that we are only pretending to be human, just as the soldiers are only pretending to be alike. Magical training involves leaving human society and going off by yourself to follow your intent.

Magical training requires erasing your sense of self, which – when you analyze it thoroughly – you discover is, at root, nothing more than self-pity in one guise or another. It takes losing lots and lots of self-pity to even be able to see and understand this most vital point: that that's all "you" are – just your self-pity. Things don't happen "to you", they just happen, period. The "to you" part – your sense of a "self" that things are happening to – is nothing more than self-pity. This is why you have so much less sense of self when you are dreaming than you do when you are awake: dreaming is too intense and NOW for you to be able to bring much self-pity to bear upon it. Also, you're alone in dreaming; whereas in waking you have everyone around you striking or stroking or in one way or another tugging at and propping up your self-pity. The practice of magic aims at erasing the barrier between dreaming and wakefulness, which is achieved by erasing self-pity in the waking state (which involves telling society and everyone around you to buzz off); and by cultivating lucid dreaming while asleep.

Master magicians are still capable of functioning in the thought form realm, just like average people. But magicians also operate on pure light fibers. Carlos Castaneda's teacher don Juan called waking mind *tonal*, or the 1st attention; dream mind *nagual*, or the 2nd attention; and dreamless sleep the 3rd attention. A master magician can operate in all of these realms. Actually, it's more difficult to go from 1st to 2nd than from 2nd to 3rd. To get to the 2nd attention you just have to lose your mind – your sense of importance. But to get to the 3rd attention you have to lose your memory – your sense of familiarity. However, if you've already lost your mind, that isn't so difficult.

In Castaneda's nomenclature *nagual* is roughly equivalent to *primary tincture* and *tonal* is roughly equivalent to *antithetical tincture*:

"At the time of birth, and for a while after, we are all *nagual*. We sense, then, that in order to function we need a counterpart to what we have. The *tonal* is missing and that gives us, from the very beginning, a feeling of incompleteness. Then the *tonal* starts to develop and it becomes utterly important to our functioning, so important that it opaques the shine of the *nagual*, it overwhelms it. From the moment we become all *tonal* we do nothing else but to increment that old feeling of incompleteness which accompanies us from the moment of our birth, and which tells us constantly that there is another part to give us completeness." (*Tales of Power*)

What don Juan termed "losing the human form" is a matter of losing your memory, or a big part of it. It's when you start losing your memory that you really enter the realm of dreamless sleep, but from a position that starts from wakefulness. This is accomplished by recapitulating your inventory of life memories, and is facilitated by gazing techniques and the cultivation of lucid dreaming.

The goal of magical training is to find your true purpose by learning how to recognize and act on your own true feelings. Magical training is designed to liberate your senses from the bondage society puts on you: to learn (or relearn) how to feel with your eyes, nose, ears, etc.; as well as to liberate yourself sexually from the bondage which society puts on your sexual energy. These exercises serve to free your waking mind from the importance coverings which society puts on your light fiber energy to channel and suck it.

The next step, then, is to free up your light fiber energy which is pinned down by the very fact of your being human (and mammalian, and animal, and multicellular, etc.). A master magician who is entering into the 3rd attention (i.e. dreamless sleep, where there aren't any thought forms and no familiarity at all) is not even human anymore, nor is he an animal. He no longer has physicality. This is described by Carlos Castaneda, and also in the writings of Sri Aurobindo, et. al.

The difference between memory and mind is that where waking mind is proper to a given lifetime and dream mind is proper to a given individual, memory is universal. That is how e.g. spirit guides can access your memories: they can get in beside you in your memories (rather like what you do to yourself when you run recapitulations). But even though spirits can tell what you are thinking at a given moment, they can't "share" the process with you. Another way of looking at it is, memory consists of light fibers, feelings; whereas mind consists of thought forms. It is easier to change your mind than to change your memories (and desires). It is easier to channel thought forms, and to banish them – i.e. to manipulate thoughts; than it is to run past life regressions or recapitulations – to manipulate feelings. Maybe "easier" isn't the right word; maybe "less profound" is better said.

All the pressure that's brought to bear on each moment is what we call memory. It's the weight of the universe on each individual creature's shoulders – the record of every decision that's ever been made. Of course, some lines of memory are more important to a given individual than others; some have a more direct bearing upon a given moment or a given lifetime than others. But it must be borne in mind that the whole kit and kaboodle is weighing upon each individual human, animal, plant, cell all the time. Each individual organism selects a piece of the whole to symbolize the whole, and that piece is everything the organism considers *familiar*.

Just as importance selects what mind will pay attention to and what it will ignore, so too does familiarity select what memory it will recall and what it will forget. Familiarity selects one line of memory and calls that one its history (*Will*), its own experience. This is easiest to see in dreams. If you are attentive to your dreams you will notice (not while still dreaming, but after you awaken) that in dreams which refer to previous events which supposedly occurred in the same dream, the so-called "previous events" are conjured up ad hoc, on the fly; and the sense you have that they occurred previous to what is happening now in the dream is due to a covering or gloss of familiarity which is conjured up at the same time as the so-called "previous events". In other words, your "personal history" in dreaming is completely random, but each moment's thought form – as it pops into existence in your conscious awareness – carries with it a feeling of familiarity – a sense that there was a coherent backstory which led up to this particular moment in "time". And similarly with your waking experience: it is merely your feeling of familiarity which creates your personal history from moment to moment. What the practice of recapitulation does is peel the familiarity gloss off each memory to which you've glued it.

We call familiarity a sense rather than a feeling because it is not really a feeling, but rather is the basic matrix of all feelings, just as importance is the basic matrix of all thoughts. All memory starts out as mind. Actually, this is not really true, since memory consists of light fibers, or feelings; but they are light fibers trapped or held down by thought forms. And this memory almost has a will of its own, an inexorability or weight that moves like a glacier. The point is that this great mass of memory arose, like mind, thought form by thought form. Death is the basic thought form, the one that separates organic from inorganic life. Inorganic life "willed" or intended organic life into being, just as one-celled life willed more complex forms into being.

Death doesn't exist in your *Daimon*, the totality of yourself. Death qua death is proper to waking consciousness; whereas dream consciousness is, of itself, death. It's similar to a fish not really knowing what water is, but only knowing what being taken out of the water is – i.e., death. In the same way, dreaming to you is like water to a fish – you are at one with death there; and waking is like being taken out of the water. It's a rather unpleasant sensation, and the way society teaches you to deal with the discomfort of waking consciousness is to put your attention on (think about) something else – something more important. The practice of magic, by contrast, deals with the discomfort of waking consciousness by dreaming it; i.e. by letting go of it, unclenching, and dying every minute.

* * * * *

Change

Castaneda distinguished between reason – the consciousness of modern humans; and silent knowledge, which was the consciousness of ancient humans. Reason represents an entirely different use of the faculty of memory than silent knowledge does.

"The strong, sustained emotion of fighting for his life had caused his assemblage point to move squarely to the place of silent knowledge [direct experience of both here and there]. ... as he explored his split perception, he discovered its practical side and found he liked it. He was double for days. He could be thoroughly one or the other. Or he could be both at the same time. When he was both, things became fuzzy and neither being was effective, so he abandoned that alternative. But being one or the other opened up inconceivable possibilities for him. While he recuperated in the bushes, he established that one of his beings was more flexible than the other and could cover distances in the blink of an eye and find food or the best place to hide." – Carlos Castaneda, *The Power of Silence*

The suppression of silent knowledge ("doubleness") in infancy in favor of reason is like the suppression of ambidexterity in favor of right- or left-handedness: it is an increase of focus at the expense of awareness. Silent knowledge entails knowing and making decisions based on gut-level feeling or intent; that is to say, direct knowing rather than thinking. It is the mode of consciousness used by our hunter-gatherer forebears as well as by animals – it enables hunters to zero in on what prey is out there and how to stalk them by tuning into the animals' awareness; and it enables gatherers to tune into what plants are out there (even outside the field of vision) and how to use them.

Memory also exists in the realm of silent knowledge; i.e. learning also takes place there, but it is done without thought or its corollary, thought forms. Each light fiber is in fact a memory or a desire; there is no difference between memory or desire and feeling. A feeling is a memory or a desire – they are just two different ways of looking at the same phenomenon.

It is the faculty of mind which, by creating thought forms, splits memory / desire from pure feeling. For one thing, mind makes memory happen in terms of thought forms of the past and desire happen in terms of thought forms of the future. Mind makes desire a longing for (or fear of) the future, and memory a nostalgia for (or anger at) the past. But there is no past or future; this is just the action of mind. All there are, are light fibers. That's all that "exists".

Mind is a method of organizing light fibers. Most animals have some faculty of reason or mind: animals organize their light fibers in a more or less mental way, even if they don't think or reason in the same way humans do. However, plants don't do this. They don't have to: they're rooted right on the spot (here and now). There's no need for organizing to find where one's next meal will come from – either it comes or it doesn't, so there's no need to think about it, to worry about a past or future. Nor, as a result, do plants die in the same way that animals do – they exist more on what humans would consider a *Creative Mind* level – have very little sense of individuation. To plants, dying is more like what cutting our hair or nails is to us – no biggy.

Memory is the record of change. It's a way of keeping track of change. Memory can be compartmentalized into sets of thought forms roughly corresponding to the evolution of consciousness:

Individual memory, which we have arbitrarily divided into three levels or lower *Faculties*, is the set of thought forms of a particular human being – the set of all probable realities related to a given life and the set of all past and future lives of an individual, which can be accessed through past life and probable reality regressions, and recapitulation.

Human memory is the set of all thought forms created by all humans in all incarnations, which we have termed *Creative Mind*, and which can be accessed by listening to the Voices of the Ancestors.

Life memory is the set of all thought forms created by all incarnations of organic life.

Spirit memory is the set of all thought forms created by all incarnations of inorganic life (e.g. rocks, mountains, the earth, the sun, the stars, etc.). It was the push of spirit memory that created life memory, and life memory that created human memory, and human memory that created individual memory.

Every thought form which you create at any given moment is the sum total of all these memories pushing forward. Each individual thought form, each moment, is pushed along by the weight of all these interacting levels of memory. It isn't happening in linear time: time is something which mind conjures up to help keep track of memory. In fact, the thing is more like a three-ring circus (actually infinite-ring circus); but we pretend the acts are unfolding sequentially. Nonetheless there is an evolution of sorts going on, but there is no obvious way of determining which way it is going. It is no more correct to say that we evolved out of one-celled beings than it is to say that we are evolving into one-celled beings. That is merely our own prejudice because we feel we are superior to (more important than) one-celled beings, so we must tell ourselves that we evolved out of them. Without a sense of importance time has no direction: it doesn't exist, just as time doesn't exist in the dream state.

While time is sequential in dreams, that's only in the most shallow stage of dreaming, which has been imbued with the prejudices of waking consciousness. Just as at the beach the ocean is full of the filth and detritus of shore life, so too do shallow levels of dreaming, at the border with waking consciousness, involve thought forms. But deep dreaming, like the open ocean, is clean and free of the thought form clutter of wakefulness, including sequential time.

Actually, what is going on isn't an evolution at all in the sense that it will ever get anywhere in particular (back to some equilibrium state from which, presumably, it started or big-banged). It's just all happening, that's all, and if we want to believe that it's all going back to some Godhead or Nirvana, that's okay, but it's only a concept. The point is that there isn't any future or past, memory has as much to do with the future as the past. The future pulls the past along just as the past pushes the future ahead.

What we perceive as time would better be characterized as *change*; and all change is, is a movement from one level of memory to another – in the case of human life, from one of the *Four Faculties* to another. Thought forms are actually all rather random: the set of all probable realities for a given lifetime branches out in all directions – there's an infinite number of ways that the next moment could happen. Maybe the next thing that will happen is a brick hitting you on the head, or a madman shooting you from behind, or sudden illumination. Anything which is possible is equally real and happening somewhere out there. The goal of magic is to be able to reach out to and grab onto the probable realities that will take you where you want to go; but in fact everyone does this all the time (selects thought forms which will reinforce whatever images or desires they are reaching for). The goal is to do this with a modicum of intelligence instead of compulsively and neurotically reaching out to repeat old memory patterns. Memory has to be fluid – it can't be pinned down to thought forms which are fighting change.

All change is, is difference. Change and difference arise together – they are the same phenomenon viewed from two points of view, dynamic and static. As mentioned previously, change is one of the two facets of memory (the other is stasis). Memory in its dynamic aspect is change, and in its static aspect is difference, or separateness. A given set of thought forms – a level of memory – can be viewed as a file full of records (static – ROM) or as a sequence (dynamic – RAM). If looked at from above (just as you look at all the memories of your lifetime in the recapitulation or *Return* immediately after your death), you see them all at once, as a certain *feeling*: the overall, sum-total feeling of a given lifetime. This is how you feel about a given lifetime after you run a regression of it. Each lifetime has a certain feeling to it, just as a symphony or poem has a certain feeling to it, as a whole. But in the course of being alive in a given lifetime, you see the set of thought forms that make up that lifetime in sequence – one at a time – just as each individual passage in a symphony or poem has its own individual feeling. You experience the feelings that make up that lifetime individually instead of all at once. It's just a different way of experiencing the same set of feelings – as change (dynamically, one-at-a-time) instead of all at once (statically). And the particular character of the thought form material available, the limits placed upon it, is what we call "memory".

Basically, the sky is the limit on memory, and the amount of memory available to us as humans is a tiny fraction of everything that's going on out there in the universe. What we call the Akashic Records, which may be defined as the sum total of everything you could ever possibly conceive of or experience on any level whatsoever, is just a drop in the bucket of what is *really* going on out there.

* * * * *

Familiarity

Pure time and pure space, pure subjectivity and pure objectivity ... are abstractions or figments of the mind.

Space and time do not actually exist. Rather, what you take to be linear time is your own internal sense of *importance*. It is the feeling of importance which enables you to focus your attention on one thing at a time (instead of everything at once – as infants perforce must do); which in turn creates the illusion of a linear sequence of succeeding now moments – of happenings in your life unfolding in linear time.

In like fashion, what you take to be space is your own internal sense of *familiarity*. Your feeling that things are familiar – that what is happening this moment bears any relation whatever to what was happening a moment ago – is the basis of your belief that what you are experiencing is *real* (in both waking and dreaming). Thus where importance reifies time for you, familiarity reifies space; and the two taken together reify "you". Without the glosses of importance and familiarity you would feel as though you were plummeting through a void in which nothing makes any sense whatsoever (which is in fact the truth of the matter). The practice of magic is merely a means of awakening to and dealing with this truth.

Note that the foregoing contradicts WBY's fourth proposition: *The emotional character of a timeless and spaceless spirit reflects itself as its position in time, its intellectual character as it position in space. The position of a Spirit in space and time therefore defines character.* Here we say that the illusion of position in time is basically a mental (thought form) production; whereas the sense of being oriented in space is an emotional (light fiber) matter. Just because WBY was the first to channel and publish information on this System doesn't mean that his version of the System is canonical, or even correct in all its details. Like any "scientific" theory WBY's System is amenable to amendment by other channels.

There is less familiarity present in the dream state than in the waking state, which is why dreaming is more ineffable than being awake. As you operate more and more on your true purpose in life rather than on your customary moods (learned from your parents and society), you sense that the world you live in is in fact highly unstable: that death is breathing down your neck every minute and that there are no sureties or protections; that really nothing is familiar; that the phenomenal world is just a passing shadow. Things just get weirder and weirder. As Carlos Castaneda put it (in *A Separate Reality*):

"When you *see* there are no longer familiar features in the world. Everything is new. Everything has never happened before. The world is incredible!"

"Why do you say incredible, don Juan? What makes it incredible?"

"Nothing is any longer familiar. Everything you gaze at becomes nothing! ..."

"Do things disappear? How do they become nothing?"

"Things don't disappear. They don't vanish, if that's what you mean; they simply become nothing and yet they are still there."

. . .

"It doesn't matter whether you like or dislike the guardian. As long as you have a feeling toward it, the guardian will remain the same, monstrous, beautiful, or whatever. If you have no feeling [of familiarity] toward it, on the other hand, the guardian will become nothing and will still be there in front of you. ... You thought it was ugly. Its size was awesome. It was a monster. You know what all those things are. So the guardian was always something you knew, and as long as it was something you knew you did not *see* it. I have told you already, the guardian had to become nothing and yet it had to stand in front of you. It had to be there and it had, at the same time, to be nothing."

Customary moods are not your feelings at all, but rather your thought forms' feelings, which we term *importance coverings*. Customary moods are basically what are shown in the interpretations for the 28 lunar phase types. Customary moods are what anchor your familiarity, your sense of being in a stable environment in which things are more or less predictable. Familiarity in everyday life is the same thing as routine / habit – the *Will* level.

Animal memory is closer to the pure principle of memory than is human memory, which is contaminated by conceptual thought forms. When something threatening happens to an animal, it will remember the place where the event occurred and avoid it in the future (create a thought form of "avoidance-of-this-place"); and if the event occurred because the animal broke its customary routines (out of curiosity, or hunger, or whatever) the animal will remember "don't do that again." But the actual circumstances of the threatening event won't be remembered as such – what is remembered is the feeling of threat rather than the thought form happening, which is what humans tend to remember. Humans remember the events – the external circumstances (the thought forms) – more than the feeling they felt at that moment.

The animal's awareness, as it approaches a place where something threatening occurred, will feel as though the place emanates a feeling of threat, so the animal avoids it automatically. There won't be as much awareness in an animal – as there is in an adult human – as to *why* this feeling of threat is associated with this place – i.e. what happened there. The animal just takes a light fiber (in this case, fear of a threat) and pins it to a sensory thought form (the scene of the event). Infants do the same thing, until they learn how to talk and think, which is why it is so difficult for us adults to consciously remember the events of early childhood (e.g. there is a greater tendency to block the recapitulation of early childhood memories; or to change the thought forms inculcated at that time; because of the automatic avoidance mechanism).

Adult human processing is more refined and elaborate: adult humans have more focused, detailed consciousness than do animals or infants. It's not that our senses are any sharper – quite the contrary – but rather that we objectify what our senses tell us more than animals or infants do; we feel more estranged from our environment than animals or infants feel. Animals are not as separated as are (modern) humans; they don't have their waking consciousness as highly polished as we do.

Another way of saying this is that animals and infants are more caught up in the dream than adult humans are: we've learned to separate ourselves from it enough to *think* about it. This is what humans learned from demons – we didn't figure this out for ourselves; and it took millennia to do it: the transition from Lower to Upper Paleolithic to Neolithic humans, is the development of the conceptual thought form from the sensory thought form; the final separation of waking from dreaming (or better said, the quintessential embellishment upon the dream) – the development of thinking and increased self-consciousness (sense of self, or sense of separatedness) which enables thinking. This step up from animal to human consciousness is thus a move away from the *primary* and towards the *antithetical*; and the next step – from waking to lucid dreaming as the quotidian consciousness of humankind – is a move back towards the *primary*. So, at this point in human history we are sort of Phase 15-ish.

It is your customary moods which make your everyday life familiar and give you a sense of stability. Unfortunately, customary moods are not an accurate response to what is actually happening in your life. Customary moods are primarily concerned with a fantasy world of a past which never happened – which only exists in your images of what could have been; together with a future which will never happen – which exists only in your fantasies of what could be. Your true purpose in life, on the other hand, is concerned with what you know in your heart of hearts beyond any shadow of a doubt. Customary moods are a cover to hide your fear of death.

Fear acts like glue in the sense of being a point of constant reference or touch with your lower self, or *Will*, the basic business of which is to secure the self. It keeps your lower self buzzing from moment-to-moment. Fear is brought in to witness the constant flow of waking consciousness. Fear is programmed into an infant by the adults around him, who tend to regard their job as complete when the young one is afraid of all the same things that they are afraid of. Not just humans do this; all animals which raise their young base their training upon fear. According to a person's own native temperament – and his or her training (which, from an astrological point of view, are but two sides of the same coin) – the young one tends to develop a pattern of reactions (such as obeisance, anger, withdrawal, attack, etc.) which are triggered by fear. These reactions are termed "conceptual thought forms" – thought forms with coverings of shame or glory – in contradistinction to sensory thought forms (or qualia, the feeling with which sensory impressions are associated).

Originally, each set conceptual thought form (conditioned reaction) was developed in response to a specific need at a specific time, i.e., at some actual moment in time the decision was made to react in this way to an actual situation, and ever since then the same reaction is automatically repeated whenever a similar situation occurs. This pattern of fear and set response persists long after the original purpose it served is superseded, thus contradictions develop between current adult needs and thought form patterns set up in early childhood.

What makes early childhood so crucial here is its remoteness in memory. The patterning of fear goes on throughout life, but patterns developed in adult life can easily be reversed. For example, if someone has been hurt in relationship, they may swear never to love again; but this decision is easy enough to reverse the next time they fall in love. Decisions made in early childhood, however, are made at a time before the adult pattern is complete, when it's still in the bits and pieces stage, and decisions are not arrived at in a consciously-directed fashion. This is why it is so difficult to remember events from infancy or early childhood: because babies, like animals, experience events more as feelings than as concepts; and in our society we are trained to repress feelings and experience the world as thoughts (conceptual thought forms). We remember "events" but not the feelings associated with those events. Therefore, trying to remember when fear patterns were originally set up is difficult since the thing is a wisp of feeling – the way animals do it – rather than a logical sequence (although each fear pattern has its own logic). The task of remembering is further complicated by the fact that the dynamics of fear include a masking of torpor or dullness which effectively prevents examining things clearly (and tends to block recapitulation of emotionally charged memories); thus you seem to be swept along by the fear and powerless to oppose it. This moment-to-moment fear is what we have called the lower self (and W.B.Y. calls *Will*). The fear glue is also what keeps society upon its pillars, with everyone marching in step; it's what makes civilization something other than a loose mob of amoral individualists, all moving in different directions. But it also makes them miserable.

Everything in the universe is one. It's all connected. Although it appears to seers to consist of individual strands of light fibers, this is indeed just an appearance. Seers tend to see individual strands because that is still familiar. To see the universe as it really is, is to see it without any familiarity at all. As Roshi Philip Kapleau said (in *Three Pillars of Zen*):

"Through zazen the first vital truth – that all component things are ephemeral, never the same from one moment to the next, fleeting manifestations in a stream of ceaseless transformation – becomes a matter of direct experience. ... Each thing *just as it is* takes on an entirely new significance or worth. Miraculously, everything is radically transformed though remaining as it is."

This entails a cessation of the act of seeing, since seeing – the visual sense – is still part of a familiarity inventory. Seeing arises on the dream plane: it's a form of familiarity. Familiarity stabilizes dream consciousness just as importance stabilizes waking consciousness. No matter how ineffable the dream plane may become, there's still always some sense of familiarity about it because there are still feelings being felt. Even if the dream is a complete horror show, the feeling of fear is quite familiar, and so reduces the dream to something familiar – i.e. makes it something known.

Only in dreamless sleep do you encounter the unknown. There is no familiarity there, no points of reference whatsoever, hence no way of relating what goes on there to dreaming or waking consciousness. What goes on in dreamless sleep is neither thinking nor feeling, but something much more fundamental than either of these activities. Since there's no way to describe it, we'll refer to it as the unknown. However, the unknown also goes on in dreaming and waking consciousness.

You go into dreamless sleep every night, but not consciously (knowing what you are doing). You gingerly thread your way through dreamless sleep following your feeling of familiarity. You don't let go of that thread – you cling to it till death do you part. Master magicians, on the other hand, just leap blindly into dreamless sleep: they use the threads to launch themselves, but then let go of them and fly free (whereas most people cling and cling to threads that hold them back and bring them down).

It is not possible to enter into the pure love of dreamless sleep still holding the threads which connect you to all your lifetimes and realities. Only through recapitulation can the main thread – the one which binds you to this lifetime, and thence to all of them – be severed, and the clinging ended. Clinging is the force of shame on a waking level (to be crazy is to be truly without shame); and clinging is the force of familiarity on a dream level. On a level of dreamless sleep, there is no clinging, just union, love.

When you're awake you're basically thinking most of the time, though you still feel feelings. Actually, feelings underlie all the thinking, but only pop up every now and again. Similarly, in dreams you're basically feeling most of the time, though you still do the unknown. You still do the unknown in waking consciousness also, but waking consciousness is even further removed from the unknown than dreaming is. And just as feelings occasionally pop up when you're awake, so too does the unknown occasionally pop up in dreams (as for example, when you have prophetic dreams; or dream wars with other people). It occasionally pops up in waking life also: orgasm is close to the unknown, as are psychotic episodes such as nervous breakdowns, and trips on psychedelic drugs. Any time you are totally cut loose from your wonted psychological moorings – i.e., at major discontinuities (loss of familiarity or *Critical Moments*) in waking life – you are experiencing something of the unknown. Actually, the unknown is going on all the time: just as feeling is going on all the time you are awake but you mask it with thinking, so too is the unknown going on all the time but you mask it with feeling (in dreams) and thinking (in waking life).

There's no point in talking about the unknown since there's no way of describing it, but it's something we all do, just as we all feel and think. The closest we can come to characterizing it is with the word "intent", but in this sense intent means something that transcends both thinking and feeling.

Now just as importance makes thinking possible, so too does familiarity make feeling possible. It's the basic feeling, just as importance (that whatever you are thinking about is important – important enough to deflect your attention from the now moment) is the basic thought. Consider a feeling that you have never felt before, that you're feeling now for the first time. Recall the first time that you ever felt e.g. orgasm, or grief, or terror. That was the first time you ever felt that feeling in this lifetime; before that it was not a part of your current familiarity inventory. That's what every moment is like for master magicians – it's as though they feel every feeling for the first time. They are completely mind-blown every minute since they have no point of reference for anything.

This is the difference between real magic, and the image most non-magicians have about magic: master magicians don't *control* anything; they have just mastered adaptation and improvisation. What they can do that the average person can't do is spot opportunities and pitfalls in the midst of total chaos and insanity, and act on that knowledge with *intent* – direct gut-level knowing and acting. Thus master magicians can bring the unknown to bear on everyday decision-making.

In waking when you are facing or have narrowly escaped death; or when your whole world and all of its supports are crumbling, as e.g. when you're being called on the carpet by your boss; or have just been told by your lover to get lost; or are being arrested by the Gestapo – any time the carpet is pulled out from under you and you feel that plunging feeling in the pit of your stomach – you experience a temporary loss of familiarity.

Now imagine what life would be like if you felt that disoriented sense of nothing to cling to, all day long every day. That's what master magicians feel. They feel as if they are in free-fall with no supports and no security, every single minute. For them, nothing makes any sense: there are no reasons why for anything. They have to grasp each moment anew, be on the *qui vive* every second. There's nothing they can take for granted or rely upon except their own intent. This is what Castaneda's teacher don Juan meant about using death as an advisor: feeling yourself to be in the presence of death, facing your death squarely, every minute of every day.

The point is that there is no time and there is no space. These are illusions, *maya, samsara*. All there really are, are importance and familiarity, which your social training reifies as the concepts of time and space. Clocks and rulers don't mean nothing – the fact that you can quantify something doesn't imply that it actually exists; just as medieval scholastics debating how many angels can dance on the head of a pin doesn't imply that any of that exists.

Just as thinking can exist without importance (in lucid dreaming, for example), so too can feeling exist without familiarity. Feeling without familiarity is like a cold detachment: you feel something, but can't pin it down as being a good feeling or a bad one; a desirable feeling or an undesirable one; a pleasurable feeling or a painful one; etc. Carlos Castaneda was always finding himself thrust into this state – of feeling feelings for which he had no point of reference. This led to his attempts to describe his feelings as "a pleasurable anguish" or similar nondescriptive descriptions. Or his feeling as bodily sensations things that happened outside his body, as when he felt doubled up in a hammock when he was physically seated on the floor. Similarly, the weird physical sensations which people so often experience when meditating are feelings which have no familiarity covering, so people invent one on the spot (feel as though they are e.g. tilted or upside down – they put this sort of interpretation on a feeling for which they have no reference in order to reduce it to familiarity). Just as your importance insists on preserving your sense of continuity by papering over all discontinuity, so too does your familiarity insist on rendering even thoroughly unfamiliar feelings familiar.

To experience the world without a filter of familiarity is to feel that everything is completely unknown all the time. Average people base their decisions on that which they think and that which they know. They can't make decisions in the face of the unthinkable and unknowable. They have to make decisions based on what they've been taught (to think) and on what they are familiar with (what they feel). They don't know how to act on intent, making decisions on the spur of the moment as a gut response involving no thought and no feeling. Of course, on rare occasions in the course of an average lifetime some people do experience true intent, as when they make some split-second decision of a life-or-death nature as a true leap into the unknown. Indeed, some people deliberately seek such experiences for the heady thrill of leaping into the unknown. But master magicians leap into the unknown every instant of every day. Even if to all appearances they're just sitting there placidly, what they are experiencing is intense, ineffable, indescribable, incomprehensible.

The only way to deal with the unknown is with sobriety. Otherwise it is too disorienting to handle – you become thoroughly caught up in it. There's no point in learning how to let go of waking mind (everyday reality) just to become caught up in some other reality. You're not out to shift from one line of memory to another; you're trying to learn how to experience different lines of memory (different realities or worlds) without being caught up in any of them. And the minute that something becomes familiar, you become caught up in it: in a hell world you become caught up in fear and anger; in a heaven world you become caught up in pleasure and enjoyment. All these feelings are familiar. When you are feeling a familiar feeling, whether enjoyable or painful, you are caught by the feeling – just as thinking that something is important is enough to make it an obsessive thought. The only antidote for familiarity is sobriety. Most people don't have a sober moment in their entire lives after infancy – a moment in which they aren't driven by feelings or thoughts "beyond their control".

True sobriety is only possible after you die, which is why all magicians have to literally die (and hopefully resuscitate – a near-death experience). Until you die, all "you" are is death watching itself. When you die you unite with your death, and the "two of you" are then watching together. You become death, you unite with your death: instead of being something which is being watched, you become the watching itself. There's still a sense of a detached perceiver perceiving, a higher self, but there's no longer a sense of stake in anything, no eagerness to prove anything, no importance in anything, no lower self. The things which happen in your life happen as if by themselves, with no volition of your own. You aren't striving for or against anything – there's no one there, no person who can be pushed and pulled by his or her ties to the world – by desires, moods, beliefs.

Memory can be accessed randomly: theoretically you can pop in or out of any world or reality anywhere in the Akashic Records that you want to (my teacher don Abel Yat could do that – make astoundingly specific, accurate predictions out of thin air). But familiarity pins it all down to ROM – not only to your birth, but backward through the evolution of the human race, back to your single-celled memories.

Just as waking mind is undergirded by importance, so too is dream mind undergirded by familiarity. Just as importance selects what you will think about, so too does familiarity select what you will feel. Actually desire and memory are the same thing – two different ways of looking at the same phenomenon. The separation of the two into two different terms is a convenience. Desire hasn't "happened yet" in your thinking, so you view the importance coverings on your desires as expectations rather than as moods. Expectation isn't as heavy as mood: you usually give yourself a greater sense of free play with your desires than you do with your memories.

Familiarity takes many forms: you feel it as regret, triumph, hurt, etc. Your moods are a cover you put over your true memories. Your true memories are always cold, detached, and analytical; more importantly, they are always *new* (which is why the practice of recapitulation is such an eye-opener). True memory is always a source of wonder, not a closet stuffed with unhappy reminders. However, to arrive at true memory it is necessary to get rid of all sense of familiarity. This is the purpose of the magical practice of disrupting routines, as well as of recapitulation.

To become a magician you have to cultivate the feeling of unfamiliarity, just as you have to cultivate the feeling of non-importance. You do this through some of the same techniques (i.e. resorting daily to tree and water spirits). Also, it's important to break up routines, to make trips to new places, to get involved with new people, to engage in new and unfamiliar activities. You break up importance by just learning not to give a damn about things; similarly you break up familiarity by doing new things all the time instead of the same old thing. The two work in tandem – it's important to do the same thing all the time, and doing the same thing all the time makes it important – ergo they must be deconstructed together.

Comfort is the greatest enemy of freedom. Comfort is true slavery. A prisoner would prefer to remain in Auschwitz because it is comfortable rather than make the effort of trying to escape. Even dying in the attempt would free him from his suffering and bondage, so there's no way he can lose anything; but just as Frankl said, man is an animal who can get accustomed to anything. It is also true that man is also an animal who can take comfort in anything. To take comfort e.g. in self-pity or self-righteousness is absurd – these are terrible feelings to take comfort in. And yet most people hug them to their bosoms. They would rather feel the good old familiar feeling of self-pity than be "uncomfortable" in some unfamiliar feeling. This is another reason for the exercise of following feelings as explained in my book *Magical Living*: naked walks and dives into water at midnight. Always the new. You have to learn to seek it, to be undaunted, to relish the feeling of unfamiliarity. It's the only way to overcome the tyranny of memory (just as cultivating non-importance is the way to overcome the tyranny of mind).

Master magicians still have personalities in the same sense in which they have bodies. When you are in Germany, you speak German. So too when master magicians act in the world of people they have to speak their language: have a personality people can relate to (liking them or disliking them, loving them or fearing them, etc.). So master magicians put on personalities so that other people can have some point of reference in order to deal with them. But in their natural, unhooked, state, even if they're physically present other people wouldn't even notice that they're there, anymore than they notice the pebbles on the road beneath their feet. To unhook yourself from other people, from the world of humans, means to erase all sense of familiarity. This is the purpose of recapitulation.

The purpose of recapitulation is this: if you can peel off the feeling of familiarity from just one lifetime, then you're in a position to be free of the feeling of familiarity from all of them (just as if you can peel off the feeling of importance from just one person – if you can truly open your heart to just one person by dethroning the feeling of self-importance that separates you – then you are in the position of opening your heart to all people and things). You peel off the feeling of familiarity by recapitulating all of your life memories.

That's why a master magician can have two memories of the same event (two different events occupying the same space in time). What keeps you glued into one track or lifetime is the sense of familiarity. Breaking that track is to feel all of your lifetimes and probable realities at once – thus it's possible to have two memories of the same event.

What makes the world of waking consciousness a drab, dull place is familiarity. Familiarity breeds contempt. That is a true statement. Familiarity is a way of grabbing onto the world, of grabbing onto other people, of clinging to them and bringing them down. Familiarity is a bringdown.

Just as lucid dreaming is a state in which things are separated, but there is no (or minimal) importance, so too is lucid dreaming a state in which things are known, or recognizable, but are thoroughly unfamiliar. To remove the familiarity from everyday life is to enter into the state of lucid dreaming while still awake (which is the purpose of many magical techniques such as gazing and astral projection).

Getting rid of familiarity is getting rid of control. You can only control things – your environment, other people – by making them familiar. Making things familiar is to control them. The waking state is controllable only as long as it seems familiar. The trick to magic, then, is to be quite comfortable with everything out of control, as it were. When things are out of control, are unfamiliar, then you are dreaming. The more out of control you let your daily life be, the more you are actually dreaming rather than being awake.

Although regressions techniques start out from a position in wakefulness, actually when you are running past life regressions or recapitulations you are not in a state of wakefulness. You are closer to being in the dream state, depending on how vivid your impression is. When you are no longer controlling a regression, when you let what will happen happen in a regression (as you do when dropping off to sleep, when you let the hypnagogic images come without trying to direct the action yourself) then you are in the dream state, even if you started out being awake. This is also the goal of magical techniques such as Creative Visualization, gazing, and astral projection: to enter into a dream state from a position that begins in wakefulness. The point is that the more vivid you can make a visualized image – the more vivid you can make your "mind's eye" – the closer to being in the dream state you are.

It is memory which pegs you into the dream state, just as it is mind which pegs you into the waking state. Familiarity is the glue which binds you to both.

* * * * *

The Akashic Records

"Now as I beheld the living creatures, behold one wheel at the bottom hard by the living creatures, at the four faces thereof. The appearance of the wheels and their work was like unto the color of a beryl; and they four had one likeness; and their appearance and their work was as it were a wheel within a wheel." – *Ezekiel* I:15 – 16

"Pisces 12: A very large disk consisting of circles of light with dark grey interspaces. These circles resemble wheels within wheels, which I find on closer examination to be spiral, all revolving." – Charubel, *The Degrees of the Zodiac Symbolized*

What these seers were seeing and trying to describe is the organization of the universe (the thought form part of it anyway); namely, the Akashic Records: swirling spiral chains of thought forms; infinite lines of scene after scene after scene stretching to infinity, in an infinity of sequences, which from a distance resemble whirling helical gyres made of filaments of living light – light which glows with awareness, which exudes awareness. And if you turn in the opposite direction you can see of what the *Daimon* is made: swirling light fibers of an individual's memories (feelings) being sucked into a vortex or whirlpool.

The image given to W.B.Y. was that of two interpenetrating gyres (conical spirals) twirling this way and that; the image given to me (and also to Busteed, Tiffany and Wergin) was that of wheels within wheels, and wheels upon wheels – i.e. cycles within cycles within cycles, all spinning this way and that. But in fact these images are merely images, because there is NO order or regularity in the universe. Your perceptions are orderly and regular, but that has nothing to do with the actual universe, which is utterly chaotic. Your perceptions are of order and regularity, but – contrary to what you have been taught – they are not perceptions of the universe. For example, what you perceive as the linear sequence of time is actually the shift of attention between different levels of memory – shifts of attention from one of the *Four Faculties* to another.

The reason the spirits suggested these images (gyres or wheels) is to represent time as intersecting cycles rather than as a straight line. These models of time are no more correct than the complete, well-ordered field continuum model because the universe, being utterly chaotic, cannot be modeled except by chaos. Nonetheless the gyre or wheels-within-wheels models are closer to the truth than the linear model because they are more representative of what is actually going on than is the linear model. The linear model describes time in waking consciousness, wherein all you are dealing with is a single sequence of personal history and future (*Will*); but this model fails when you go beyond that and enter the realm of dreaming, wherein you are considering all past and future lives and probable realities (*Mask*) – the totality of your being rather than one particular ramification of it (*Will* = this present lifetime). Thus the gyre and wheels-within-wheels are more inclusive or encompassing models of time than is linearity.

The part of the Akashic Records which is available to us as humans is accessed by the faculty which we call memory. Memories (the thought form components at least) are not stored in the physical brain, as materialists believe. They are stored in the Akashic Records. The physical brain accesses the Akashic Records in the same way that the eyes access certain wavelengths of light and the ears access certain wavelengths of sound. This is how "idiot savants" and geniuses perform their miracles: they enter into heightened awareness to "read" the (music, mathematics, whatever) directly from the Akashic Records. It's quite analogous to cloud computing – the brain accesses the Akashic Records in the same way that individual computers access the internet. But the information is not in the brain – it's in the Akashic Records; just as in cloud computing the information is not in the computer but on the internet. The overall effect creates the illusion of a physical world surrounding you, but in point of fact the individual memories being accessed – out of all the probable realities possible – are determined largely at random, in *a Record where the images of all past events remain for ever "thinking the thought and doing the deed". They are in popular mysticism called "the pictures in the astral light."*

"... suddenly the 'me' I knew and was familiar with erupted into the most spectacular view of all the imaginable combinations of 'beautiful' scenes; it was as if I were looking at thousands of pictures of the world, of people, of things.

"The scenes then became blurry, I had the sensation that they were being passed in front of my eyes at a greater speed until I could not single out any of them for examination. Finally it was as if I were witnessing the organization of the world rolling past my eyes in an unbroken, endless chain." – Carlos Castaneda, *Tales of Power*

The internet is a thought form representation or symbol for the Akashic Records. And, as you can also do with the internet, you can access the thought forms of memory stored in the Akashic Records in one of two ways: dynamically (sequentially, as you do in everyday life) or statically (all at once, as you do when you recapitulate all of your life memories at the *Return* the moment you die). But in fact the entire body of the Akashic Records is not only available right there at every moment in time, it is actually pressing on it. It's not creating it per se (it is the action of mind to create thought forms); but rather the weight of the Akashic Records provides the general form or matrix out of which mind can finish shaping a thought form. Mind doesn't start from scratch but relies heavily upon memory to create thought forms. There are realms in which memory doesn't exist: you can access these in moments of ecstasy, but you can't create thought forms in these moments. Even as low a level of ecstasy as climactic orgasm is so "NOW" that there's not enough room (separatedness) for much memory to bear upon it.

Everything that ever was or ever will be or could have been or could be – here, there, or anywhere in this universe or any universe – makes up the Akashic Records. The Akashic Records is a cosmic shopping mall and we are like shoppers strolling down the aisles browsing for whatever thought forms will be brought to importance in this lifetime. It's a moment-to-moment process of decision-making (intent). Déjà vu is not a "glitch in the Matrix" (as the materialists would have it), but rather an adventitious accession of the Akashic Records.

Consider average people who dream of becoming famous artists or musicians, or fabulously wealthy, or just happily married with a family; but every attempt to make these dreams come true in the "real" world leads to nothing but disappointment. Obviously, they were not meant to realize these dreams – at least not in this probable reality. In other probable realities, yes – those dreams came true; and it is the beckoning of these probable realities which motivate them to formulate images of these dreams coming true in this probable reality.

Another way of looking at it is: every moment of your life you spin the magic wheel of fortune; and, if you are patient and dogged enough through enough lifetimes of repeating that intent, the wheel of fortune will stop on the probable reality in which your dream comes true. It's like catching the brass ring on a merry-go-round – all a matter of desire and timing.

Mind is guided, or nudged along, by memory, and at the same time it imposes a temporality or linear march of time on memory. Mind cannot exist without memory (it cannot organize something in sequence if there is nothing to organize); but memory *can* exist without mind (the thought form bank exists as a whole and can be experienced as a whole in lucid dreaming, after death, and even in very poignant moments in waking consciousness, without any sense of temporal sequence or "time").

To say that the Akashic Records are pressing upon each new moment is to say that the thought form you create at each moment of "time" includes your memory of what one-cell creatures feel; which led them to evolve into more complex life forms – animals, vertebrates, mammals, primates, and then into humans – with the memories of all those feelings; as well as all of the feelings you have ever felt in all of your own incarnations as a human; together with the feelings you felt at each moment in your present lifetime and all of its probable realities. All levels of memory, striving, hope, aspiration, fear etc. come to bear upon each new moment in your life, help to shape it out of material that is familiar. Life isn't a zing-zing-zing from one incomprehensible scene to another – it has an orderly progression to it, which is what we mean by the principle of mind. Mind is thus a more specialized facet of memory – the cutting edge, as it were.

Even rocks have memory, but they don't have mind. They have feelings, but they don't create thought forms in the same sense in which we humans do. They don't have what we would consider a sense of time. Note that rock spirits are not the same thing as the innate spirit of the rocks which they inhabit. There are spirits who possess a rock, or tree, or body of water in the same way that spirits can possess humans (or that human "souls" possess their bodies). But a rock itself has a proper spirit (just as a human body has a proper spirit apart from the "soul" inhabiting it), which is a feeling that can also be characterized as memory. Rock memory is not organized sequentially: if you pick up a rock and smash it to the ground in anger, the rock (or all of its pieces) will "remember" that feeling of anger, but not as part of an ordered sequence. So while inorganic life has a faculty of memory, it doesn't have mind – it doesn't create thought forms. What you conceive of as a "rock" – the sum total of properties which you classify as "rockness"; the way you know that something is a rock – i.e. your learned "rock" thought form; is completely your creation and has nothing to do with the actual rock, or anything that rock is feeling.

Look at it this way: the inverse square law (gravity, magnetism etc.) is a fabrication. It doesn't describe anything that is really going on in the universe. It wasn't even true of anything until Newton came along and made it true. Of course, Kepler, Copernicus etc. were also pushing that idea along, it didn't start with Newton. He didn't conjure that thought form up out of thin air, but based it on things other men had done before him. That's what is meant when it is said that memory is the shaper of thought forms on which mind puts the finishing touches. The future pulls the past along: it was just as much Newton trying to do what Newton tried to do which influenced Kepler to do what Kepler did, which called upon Copernicus to do his thing, as it was the other way around. Humankind was pushing along in the direction of making an inverse square law describe a certain type of light fiber, on which it had pasted the thought form of "gravity". But it could have just as easily pasted other thought forms on that same light fiber, and organized other bodies of thought forms (other evolutions or bodies of memory) to describe the same phenomenon.

Magic, for example, is a wholly different way of organizing basically the same thought form material as materialistic science. A master magician can fly, read thoughts, communicate over long distances, etc. A materialistic scientist can also do some of these things, but he needs a machine to do them. He needs the prop of a machine thought form to perform these dream tasks because in his conscious, accessible memory humans can only do these things with machines. But there are other possibilities of memory, other lines of memory which can be accessed, in which these feats can be performed as acts of intent, or magic, but still within the basic context of human memory. And there are other levels of memory which can be accessed (that of cellular and even molecular feeling) which are even weirder. But all these memories press upon, or shape, the present moment. The Wright Brothers, Alexander Graham Bell, Thomas Edison, were all reaching out along one particular line of memory; but they were influenced by other lines of memory (the racial memory that humans – albeit magicians – can fly, communicate at a distance, see in the dark, etc.). Which in turn is based upon memories of other possibilities of experience. The whole thing is a turning wheel, with wheels within wheels. And although it's evolving, it's not going anywhere in particular.

The point is that although memory starts out as mind (a light fiber pinned down to a thought form), it soon takes on a will of its own. The human race and its evolution is as much the product of collective memory, as collective memory is the product of the human race (which duality is symbolized by the two interpenetrating cones or gyres).

The collective memory of the human race (*Creative Mind*) forms and informs each new thought form created by any individual human; and each thought form gives a little tug to the direction that collective memory is heading in, just as each drop helps fill a bucket. Memory is an anchor that holds you back in a sense, but also stabilizes your experience – grooves it – by providing you with a feeling of familiarity. Without an underlying feeling of familiarity – routine, habit – everything would be truly bizarre. Familiarity is what ties everything together for you, gives you a sense of continuity, etc. Familiarity is to memory what importance is to mind – it stabilizes it. Without a feeling of familiarity everything would be like new every instant. Even a baby has a sense of familiarity to stabilize him, otherwise he'd be completely disoriented.

Master magicians, unlike average people, have no sense of familiarity. They find every minute totally disorienting. They just don't freak out about it as an average person would since they've gotten used to it. They've learned to operate without a sense of self or center, in an environment that is totally unfamiliar. In other words, they have familiarized themselves with the unfamiliar. They use familiarity just like everyone else uses familiarity, to steady themselves, to provide a springboard to action. But they don't cling to familiarity and go bananas when they find themselves in a thoroughly unfamiliar and disorienting situation.

At the Critical Moments – if I may extend the term to all wheels – mans will is free. In so far as he has attained Unity of Being mans will is free, & he sets himself free altogether from the whirling, or enlarges his gyre, between those moments destined or fated – automatic. He is free at a critical moments because then & then only does he can be satisfied with 'nothing but the whole Daimon*' whether understood as object of desire or object of thought, & <not> all separated objects of its desire or thought; its* *symbols or surrogates* [i.e. thought forms] *lead to dissatisfaction or rejection & so into the whirling.*

– (W.B.Y., *National Library of Ireland manuscript 30,319*)

Carlos Castaneda describes the direct experience of the *Daimon* (in *Tales of Power*) as follows:

"Then I exploded. I disintegrated. Something in me gave out; it released something I had kept locked up all my life. I was thoroughly aware then that my secret reservoir had been tapped and that it poured out unrestrainedly. There was no longer the sweet unity I call 'me'. There was nothing and yet that nothing was filled. It was not light or darkness, hot or cold, pleasant or unpleasant. It was not that I moved or floated or was stationary, neither was I a single unit, a self, as I am accustomed to being. I was a myriad of selves which were all 'me', a colony of separate units that had a special allegiance to one another and would join unavoidably to form one single awareness, my human awareness. It was not that I 'knew' beyond the shadow of a doubt, because there was nothing I could have 'known' with, but all my single awarenesses 'knew' that the 'I', the 'me', of my familiar world was a colony, a conglomerate of separate and independent feelings [light fibers] that had an unbending solidarity to one another. The unbending solidarity of my countless awarenesses, the allegiance that those parts had for one another was my life force.

"A way of describing that unified sensation would be to say that those nuggets of awareness were scattered; each of them was aware of itself and none was more predominant than the other. Then something would stir them, and they would join and emerge into an area where all of them had to be pooled in one clump, the 'me' I know. As 'me' 'myself' then I would witness a coherent scene of worldly activity, or a scene that pertained to other worlds and which I thought must have been pure imagination, or a scene that pertained to 'pure thinking', that is, I had views of intellectual systems, or of ideas strung together as verbalizations. In some scenes I talked to myself to my heart's content. After every one of those coherent views the 'me' would disintegrate and be nothing once more. ... I longed for the 'unknown' where my awareness was not unified."

How could it be that you are, at root, a cluster of separate awarenesses when it seems to you that you are so unified? Think about this analogy: when a sufficient number of the cells in your body require water, "you" feel thirst. Actually, that's all "you" are or ever could be: the momentary union of a bunch of disparate tendencies or feelings which unite intents for an instant to achieve a common purpose, just as soldiers submerge their individualities to achieve a common purpose. And when that purpose is achieved, everything dissolves once again. What you really are is like a pointillist painting, like *Sunday Afternoon on the Island of La Grande Jatte*, which seems to make some kind of sense – which seems to be familiar – but all it really is, is a bunch of dots.

This is the real reason for the magical practice of resorting to trees every day: to reconnect with what you really are. Whether you know it or not, your body is made up of infinite imprints, relatively few of which you are consciously aware of. What actually happens to your body when you sit by a tree is that it begins to disintegrate. Your body actually falls apart, even though on a conscious level you are totally unaware of this. Love is also an actual disintegration of your cells and molecules: love recharges your molecules on one level; but on a more profound level it rearranges the molecules, and it composes them in another form. Love's manifestation sitting next to a tree, or falling in love with a person or a pet, are manifested outside your molecules; but the actual miracle is that love manifests from "without" before it is even able to manifest in your physical, bodily world.

Here is another way of thinking about it: you actually see two very different scenes every passing moment through your two eyes, and yet you are somehow able to blend them together and are consciously aware of only one scene (unless you are too drunk or drugged to keep the two views separated). This blending faculty you learned as an infant; newborns still do see two scenes, and they have little sense of themselves as separated, isolated, individual beings in consequence. Infants see two of everything, so there are two things going on moment-to-moment which compete for attention in an infant's visual awareness. As a result, infants have no sense that there's only one of them watching the show – they have no sense of a unified self-at-center (a single, separated witness) as adults have. It is the socialization process which teaches the infant how to create one unified witness (being) out of two distinct beings.

In the same way that you are somehow able to blend two distinct visual scenes into one view in your attention, so too are you able to blend a zillion separate awarenesses into one overarching consciousness which you feel as "you". This is what is meant by focus – focus is achieved by ignoring information, screening out the fact that there is not a single view going on, but multiple views. We call this focus importance; it is what creates your lower self (*Will*), your sense of separatedness.

You have learned how to do this blending or uniting of separate awarenesses into one being as part of your evolutionary heritage since you were a one-celled being. These zillion separate awarenesses are what we have termed light fibers – which are apprehended as feelings – which tend to agglomerate or agglutinate here and there in the universe. Where groups of light fibers agglomerate they start issuing thought forms – a separation between observer and observed – i.e. a separated being. But actually all that you are is a momentary focus – a momentary conjunction of disparate tendencies that for a fleeting instant have a solidarity, and then disperse once again; but to you it seems like lifetimes and lifetimes. But all you really are, is a mayfly caught up in wheels within wheels.

The "unbending solidarity" which these awarenesses have for one another is what Castaneda termed his life force, what W.B.Y. termed *Deception*, and which we term *striving*. Striving is the sum total of the changes which all the zillion separate awarenesses are going through. Striving is what animates the swirl of the thought forms in the Akashic Records – what you take as time. Striving is the real cause or source of what is going on; moreover, this constant change and flux is completely random and chaotic.

For example, evolution has nothing whatsoever to do with competition for scarce resources, as the materialists would have it. By buying into the linear time fallacy, all of materialistic science is completely off the bat – it's all a bunch of *post hoc ergo propter hoc* hooey: trying to explain the inexplicable by coming up with reasons why things are the way they are, when in fact there is *no* reason whatsoever why *anything* is the way it is. There's no reason, period. So to try to conceive of it at all we focus on arbitrary levels, and divide the lowest (most "recent" or "closest") levels of movement – those relating to humanness – into four, which are the *Four Faculties* or moods. But this is merely a convenience to enable us to get a handle on the unspeakable.

The world is completely new, startlingly new and unrecognizable, every instant. To you it seems that this present moment is similar to a moment ago. But this is a falsehood: every moment is a whole new ballgame, with completely different rules. Familiarity is a gloss or lie you tell yourself that what is happening at this moment bears any resemblance whatsoever to what was happening a moment ago. It makes you focus upon the features of "reality" which do seem to persist – the thought forms. Thought forms have no persistence either: what they have is a little built-in tape recorder saying over and over "I persist! I persist! Look, ma, I persist!" Listening to this tape recording occupies your total attention, so that you never look around and notice that nothing persists, that every passing moment is utterly baffling and ineffable, that the entire universe is exploding into being and dissolving again into nothingness with each passing instant of "time". Familiarity is the basis of your sense of separatedness. Without familiarity you dissolve into what you actually are – a zillion separate awarenesses.

"Your perception unfolded its wings when something in you realized your true nature. You are a cluster. This is the sorcerer's explanation. The *nagual* is the unspeakable. All the possible feelings and beings and selves float in it like barges, peaceful, unaltered, forever. Then the glue of life binds some of them together. ... When the glue of life binds those feelings together a being is created, a being that loses the sense of its true nature and becomes blinded by the glare and clamor of the area where beings hover, the *tonal*. The *tonal* is where all the unified organization exists. A being pops into the *tonal* once the force of life has bound all the needed feelings together. I said to you once that the *tonal* begins at birth and ends at death; I said that because I know that as soon as the force of life leaves the body all those single awarenesses disintegrate and go back again to where they came from, the *nagual*." (Carlos Castaneda, *Tales of Power*)

The repose of man is the choice of the Daimon, *and the repose of the* Daimon *the choice of man; and what I have called man's terrestrial state the* Daimon*'s condition of fire.* – (W.B.Y., note to *Per Amica Silentia Lunæ*).

All any sentient being is at any given moment of time is a set of tendencies this way and that; and the force which makes them appear to be a single, separated, being persisting in linear time is *death*. Death is what keeps separated beings separated. First there's birth, and then this happens, that happens, and the other happens; and then there's death. That personal history, or album of thought form snapshots, is made of death; that is to say, the collection of thought forms apparently taking place in linear time – which separated beings perceive as their lives – that matrix of individuality, is just death. That's all death is: the sequencing of an arbitrary collection of thought forms. Many of those same thought forms are bound up in other collections with other deaths and those are what we have termed probable realities (*Body of Fate*), and past and future lives (*Mask*). Death is what keeps these thought form collections or lines of memory separated.

The question arises, if nothing in the universe persists for more than an instant, why then do beings seem to persist? The answer is familiarity: just as individual thought forms have a gloss of importance which keeps them separated, so too do chains of thought forms have a gloss of familiarity which keeps them in sequence. Familiarity is a feeling; linear time is how mind apprehends or interprets this feeling. If you can get back to feeling the original feelings underlying the sequences of thought forms which you term your "lifetimes", then you don't need as much of a sense of linear time to keep them separated.

The real movement or emanation lies beneath the thought forms of striving. Although it seems to you that you persist in time and space, in fact you are in a constant flux as all the zillion separate awarenesses which make you up go hither and thither. All you are at any given moment are tendencies this way and that, like schools of fish that momentarily are oriented in the same direction. The tendencies this way and that you apprehend as the *moods* which inform the moment (mold the thought forms which you create, i.e., the events which happen to you in your life). These tendencies in turn are influenced by the complete pattern of evolutionary memory of all the thought forms which have ever existed and ever will exist; namely the Akashic Records.

*I need some mind that, if the cannon sound
From every quarter of the world, can stay
Wound in the mind's pondering,
As mummies in the mummy-cloth are wound;
Because I have a marvellous thing to say,
A certain marvellous thing
None but the living mock,
Though not for sober ear;
It may be all that hear
Should laugh and weep an hour upon the clock.*

Glossary

Active Imagination – a technique devised by Carl Jung for consciously interacting with our thought forms (described at length in *Thought Forms*)

Akashic records – set of all thought forms that ever have been or ever will be or ever could be. All that is knowable by any sentient being. These are accessed by the RAM capabilities of the physical brain, in the same way that the physical eye accesses certain wavelengths of light

Antithetical (tincture) – sense of Separatedness; self-consciousness, self-awareness. It is Separatedness which makes mind possible (when we apprehend via mind, things seem to be separated from us; i.e. happening to an "us")

Automatonism – "automatic pilot" – the compulsive, incessant inner dialogue or rumination which occupies a person's attention most of the time they are awake

Beatific Vision – (called *Stopping the World*, *Kensho*, *Satori*, *Samadhi*, in other traditions) a peak moment when "the world" dissolves into a state of selflessness and timelessness

Body of Fate – the set of probable realities which branch off from this present lifetime; a person's spontaneous motivations in everyday life

Chaldean Order – of the planets: Saturn, Jupiter, Mars, sun, Venus, Mercury, moon. It is the basis of various astrological techniques such as the Firdaria and the Planetary Hours, from whence derives the order of the days of the week

Closing and **Opening of tinctures** – occurs between the moon-ruled and Saturn-ruled phases (at the disjunction in the Chaldean cycle), at which point the interpretations take an *antithetical* turn (in a *primary* quarter) or a *primary* turn (in an *antithetical* quarter). *N.b. this*

definition of the closing and opening of the tinctures differs from that used in A Vision

Cognition – making sense of what is perceived; the sense that what is happening is familiar (recognizable) and important (makes sense)

Complementary planetary rulers – the pairs of planets Venus-Mars, Mercury-Jupiter, and moon-Saturn complement each other since they rule opposite zodiacal signs

Conceptual thought form (meme, schema control unit, agent) – a thought; a conditioned pattern of behavior or reaction (learned from parents and society); a position which is being defended, which has a logic, a rationale, and a will to live all its own

Creative Mind – Collective unconscious; the body of knowledge we can draw upon by virtue of our humanity which is communicated to us in the voices of our ancestors; a person's societal conditioning in everyday life

Critical Moments or **Initiatory Moments** – peak experiences when the higher *Faculties* break through *Will* and reveal something of the *Daimon* (a person's true purpose in life)

Customary moods – the habitual moods invoked by our customary internal dialogue (conceptual thought forms).

Daimon – "oversoul" or sum total of who a person is on all levels of human memory: present life history and future + probable realities of same + past and future lives + ancestral and human inheritance

Dream consciousness consists primarily of sensory thought forms

Dreamless sleep consists primarily of feelings (light fibers). It is the deepest level of sleep, on which we make direct contact with our *Daimon*

Familiarity – recognition; routine; habit; the feeling that what is happening now resembles something that happened previously

Faculties (*Will, Body of Fate, Mask, Creative Mind*) – 1) four levels of human memory: present life history and future, probable realities of same, past & future lives, ancestral and human inheritance; 2) four levels of human communication; 3) four levels of motivation which shape / impinge upon people's incessant inner dialogue or rumination (and thus how they define their world)

Gyre – helical spiral

Human form – our human memory (customary moods; the light fibers which tie us to our fellow humans)

Importance – the feeling of urgency, of being driven; of something being more important than paying attention to the now moment

In phase – following one's true purpose in incarnating into this life

Intent – feeling, the stuff of dreamless sleep, just as sensory thought forms are the stuff of dream consciousness and conceptual thought forms are the stuff of waking consciousness. Our intent is our true feelings; our innate sense of what is right and true; of who we are and what we must do

Interchange of Tinctures at Phases 1 and 15, at which points the power of the tinctures culminates (*primary* at Phase 1 and *antithetical* at Phase 15) and begins to decline

Inversion of Tinctures at Phases 8 and 22, at which points the balance shifts to the opposite tincture (*antithetical* at Phase 8 and *primary* at Phase 22)

Light fiber – feeling, intent (which to psychic vision appears as fibers of living, aware light)

Lucid Dreaming – dreaming in which we are consciously aware of the fact that we are dreaming. It is the next step in the evolution of human consciousness (after waking consciousness) – i.e the consciousness of the future

Mask – set of all of a person's human incarnations (past and future) in all realities; everyday decisions taken in response to karmic imperatives from other incarnations

Nagual – (*Antithetical* experience); cognition without importance or familiarity

Out of phase – straying from one's true purpose in incarnating in this life

Planetary hours – an ancient Chaldean system for choosing propitious times to act based upon which planet rules each hour of the day

Primary (tincture) – sense of union, direct experience (without the gloss of a "self" to whom things are happening)

Principles (*Husk, Passionate Body, Spirit, Celestial Body*) – four levels or ramifications of dream consciousness (just as the *Faculties* represent four levels or ramifications of waking consciousness), which refer to the after-death state (just as the *Faculties* underpin the waking state)

Probable reality – a "parallel reality" which branches off from this lifetime whenever a person makes a decision

Recapitulation – a technique for reliving memories from this present lifetime

Return or Review – the recapitulation of all the memories of a lifetime at the moment of death

Sensory thought form (qualia) – sensory or extrasensory perception of the now moment: sight, sound, smell, taste, or feeling (either physical or nonphysical). Sensory thought forms have a high proportion of feeling to them, such as the sight of a beautiful woman; the smell of roses; the roar of the ocean; the feel of slime

Silent knowledge – cognition and decision-making based upon direct knowing rather than thinking

Synodic cycle – a planet's orbit around the sun as seen from the earth (as opposed to sidereal cycle – a planet's orbit around the sun as seen from a fixed point outside of it)

Thought form – moment-to-moment awareness; observer / observed duality; the content of each moment's awareness is a thought form (sensory when we are being mindful and conceptual when we are acting mindlessly)

Tincture – the state of being focused (*primary*) or aware (*antithetical*)

Tonal – (*Primary* experience); the socialized person – cognition via a gloss of a "self"

Waking consciousness – consists primarily of conceptual thought forms

Will – set of memories from this present lifetime; personal history and future

Bibliography

Hashem Atallah (trans.), *Picatrix*, Ouroboros Seattle 2002
Marilyn Busteed, Richard Tiffany, Dorothy Wergin, *Phases of the Moon*, Shambhala Berkeley 1974
Carlos Castaneda, *Tales of Power*, Simon and Schuster NYC 1974
Carlos Castaneda, *The Active Side of Infinity*, HarperCollins NYC 1998
Viktor Frankl, *Man's Search for Meaning*, Beacon Press Boston 1959
Philip Kapleau, *The Three Pillars of Zen*, Doubleday NYC 1980
Allan Kardec, *The Spirits' Book*, LAKE São Paulo
Neil Mann, Yeats's A Vision: *Ideas of Man and God*, unpublished dissertation, Oxford 2002
Neil Mann, www.yeatsvision.com (excellent general introduction to *A Vision*)
Mann, Gibson, Nally, *W.B. Yeats's* A Vision - *Explications and Contexts*, Clemson 2012
Michael Newton, *Journey of Souls*, Llewellyn St. Paul 1994
Jane Roberts, *Seth Speaks*, Bantam NYC 1974
Armando Torres, *Encounters With the Nagual*, First Light Press 2004
Chelsea Quinn Yarbro, *Messages from Michael*, Caelum 2005
William Butler Yeats, *A Vision* , MacMillan NYC 1937
Gary Zukav, *The Dancing Wu Li Masters*, Bantam 1980

Appendix I: W.B.Y.'s Keywords for the Influence of the *Faculties* Upon the Phases

The following table gives the keywords found in *A Vision*, transposed according to the rules found therein (so that the keywords for *Mask*, *Creative Mind*, and *Body of Fate* are listed according to the phase to which they apply rather than – as in *A Vision* – the phase from which they are derived. These rules are the same as those used in constructing the Chaldean Rectangles described earlier, so will not be repeated here).

19 The assertive man	T: 5<CM 25 Conviction F: 5<BF 11 Domination	T: 11<CM 19 Emotional intellect F: 11<BF 5 The Unfaithful	25 Enforced failure of action

As an example, Phase 19's *Will* is *The Assertive Man*: *When this man lives according to phase, he is now governed by conviction, instead of by a ruling mood* [as is the tyrannical Phase 5], *and is effective only in so far as he can find this conviction. ... The strength from conviction, derived from a* Mask *of the first quarter antithetically transformed, is not founded upon social duty, though that may seem so to others, but is temperamentally formed to fit some crisis of personal life. ... The* Creative Mind *being derived from Phase 11, he is doomed to attempt the destruction of all that breaks or encumbers personality, but this personality is conceived of as a fragmentary, momentary intensity. ... The* Mask *is derived from that phase where perversity begins, where artifice begins* [where the *primary* tincture opens in the middle of an *antithetical* quarter], *and has its discord from Phase 25, the last phase where the artificial is possible; the* Body of Fate *is therefore enforced failure of action, and many at this phase desire action above all things as a means of expression.*

Table of W.B.Y.'s Keywords for the Influence of the *Faculties* Upon the Phases

< indicates "modified by"

Will	Mask	Creative Mind	Body of Fate
1	15 No description except	1 Complete plasticity	15
2 Beginning of energy	T: 16<BF 28 Player on Pan's Pipes F: 16<CM 14 Fury	T: 28<BF 16 Hope F: 28<CM 2 Moroseness	14 None except monotony
3 Beginning of ambition	T: 17<BF 27 Innocence F: 17<CM 13 Folly	T: 27<BF 17 Simplicity F: 27<CM 3 Abstraction	13 Interest
4 Desire for primary objects	T: 18<BF 26 Passion F: 18<CM 12 Will	T: 26<BF 18 First perception of character F: 26<CM 4 Mutilation	12 Search
5 Separation from innocence	T: 19<BF 25 Excess F: 19<CM 11 Limitation	T: 25<BF 19 Social intellect F: 25<CM 5 Limitation	11 Natural law
6 Artificial individuality	T: 20<BF 24 Justice F: 20<CM 10 Tyranny	T: 24<BF 20 Ideality F: 24<CM 6 Derision	10 Humanity
7 Assertion of individuality	T: 21<BF 23 Altruism F: 21<CM 9 Efficiency	T: 23<BF 21 Heroic sentiment F: 23<CM 7 Dogmatic sentimentality	9 Adventure that excites the individuality

< indicates "modified by"

Will	Mask	Creative Mind	Body of Fate
8 *War between individuality and race*	22 T: *Courage* F: *Fear*	22 T: *Versatility* F: *Impotence*	8 *The beginning of strength*
9 *Belief takes place of individuality*	T: 23<CM 7 *Facility* F: 23<BF 21 *Obscurity*	T: 21<CM 9 *Self-dramatisation* F: 21<BF 23 *Anarchy*	7 *Enforced sensuality*
10 *The image-breaker*	T: 24<CM 6 *Organisation* F: 24<BF 20 *Inertia*	T: 20<CM 10 *Domination through emotional constriction* F: 20<BF 24 *Reformation*	6 *Enforced emotion*
11 *The consumer. The pyre-builder*	T: 25<CM 5 *Rejection* F: 25<BF 19 *Moral indifference*	T: 19<CM 11 *Moral iconoclasm* F: 19<BF 25 *Self-assertion*	5 *Enforced belief*
12 *The Forerunner*	T: 26<CM 4 *Self-exaggeration* F: 26<BF 18 *Self-abandonment*	T: 18<CM 12 *Subjective philosophy* F: 18<BF 26 *War between two forms of expression*	4 *Enforced Intellectual action*
13 *The sensuous man*	T: 27<CM 3 *Self-expression* F: 27<BF 17 *Self-absorption*	T: 17<CM 13 *Subjective truth* F: 17<BF 27 *Morbidity*	3 *Enforced love of another*
14 *The obsessed man*	T: 28<CM 2 *Serenity* F: 28<BF 16 *Self-distrust*	T: 16<CM 14 *Emotional will* F: 16<BF 28 *Terror*	2 *Enforced love of the world*

< indicates "modified by"

Will	Mask	Creative Mind	Body of Fate
15	1 No description except	15 Complete beauty	1
16 The positive man	T: 2<CM 28 Illusion F: 2< BF 14 Delusion	T: 14<CM 16 Vehemence F: 14<BF 2 Opinionated will	28 Enforced illusion
17 The Daimonic man	T: 3<CM 27 Simplification Through intensity F: 3<BF13 Dispersal	T: 13<CM 17 Creative imagination through antithetical emotion F: 13<BF 3 Enforced self-realization	27 Enforced loss
18 The emotional man	T: 4<CM 26 Intensity through emotions F: 4<BF 12 Curiosity	T: 12<CM 18 Emotional philosophy F: 12<BF 4 Enforced lure	26 Enforced Disillusion-ment
19 The assertive man	T: 5<CM 25 Conviction F: 5<BF 11 Domination	T: 11<CM 19 Emotional intellect F: 11<BF 5 The Unfaithful	25 Enforced failure of action
20 The concrete man	T: 6<CM 24 Fatalism F: 6<BF 10 Superstition	T: 10<CM 20 Dramatisation of Mask F: 10<BF 6 Self-desecration	24 Enforced success of action
21 The acquisitive man	T: 7<CM 23 Self-analysis F: 7<BF 9 Self-adaptation	T: 9<CM 21 Domination of the intellect F: 9<BF 7 Distortion	23 Enforced triumph of achievement

< indicates "modified by"

Will	Mask	Creative Mind	Body of Fate
22 Balance between ambition and contemplation	8 T: *Self-immolation* F: *Self-assurance*	8 T: *Amalgamation* F: *Despair*	22 Temptation versus strength
23 The receptive man	T: 9<BF 7 Wisdom F: 9<CM 21 *Self-pity*	T: 7<BF 9 Creation through pity F: 7<CM 23 *Self-driven desire*	21 Success
24 The end of ambition	T: 10<BF 6 Self-reliance F: 10<CM 20 *Isolation*	T: 6<BF 10 Constructive emotion F: 6<CM 24 *Authority*	20 Objective action
25 The conditional man	T: 11<BF 5 Consciousness of the self F: 11<CM 19 *Self-consciousness*	T: 5<BF 11 Rhetoric F: 5<CM 25 *Spiritual arrogance*	19 Persecution
26 The multiple man also called The Hunchback	T: 12<BF 4 Self-realization F: 12<CM 18 *Self-abandonment*	T: 4<BF 12 Beginning of the abstract supersensual F: 4<CM 26 *Fascination of sin*	18 The Hunchback is his own Body of Fate
27 The Saint	T: 13<BF 3 Renunciation F: 13<CM 17 *Emulation*	T: 3<BF 13 Supersensual receptivity F: 3<CM 27 *Pride*	17 None except Impersonal action
28 The Fool	T: 14<BF 2 Oblivion F: 14<CM 16 *Malignity*	T: 2<BF 14 Physical activity F: 2<CM 28 *Cunning*	16 The Fool is his own Body of Fate

Appendix II: The Critical Degrees

As helpless as baby kittens are, when a stranger approaches they hiss and spit and kick up a fuss, and make a fine show of bravery. Human beings are rather frail creatures too, with great pretensions. Behind all their hissing and spitting they possess a sheer gumption which is peculiarly human and is most noticeable in moments of stress and harassment. In the horoscope it is shown by the critical degrees.

The critical degrees are 28 points spaced 12°51' apart, beginning at 0° Aries: 0°, 12°51', and 25°43' of Cardinal signs; 8°34' and 21°26' of Fixed signs; and 4°17' and 17°09' of Mutable signs. This is a division of the zodiac by 28 (since 360/28 = 12°51'), which is symbolically the moon's orbital period (for detailed information on the 28 lunar mansions, with particular regard to talismanic magic, see Chapter IV of *Picatrix*). The critical degrees are "lunar" in the sense that this area of life is never stable – there is always some question or problem about it. Any natal planet or horoscope angle that lies within an orb of one degree of any of these points is considered to be critical. Where you find a critical planet or angle in the chart, you find a good deal of hissing and spitting in the life.

Critical degrees can be considered to symbolize one's abstract purpose in life. Only the pursuit of an abstract purpose (*Mask*) can sufficiently ennoble and elevate our lives above humdrum routine and endless suffering and give us the courage to overcome when everything seems out to crush our spirit. This is what planets conjunct critical degrees show: one's abstract purpose in life. An absence of critical degrees implies the lack of an abstract purpose (beyond getting through the daily grind & indulging oneself evenings and weekends).

"Abstract purpose" (also arts, crafts, invention) doesn't necessarily mean something good – it can be seeking enlightenment, or getting to heaven; or it can mean upholding one's social superiority by extirpating "inferior races"; or saving the environment; or promulgating a proletarian revolution. The point is that having a dominant purpose in life beyond grubbing out a living is the only way to get on top of life – to face the waves and breakers of life dead on instead of being bobbed up and down and thrashed around. Planets conjunct critical degrees put the area of life symbolized by that planet on hold (in a material sense) so that the spiritual can flower. So, it is possible to get a clue to your abstract purpose by looking at which planets are critical (and why things are so difficult in these areas from a material point of view).

In a sentence, the meaning of the critical degrees (whether conjunct a planet in the natal horoscope; or a critical degree line on the earth in an astrolocality map) is good for spiritual things and bad for material things. Critical degrees show a cosmic restraint: natives will experience obstruction and frustration here (depending on the planet involved) until they learn to surrender their own will in this particular area of life. By denying satisfaction in external circumstances, natives are forced back upon their own resources: they have to find satisfaction within themselves. These degrees are neither benefic nor malefic: they deny external satisfaction, but increase self-reliance. There is an obstinate struggle here against hampering and isolating circumstances – usually self-created – and also a great reserve of fortitude and strength.

This strength is especially apparent when a planet or angle comes to conjunction with a critical degree by secondary (day-for-a-year) progression. Except for the progressed moon, whose effect is much weaker, there is usually a preceding month or months of personal limitation and frustration. Then, within a few weeks of the time after the progression is exact, a crisis occurs. The situation calls for a transcendence – moving up to a new level of grasp and control. The real significance of these critical moments in life is often properly understood only in retrospect over a period of months after the event.

Generally, your critical planets and angles reveal not only where you fume, but also where your greatest potentials lie. They are your true points of touch with the depths of your own humanity.

When there is a **Preponderance of planets conjunct critical degrees** (four or more) in your horoscope, then you possess a deep sense of accountability to the world at large; yet life keeps you on a very short leash. You soon learn that even slight deviations from the straight and narrow path can have catastrophic consequences. You feel compelled to do more than is necessary because you have an acute need to justify to yourself the fact of your existence on this earth. You tend to distrust being too happy – or at least feel vaguely guilty about the idea – which gives you an air of world-weariness. You bear life's burdens with downright doggedness, which on the negative side reveals itself in a singular pigheadedness. At your best, you possess dignity and a real sense of self-worth which in time can lead you to true wisdom.

If there is an **absence of planets conjunct critical degrees** in your horoscope, then you possess great flexibility and adaptability, together with an uninhibited opportunism. You tend to be rather happy-go-lucky; you get to do pretty much as you please in life because you let nothing interfere with what you want to do. At times you may use other people for your own ends and discard them when you have no further need of them. You have a gift for transplanting yourself body and soul whenever your involvements have reached a point of frustration. You have little sense of remorse or guilt, and can get away with things that most people can't because life doesn't hold you accountable. An absence of critical degrees provides a relative freedom from compulsion, which can be a great opportunity to practice self-limitation on a voluntary basis. At your best you are honorable, dispassionate, and just. At your worst, like Temple Drake or Tom and Daisy Buchanan, you tend to leave your messes for other people to clean up.

When your **natal Sun** is critical you have a strong will and determination, but very little fulfillment in life. You feel misunderstood and unappreciated, out of synch with the world around you. You have high ideals and a good heart, combined with a fierce pride and unwillingness to compromise. You are out-of-step with the world around you, but have an unwavering faith in your own worth. This is not so much a pride before people (though there can be a touchy, snobbish, or overweening tendency) as it is a pride before God. It's difficult for you to reconcile the demands that the world makes upon you with what your own inner voice is telling you to do. You tend to find real life too real, too harsh, which lends a softness and sweetness to your nature and gives you a grumpy or brooding air. At your worst you are given to self-righteousness or self-pity. Your independent disposition and belief in yourself are trimmed by a long period of servitude in which you must bend yourself to the demands of other people or the press of circumstances until the nascent humility, which is your most endearing virtue, truly flowers.

When your **progressed Sun** arrives at a critical degree your life comes to some dead end or point of futility. There may be arguments or disagreements with associates, or just an awareness of nonfulfillment with where your life seems to be taking you. Abruptly some new door opens. You make the decision to change direction in life. Filled with inspiration and a new sense of purpose, you leave the uncongenial environment to go off on your own. It's as if you can feel the hand of God guiding and directing you. In the succeeding months you may reflect upon your own limitations; you come to appreciate what it is that is really of importance to you in the working out of your destiny.

When your **natal Moon** is critical you possess good instincts and great tenacity; yet life is never a settled issue for you. You're never quite sure what it is you want out of life, so you're never quite satisfied with things as they are. You tend to hold yourself back because you have an emotional sensibility which is very easily moved or disturbed. You take everything that happens very much to heart, which on its negative side can become a tendency to sulk or pout. At your worst you are completely dominated by your moods, and the less rational they are, the more adamant you become. Your best quality is your willingness to follow your intuition all the way to the end, which endows you with a great capacity for loyalty and dedication.

The **progressed Moon**'s conjunctions with critical degrees are by no means as important or far-reaching as those of the other planets. Occurring about once a year, they are usually in effect for a day or so around the exact date they are due. Something comes up that is a bit out of the ordinary or involves you with other people in a novel way. The experience is quite engaging emotionally. It often has an oblique or indirect bearing upon your present situation in life, and thus serves as a focus for your current feelings and aspirations. The event helps you to realize consciously some of the things you may have been taking for granted heretofore. The upshot is a change of attitude as regards your current involvements and a real sense of emotional encouragement.

When your **natal Mercury** is critical you are sociable and eager to please; but you never quite seem to fit in no matter how hard you try. You are self-conscious and constantly aware of the impression you are making on other people. At times you may become too dependent on their approval or acceptance. You can be overly self-justifying in your efforts to dodge blame and reproach. There can be a sense of cheerful indifference or helplessness about you; you can be a little too pleased with yourself as a reaction against others' judgments. On the other hand, you tend to be nonjudgmental yourself, and are eager to learn and communicate. Typically your friendships cut across all lines of social class and educational background. There is a freshness, an openness, about you, which heralds a nascent innocence.

Progressed Mercury usually arrives at a critical degree on the heels of a period of inner turmoil and confusion about who you are and where you belong. Then you conceive some new idea or project with which you can identify yourself. You enter a period of great energy and activity. The situation hinges upon clear communication with other people, and you have the aplomb and self-possession to bring it off. Your fondest images of yourself seem to come true; you feel like Super-You. In the succeeding months you come to see yourself in a new light, with a new-found sense of personal prowess.

When your **natal Venus** is critical you possess an unflagging optimism and hopefulness; yet life seems to continually disappoint your expectations. You are endowed with a somewhat abashed playfulness and the eager anticipation of a child, but you are extremely vulnerable emotionally and susceptible to being imposed upon or taken advantage of. Actually you victimize yourself with a childish impatience and refusal to allow things to run their course – such as waiting for Mr. or Ms. "Right" to come along, and pouncing on any likely prospects. You may not be looking for give-and-take in an intimate relationship so much as for security and a sense of stability. On your positive side you have a nurturing impulse towards your fellows. You are a delight to know because you are spontaneous, full of adventure, and possessed of a wide-eyed curiosity about the world.

Progressed Venus usually conjoins a critical degree after a chaotic or unsettling period in which your life and relationships have seemed unsubstantial or unfruitful. Then a new possibility presents itself and you realize that you have it within you to change matters. It is a very creative, artistic, inspired period. A new beginning – sometimes an actual removal – is made. You break old alliances and make new ones. Your situation in life stabilizes and loose ends come together. In the months that follow you come to understand better the contribution which you have to make of yourself in order to find your own happiness and peace of mind.

When your **natal Mars** is critical you possess great perseverance and endurance; but you usually find yourself in a rut, stuck in the same old dead-end situations. You don't like being under pressure but often find yourself in that position because you put off decision-making or just let things slide until you're absolutely forced to make a stand. You may harbor secret ambitions or dreams of grandeur, together with a secret fear of successfully realizing them; so you tend to carry an air of frustrated intentions around with you. On the other hand, you mix your caution with bravado and panache and an exceptional amount of personal charm. You have a sense of fair play and a determination to shield and protect other people, which is the hallmark of an incipient heroism.

Progressed Mars often reaches a critical degree after a period of battering your head against a wall. Sometimes there has been illness, or disapproval and rejection by other people. Then the wall falls away. Some sort of renunciation, conversion, or self-sacrifice is required; a new commitment must be made. You may get to do something you've wanted to do for a long time, and you receive the support of other people. Succeeding months show you the futility of passive acceptance: you become more willing to stand up for yourself.

When your **natal Jupiter** is critical you possess a rather sheepish desire to be looked up to and a gift for taking charge, together with a disinclination to play at all unless you can make the rules. You are the proverbial "leader without followers": enthusiastic and eager to share, but overly set in your ways and fixed in your views so that there is a certain point beyond which you just cannot be reached. You take great delight in sheer contrariness, and there may be a vaguely patronizing or condescending air about you – or the sense that you are humoring or indulging other people. If life at times makes you feel that nothing you say or do counts, it's because you're often unwilling to give anyone else any credit. When you have learned the virtues of adaptability, the steadfastness of purpose and complete sincerity which are your outstanding qualities win you the firm allegiance of all who know you.

Since the planets beyond Mars move very slowly by secondary progression and rarely conjoin critical degrees, delineations for the progressed outer planets will not be given.

When your **natal Saturn** is critical you are gentle, sensitive, and aware; yet you tend to find life rather unresponsive and indifferent to you. You are ever the objective observer, even of yourself; this aloofness endows you with an ironic, even self-mocking, sense of humor. You tend to insulate yourself in your objectivity and resist committing yourself fully to what is going on around you. You are always conscious of yourself as an actor in the drama of life, which on the negative side inclines you to pose. If life at times makes you feel that your ideas and feelings are not being respected, it's because you tend to play at life, refusing to take it – or other people – seriously in its own right. Your best quality is your conscious determination to keep your own participation in life as clean and free of ulterior motive as possible, which is the herald of a true personal integrity.

If your **natal Uranus** is critical you are extraordinarily exacting, especially of yourself, and determined to carve out some special niche in the world wherein you are the undisputed master. You are a scrapper, with clearly defined goals in life; and you will not tolerate being crossed in your efforts to realize them. You are endowed with ingenuity and a marked originality in point of view, and you know it, which may make for unendurable smugness or complacency in your temperament. Your dogmatism and bluntness in speaking your mind often antagonize and repel others, even when you're basically right. You possess a true moral courage, ever present but particularly noticeable in the face of adversity. You are characterized by a readiness to sacrifice yourself for other people or for an ideal.

If your **natal Neptune** is critical you are easy-going and free-spirited; yet life is constantly bogging you down with entangling obligations. You sometimes give the impression that the world is faintly a nuisance – a brief and bothersome sojourn en route to some more interesting place. You are a dreamer with your own private world: some area of life in which you feel centered and at ease and in which you have everything down pat. There is often an outstanding talent or competency, even a touch of genius. But, outside your specialty, you keep relations with other people and the world generally as superficial and perfunctory as possible. It can be hard to pull you down off your cloud when an emotional commitment is called for. When you have learned to accept responsibility for the world beyond yourself, your inspiration and vision influence all who know you.

When your **natal Pluto** is critical you possess great intensity and ardor, but life is always trying to dominate you or grind you down. You are endowed with a penetrating intellect and can see very clearly through the prevailing cultural mores. You may toy with fanaticism or extremism in one form or another, but you are more of a malcontent than a revolutionary: you can get hipped on something and lose all sense of objectivity. You chafe at the normal expectations that your social milieu seeks to impose upon you, but you may be at a loss as to how to strike out on your own. You tend to meekly accept some socially approved role in life rather than seize the responsibility for your own destiny. As a result there is a seething or disgruntled air about you, a tendency to crab and complain. At your best you are endowed with great personal stake in the fate of humankind as a whole, which heralds a nascent modesty.

If your **natal Ascendant – Descendant** is critical then you alternate between great self-possession on the one hand, and a sureness of self or snobbishness of unsociable proportions on the other. Although you can be self-assertive to the point of brusqueness, the private you is often plagued with self-doubts. You both openly disdain and desperately need the support and encouragement of other people. You tend to feel misunderstood; and usually you *are* misunderstood, because you are always marching to the beat of a different drum. You constantly try to live up to some idealized image you have of yourself. You are animated by a sense of mission in life, and you resent being judged on any basis other than the terms of your own ideals; but you are apt to discount your own ulterior motives, which are quite visible to everyone else. Your best qualities are your idealism and conscientiousness, which endow you with a true nobility.

The **Progressed Ascendant – Descendant** often reaches a critical degree at the end of a long period of low self-esteem. Some situation crops up in your relations with other people which puts you in an unaccustomed and unusual position. It presents a challenge to your normal image of who you are. You must rise to the situation and get on top of it; and to do so requires that you surpass your normal expectations of yourself. A feeling of great power wells up inside you; or you simply know within your heart that you can master the situation. You assert yourself and put yourself in complete control of both the situation and your own doubts. Succeeding months give you a better estimation of where you must draw your lines, and you gain a new confidence in the power of your own personality.

If your **natal Midheaven – Lower Meridian** is critical, you possess great resolution but also a tendency towards vehemence or absolutism. Although you can be positive to the point of peremptoriness, the private you is somewhat defensive. You have a desperate need to feel that you are standing on solid ground, invulnerable to challenge. You may embrace some sort of philosophy or religion as a standard for all that is desirable and good and as an assurance of divine benediction upon your efforts. You have lofty goals and ambitions, and are inclined to regard the accomplishment of your work in life as being of much greater importance than yourself personally. The unvarnished self-aggrandizement that colors all of your actions is liable to escape your notice. On your positive side you are dependable and thorough, with a great capacity for self-discipline and a true spirit of dedication.

The **Progressed Midheaven – Lower Meridian** often comes to a critical degree at the finish of a period of hard work or intense effort, usually under the direction or for the benefit of other people. Then a new freedom of action opens up. You find yourself able to make your own choices, and you decide to change the course of your career or life's work. You accept some new responsibilities. Frequently there is some sort of travelling or moving about, but in pursuit of opportunity rather than for mere convenience. In the succeeding months you understand better how you can secure your position in life and guarantee your own independence.

BOOKS BY BOB MAKRANSKY:

Bob Makransky's **Introduction to Magic** Series:

"In this series, not only do we get an author who knows his subject inside out, but also a directness of approach often not seen in works of this kind. Not for Makransky the wishy-washy approach that attempts to soothe and reassure the reader with false promises of magical success - something about which many customer complaints arise on the Amazon website - but, rather, an honest and uncompromising study of what Magic really entails. – James Lynn Page (author of *Celtic Magic*, *Everyday Tarot* and *The Christ Enigma*)

What is Magic?, the introductory book on witchcraft:
paperback $19.95: http://www.amzn.com/1499279418
ebook $9.95:
https://www.smashwords.com/books/view/132491

Magical Living, the second volume about paganism:
paperback $16.95: http://www.amzn.com/1499279337
ebook $9.95:
https://www.smashwords.com/books/view/22860

Thought Forms, the third volume about cognitive psychology and the Mercury cycle:
paperback $24.95: http://www.amzn.com/1499267444
ebook $9.95:
https://www.smashwords.com/books/view/22859

The Great Wheel, the fourth volume about reincarnation and the lunation cycle:
paperback $24.95: http://www.amzn.com/154416355X
ebook $9.95:
http://www.smashwords.com/books/view/306020

Volume I of Bob's Introduction to Magic series:

What is Magic?

Magic is a spiritual path which is not very well understood in our society. This is because the theory and practice of magic have never before been explained clearly and convincingly, in a way that makes sense to intelligent and thoughtful people. Written in a sassy, irreverent style, *What is Magic?* discusses how such otherworldly concepts as demons, casting spells, and bewitching are just the hidden underside of everyday society – the skeletons in everybody's closet. *What is Magic?* answers the questions which all serious spiritual seekers, no matter what their spiritual path, ask at one time or another, but can never find satisfactorily answered:

1) What is the difference between faith and fooling yourself?
2) What is the relationship between altered states and normal, everyday life?
3) If you lose your desires, as many spiritual paths advocate, what zest or spice does life have left?
4) If the world is an illusion or dream, as it's said to be, then why does it seem so real?
5) Where does the world of magic – the shaman's world – take off from the world of everyday life? What and where is the interface?
6) Why is it so difficult to achieve real, permanent spiritual growth?

Contents: Spirits, Intent, The Nature of Reality, Spells, Charms & Rituals, Science Debunked, Demons, The Nature of the Self, Bewitching, Magic & Money, Death, Black Magicians & Vampires, Power Places, The Magician's God, Magical Time, Magic and Morality, Dreaming & Stalking, Magic and Sex.

"Bob is daring, willing to be offensive with his truths, and wise in the ways of words and magic. ... Bob

Makransky, I feel, has written a great treatise on magic. I urge you to enjoy it as much as I have." from the foreword by Michael Peter Langevin, publisher of *Magical Blend* magazine.

"There is a certain no-nonsensical feel to his presentation that is both refreshing and a bit disconcerting. Makransky's writing style is very different from other New Age authors, and that alone should appeal to readers looking for a bit more substance in their study of magic" – J Byrne, *Psychic Magic* magazine

What is Magic? paperback $19.95:
http://www.amzn.com/1499279418
ebook $9.95:
https://www.smashwords.com/books/view/132491

* * * * *

Volume II of Bob's Introduction to Magic series:

Magical Living

Winner of the Reader Views Reviewer's Choice Award; the Sacramento Publishers' Association Awards for Best Nonfiction and Best Spiritual book; and Mind-Body-Spirit Finalist in the National Indie Excellence Awards and the USA Book News Best Books Awards.

Contents: How to channel spirit guides, communicate with plants and nature spirits, develop your psychic vision; together with inspirational essays on managing love relationships, handling oppressive people, and dealing with hurt.

"I love this little book! ... Carry this book with you, read and reread the essays, and connect with joy. " – Kathryn Lanier, *InnerChange* magazine

"*He writes beautifully, clearly, elegantly ... he is incapable of an unoriginal thought.*" – Joseph Polansky, *Diamond Fire* magazine

"*I could not get enough! I actually read some of the essays 2 to 3 times and discovered new insights each time. ... Magical Living by Bob Makransky is an easy to read little book with a lot of surprises. A great book to revisit more than once!*" – Susan Violante, *Reader Views*

"*It's a beautiful little book to carry around for when you just want something to read at odd moments, but I suspect that, for some, it will be a book that's picked up over and over again. At times, I find myself ruminating over something I read or glance at the contents page to have something jump out at me that's relevant to the moment. I highly recommend this book to anyone with an open mind and a real willingness to look at themselves and their surroundings.*" – J Byrne, *Psychic-Magic* magazine

Magical Living paperback $16.95:
http://www.amzn.com/1499279337
ebook $9.95:
https://www.smashwords.com/books/view/22860

*   *   *   *   *

Volume III of Bob's Introduction to Magic series

Thought Forms

Contents: Astronomical and astrological explanations of Mercury's synodic cycle – its cycle of phases as it circles the sun, with tables 1900-2050; explanation of the astrological / magical view of mind (the theory of thought forms): what consciousness is, how it arose, and whither it is going; basic course in white magic with detailed instructions on: how to channel and banish thought forms; creative visualization; how to banish the black magicians in everyday life; how to cast out demons; how to use tree spirits.

"Bob Makransky is a knowledgeable, purposeful and entertaining writer." – Paul F. Newman, *The International Astrologer*

"Steady Diamond Fire *readers are well acquainted with the genius of Bob Makransky. Highly recommendable."* – Joseph Polansky, *Diamond Fire*

*"*Considerations *readers have become familiar with [Makransky's] fresh insights into different facets of astrology. In this book* Thought Forms *he is especially provocative and I strongly recommend its purchase and study."* – Ken Gillman, *Considerations*

"Thought Forms *is both highly readable and highly informative, and is very definitely worth checking out."* – Kenneth Irving, *American Astrology* magazine

"I will fully agree with the statement that 'You've never read a book like this before!' The material is fresh and woven very skillfully to conclusion. I look forward to his next installment of the trilogy." – Marion MacMillan, *SHAPE*

Thought Forms paperback $24.95:
http://www.amzn.com/1499267444
ebook $9.95:
https://www.smashwords.com/books/view/22859

* * * * *

Intermediate-level Astrology textbooks:

Topics in Astrology

Topics in Astrology is a delightful smorgasbord of three dozen essays on a wide variety of astrological topics ranging from practical, hands-on advice to technical issues to humor and satire. *Topics in Astrology* is chock-full of original tips and guidelines for experienced practitioners (it may be a bit advanced for beginners; but even they will find parts of the book fascinating).

Contents: Natal Astrology, Relationships, Transits, Progressions and Directions, Horary and Electional Astrology, Mundane Astrology, Mayan Astrology, Theory.

"The sheer scope of the work is mind boggling. Bob Makransky has thought deeply and cogently on the subject and it shows. He is one of our most prolific of astrology writers. ... In typical Makransky fashion he takes an axe to some of our most cherished assumptions. After the shock wears off, we are forced to consider what he says and go deeper in our own understanding. .... He is a beautiful writer and as always, you get a good read regardless of whether or not you agree with him. He shows aspects of Astrology that are outside the current mainstream. A very recommendable book for the serious astrological student." – Joseph Polansky, *Diamond Fire* magazine

"Makransky expounds on numerous subjects of interest to astrologers in his anthology of published articles, Topics in Astrology. *Makransky's plainspoken writing style is direct and thought-provoking. Beginners will enjoy and frequently refer to many of the articles. With his wide-ranging interests, Makransky offers something for everyone."* – Chris Lorenz, *Dell Horoscope magazine*

Topics in Astrology   paperback – Price = $22.95
http://www.amzn.com/1519765878

*   *   *   *   *

Planetary Strength – a commentary on Morinus

An essential contribution to natal horoscope interpretation. Taking as its point of departure *Astrologia*

Gallica by Jean Baptiste Morin de Villefranche (1583 - 1656), *Planetary Strength* explains the differences between the strengths conferred upon planets by virtue of their sign placements (celestial state); house placements (terrestrial state); and aspects (aspectual state). A detailed system of keywords is augmented by insightful "cookbook" interpretations for each and every planetary combination. The depth and quality of the analysis – as well as the hundreds of practical examples and tips – make *Planetary Strength* an essential reference work which both neophyte and experienced practitioners will consult every time they read a horoscope.

"*The book is beautifully written. With Makransky, whether you agree or disagree is not the issue - you will always get a good read. It is clear. He has done his homework. He makes the genius of Morinus accessible to English speakers. He shows us how to 'think astrologically'.*" – Joseph Polansky, *Diamond Fire* magazine

"*What's fascinating about* Planetary Strength *is that the author is using his own prose to describe the planets' conditions. In the introduction, he advises readers to study Morinus, but clearly Makransky's efforts are the better source. ... Try them in practice and compare these interpretations to what you might otherwise think about a planet. It may just sharpen your ability to make accurate statements about character, a person's history, and even to make predictions. And what more do you ask of astrology?*" – Chris Lorenz, *Dell Horoscope* magazine

"*This is certainly an interesting addition to reading and interpreting the translations of Morinus' original work. It is detailed and considered, and the author's knowledge and experience are evident throughout.*" – Helen Stokes, *AA Journal*

"Presenting a mixture of discussion, detailed cookbook offerings and chart examples as well as keywords and tables, this fascinating book also addresses the fixed stars. ... This fascinating book assumes a fair knowledge of astrology as well as some experience in preparing charts."
– Margaret Gray, *ISAR*

"This is a book that every beginner as well as advanced student of astrology would do well to possess. The author is extremely perceptive in his descriptions of the planets in their various strength and weaknesses ... this book would be a helpful aid to the researcher, as it would point him in the right direction." – Wanda Sellar, *Correlation*

Planetary Strength – 130 pages – paperback – Price = £ 11.99
http://wessexastrologer/product/waps001/

* * * * *

Planetary Combination

Planetary Combination picks up where *Planetary Strength* left off, explaining how the planetary influences combine in aspects and configurations to paint a picture of a person and his or her life. Descriptions of planetary configurations such as Grand Trines, Grand Squares, T-Crosses, Wedges, Fans, Rectangles, Kites, and Trapezoids provide overall schematics of people's psychological dynamics. Then, detailed interpretations for the conjunctions, sextiles / trines, squares, oppositions, parallels / contraparallels, and Mutual Receptions between the individual planets enable the practitioner to see clearly how these dynamics work out in a particular horoscope. An illuminating chapter on planetary conjunctions with the moon's nodes reveals the underlying karmic influences at work. An indispensable reference you'll consult every time you read a chart.

"While this book is nominally a series of explanations about aspects between the traditional planets, the degree of character description for each planetary pair is extraordinarily precise. An entire personality is captured within these aspects. In the same way that the author provides highly detailed character sketches for each planetary duo, he gives the same attention to configurations. In addition to the most common shapes, he also provides several pages on shapes that are not found in any other astrology text. An unusually terse and bold reference, Planetary Combination *transcends psychological mumbo-jumbo to give you the bare-naked reality of the adult Western psyche."* – Chris Lorenz, *Dell Horoscope* magazine.

"You are entering a world of verbal complexity and conceptual subtlety. There will be plenty you have not seen anywhere else. You may find Makransky's approach to astrology insightful, delightfully unconventional, or just plain weird. I applaud Bob Makransky and his publisher Margaret Cahill at Wessex Astrologer for having produced a work of originality and complexity and befuddlement, astonishment and inspiration and irritation."
– Joseph Crane, The Astrology Institute

*"*Planetary Combination *is an excellent and comprehensive summary of all the relevant chart factors. ... One has to search hard to find such material! But this is all presented, as is all of Makransky's work, with vigour, wisdom and accessibility. ... Much of the book is taken up – as we might expect – with a very generous coverage of the astrological aspects. I looked up a few of my own and they were spot on. ...* Planetary Combination *fills a gap in the current state of astrological literature. It manages to retain both a sense of firm tradition whilst feeling utterly new and fresh."* – James Lynn Page, author of *Everyday Tarot, Celtic Magic, The Christ Enigma* and *The New Positive Thinking*.

"This is one of the best books on aspects out there. He not only deals with aspects themselves, but goes deep into chart morphology. It is one thing to analyze aspects and quite another to look at the "pictures" - the forms - that the aspects make. Most books on aspects deal with the aspects of longitude. But he also includes the parallels and contra-parallels. He has an interesting discussion of orbs, values (strengths of an aspect) and mutual receptions. A student would have to read many books from many authors to get the information that is given here. As always with Bob Makransky's work, the book is interesting and well written, not for a beginner or casual reader, but fascinating nevertheless - especially for a serious student." – Joseph Polansky, *Diamond Fire* magazine

Planetary Combination – 232 pages paperback
Price = £ 17.50
http://wessexastrologer/product/wapc001/

* * * * *

Planetary Hours

Planetary Hours are an ancient astrological system for selecting favorable times to act (and avoiding unfavorable times), by assigning planetary rulers to the twenty-four hours of the day. **Contents:** instructions for finding and interpreting your birthday and birth hour rulers; electional astrology – how to use the Planetary Hours to find lucky times to act (to ask for money; to ask someone on a date or to marry; to go on a journey; to begin a new business); how to cast spells; the Firdaria, an ancient astrological prediction system; Tables of Planetary Hours for any day of the year, and for anywhere on earth from the Equator to 58° North and South latitudes.

"Bob Makransky's new book ably taps the rising vogue for traditional astrology, though eschewing the fatalism often assigned to so-called 'magical' ancient

approaches. He describes Planetary Hours (PH) as the "astrology of luck" and a method of finding empowering life moments for the proper exercise of freewill – to be yourself and not an enslaved cog of convention. ... As an introduction, this book is highly accessible." – AA Journal

"Bob Makransky has written the definitive book on Planetary Hours. It's the best book on the subject out there. It will be read and studied by future generations of astrologers. Its not just something that you read and discard. You want it in your bookshelf to refer to again and again." – Joseph Polansky, *Diamond Fire* magazine

Planetary Hours – 130 pages – paperback
Price = £ 11.00
http://wessexastrologer/product/waph001/

www.ingramcontent.com/pod-product-compliance
Lightning Source LLC
Chambersburg PA
CBHW050616300426
44112CB00012B/1529